the cinema of JAMES CAMERON

DIRECTORS' CUTS

Other selected titles in the Directors' Cuts series:

the cinema of ISTVÁN SZABÓ: *visions of europe*
JOHN CUNNINGHAM

the cinema of AGNÈS VARDA: *resistance and eclecticism*
DELPHINE BÉNÉZET

the cinema of ALEXANDER SOKUROV: *figures of paradox*
JEREMI SZANIAWSKI

the cinema of MICHAEL WINTERBOTTOM: *borders, intimacy, terror*
BRUCE BENNETT

the cinema of RAÚL RUIZ: *impossible cartographies*
MICHAEL GODDARD

the cinema of MICHAEL MANN: *vice and vindication*
JONATHAN RAYNER

the cinema of AKI KAURISMÄKI: *authorship, bohemia, nostalgia, nation*
ANDREW NESTINGEN

the cinema of RICHARD LINKLATER: *walk, don't run*
ROB STONE

the cinema of BÉLA TARR: *the circle closes*
ANDRÁS BÁLINT KOVÁCS

the cinema of STEVEN SODERBERGH: *indie sex, corporate lies, and digital videotape*
ANDREW DE WAARD & R. COLIN TATE

the cinema of TERRY GILLIAM: *it's a mad world*
edited by JEFF BIRKENSTEIN, ANNA FROULA & KAREN RANDELL

the cinema of TAKESHI KITANO: *flowering blood*
SEAN REDMOND

the cinema of THE DARDENNE BROTHERS: *responsible realism*
PHILIP MOSLEY

the cinema of MICHAEL HANEKE: *europe utopia*
edited by BEN McCANN & DAVID SORFA

the cinema of SALLY POTTER: *a politics of love*
SOPHIE MAYER

the cinema of JOHN SAYLES: *a lone star*
MARK BOULD

the cinema of DAVID CRONENBERG: *from baron of blood to cultural hero*
ERNEST MATHIJS

the cinema of LARS VON TRIER: *authenticity and artifice*
CAROLINE BAINBRIDGE

the cinema of WERNER HERZOG: *aesthetic ecstasy and truth*
BRAD PRAGER

the cinema of TERRENCE MALICK: *poetic visions of america (second edition)*
edited by HANNAH PATTERSON

the cinema of ANG LEE: *the other side of the screen (second edition)*
WHITNEY CROTHERS DILLEY

the cinema of STEVEN SPIELBERG: *empire of light*
NIGEL MORRIS

the cinema of TODD HAYNES: *all that heaven allows*
edited by JAMES MORRISON

the cinema of ROMAN POLANSKI: *dark spaces of the world*
edited by JOHN ORR & ELZBIETA OSTROWSKA

the cinema of JOHN CARPENTER: *the technique of terror*
edited by IAN CONRICH & DAVID WOODS

the cinema of MIKE LEIGH: *a sense of the real*
GARRY WATSON

the cinema of NANNI MORETTI: *dreams and diaries*
EWA MAZIERSKA & LAURA RASCAROLI

the cinema of DAVID LYNCH: *american dreams, nightmare visions*
edited by ERICA SHEEN & ANNETTE DAVISON

the cinema of KRZYSZTOF KIESLOWSKI: *variations on destiny and chance*
MAREK HALTOF

the cinema of GEORGE A. ROMERO: *knight of the living dead (second edition)*
TONY WILLIAMS

the cinema of KATHRYN BIGELOW: *hollywood transgressor*
edited by DEBORAH JERMYN & SEAN REDMOND

the cinema of
JAMES CAMERON

bodies in heroic motion

James Clarke

WALLFLOWER PRESS LONDON & NEW YORK

A Wallflower Press Book

Wallflower Press is an imprint of
Columbia University Press
Publishers Since 1893
New York . Chichester, West Sussex
cup.columbia.edu

Copyright © James Clarke 2014
All rights reserved
Wallflower Press® is a registered trademark of Columbia University Press

A complete CIP record is available from the Library of Congress

ISBN 978-0-231-16976-9 (cloth)
ISBN 978-0-231-16977-6 (pbk.)
ISBN 978-0-231-85062-9 (e-book)

Series design by Rob Bowden Design

Cover image of James Cameron courtesy of the Kobal Collection

CONTENTS

Acknowledgements   vii

Introduction   1

1 Genesis: From Short Film Visions to Low-Budget Monster Movie   29
2 *The Terminator* (1984)   35
3 *Aliens* (1986)   57
4 *The Abyss* (1989)   75
5 *Terminator 2: Judgement Day* (1991)   89
6 *True Lies* (1994)   103
7 *Titanic* (1997)   115
8 *Avatar* (2009)   129
9 Cameron's Documentaries   149
10 Cameron as Writer and Producer   153

Filmography   159
Bibliography   163
Index   173

ACKNOWLEDGEMENTS

My very first published writing about movies was back in 2001 with Wallflower Press and so I am very glad to have returned to them with this project. I would like to thank all the team there for their contributions to the realisation of this title. Thanks, too, for encouraging and insightful conversations with Steven Awalt and George Ttoouli. Finally, particular thanks to Wallflower Press's Commissioning Editor, Yoram Allon, for his long-running guidance and support in helping me bring what I was thinking about onto the page.

INTRODUCTION

On 12 June 2014 at the Arena Corinthians stadium in São Paulo in Brazil, a 29-year-old paraplegic man named Juliano Pinto walked and then kicked a football. This moment instigated the beginning of the 2014 World Cup. This moment also resonated as an achievement of invention, imagination, finance, scientific enquiry and technology that resulted in a 'real world' event, and image of that event, that echoed a central concern in the films of James Cameron; namely, the interface of the human mind and body with technology. In large part, this book will seek to explore the ways in which Cameron's films visualise and dramatise a relationship that is key to human experience and which in our current moment is becoming evermore acute as so many of us integrate digital technology into every moment of our daily lives. Cameron's films engage with the ways in which technology can transform and maximise our natural, physio-logical potential and they also construct narratives that suggest something of the limitations and perils inherent in that same allure of technology. They provide us with a range of images that have crystalised this essential conjunction of the biological and the mechanical and digital, resulting in films that assume evermore pertinence and resonance with our the lives that so many of us lead in the early twenty-first century. How interesting, then, to hear the word 'exoskeleton' used during the World Cup broadcast. Cameron has been peppering his interviews and comments on his work with such terminology since his breakthrough movie, *The Terminator*, in 1984.

This introductory chapter will map out the key strands that weave throughout the book in terms of concerns around Cameron's status as an 'auteur'; the particular film industry conditions within which he emerged as a new creative 'voice' in the early 1980s; and the overarching formal and thematic interests of each film that he has written, directed and produced. As such, the discussions that lie ahead on these pages will also seek to make connections between Cameron's movies and certain other frames of film reference. We will commence our investigations by continuing to think about the body/technology fusion.

Reflecting on what constitutes certain aspects of our humanity, Donna Haraway has noted that 'by the late twentieth century, our time, a mythic time, we are all chimeras, theorized and fabricated hybrids of machine and organism; in short, we are cyborgs' (1991). Haraway's sense of the zeitgeist offers an encapsulation of what we might propose constitutes the interests, preoccupations and allure of the films that James Cameron has written and directed since his breakthrough second feature film, *The Terminator*. His films might all be understood as explorations of the idea of the avatar to some degree. Now more than ever, the idea of an avatar has currency. As of this writing, Tom Cruise has starred in his latest science fiction movie, *Edge of Tomorrow*, a big-budget, Hollywood-produced event-movie adaptation that cinematically realises the Japanese novel *All You Need is Kill* by Hiroshi Sakurazaka. In *Edge of Tomorrow* (2014) part of the action centres on humans who wear armour that is body-encompassing, 'transforming' the person into part-machine.

When the writer/director/producer of two successively produced feature films, *Titanic* (1997) and *Avatar* (2009), finds that 'they' have conceived, engineered and marketed these products to the combined figure of around $3 billion in worldwide ticket sales *we* might be inclined to investigate further how these films have been constructed as generators of meaning. What is it that audiences have found, and continue to find, compelling in the way that Cameron makes a movie? What are Cameron's poetics? What forms of representation are at work? What is it that audiences of his films might be responding to? Inevitably, perhaps, we need to respond to the critical question of the place of the auteur in popular film. In thinking through this matter we might consider what the choices made cohere to and what associations they resonate with. This book, then, takes both a formal-aesthetic and a socio-ideological approach to his body of work.

Let us start, then, at the very end; namely, the concluding sentence of Mark Twain's novel *The Adventures of Huckleberry Finn* (1884). Here are its closing words: '…I reckon I got to light out for the Territory ahead of the rest, because Aunt Sally she's going to adopt me and sivilize (sic.) me, and I can't stand it. I been there before' (1987: 369). Huck's plain-spoken, potent declaration will resound at points later in this book. It is pertinent, but broadly stated here, to say that Twain's novel expresses what has been understood as an essential American-ness. Cameron, whilst hailing from Canada, has worked with film genres and narrative forms that have evolved within the American popular cinema.

Let us now make the imaginative leap from a literary reference to a rural, mid-nineteenth-century place to the proposed cusp of a twenty-first century, urban experience that is cinematically-sited. In the earliest part of his treatment for what eventually became *Strange Days* (Kathryn Bigelow, 1995), co-writer Cameron, in a process of establishing some sense of the not-too-distant future world (the year is 1999, the place is North America) in which he was setting the drama, wrote: 'The really big changes are all behind the scenes, in high technology, in telecommunications, in the way it's all wired up. And the average guy is barely aware of these changes. They seep into his consciousness as the new toys hit the consumer market and the new technology became part of life' (1995). Cameron's briefly-sketched image of technology entwined with human consciousness and activity is somewhat emblematic of the cinematic story-worlds that he has produced (by which we will typically mean written, directed and produced) since 1984 and which, more broadly, have seemingly become increasingly prescient in our 'real' lives. The point has variously been made that we do not live with technology but rather that we 'live it'. Each of Cameron's films dramatise, and visualise, this quality of human experience that is shared by so many of us.

Of *Strange Days*, directed by Bigelow but very much a Cameron movie in sensibility and thematic interest, Christine Cornea has commented that 'in what appears to be an updated reworking of the seminal *Peeping Tom* [1960], Bigelow attempts an exhausting critique of voyeuristic, cinematic practice whilst also suggesting that the development of more immersive technologies may result in an excessive extension of these practices' (2007: 191). The idea of the 'immersive technologies' of this Bigelow/Cameron collaboration rhymes with his most recent feature film, *Avatar*.

Making what have been predominantly science fiction films, the relatively small number of movies that James Cameron has written, directed and produced since he came to prominence in the early 1980s have, within the parameters of the Hollywood studio film format (as both industrial and ideological system), become hugely popular evocations of the formal and thematic preoccupations of the science fiction, war movie and historical epic genres. His work has arguably both affirmed and countered established conventions of mainstream representation. Allied to this has been, we might propose, an increasingly self-aware attempt on Cameron's part to couch his productions in a frame of reference much broader than merely the culture of popular film. Indeed, in the opening moments of *The Abyss* (1989), Cameron includes a quotation from Friedrich Nietzsche. We might say that at that point in Cameron's career an overt reference to literary heritage suggested an evolving trajectory for his movie stories. By the time we arrive at *Avatar*, Cameron's literary antecedents are being name-checked at every opportunity. Staying with *The Abyss* momentarily, and the Nietzsche quote from *Beyond Good and Evil* (1886) ('And when you gaze long into an abyss, the abyss gazes into you') that opens that film, it is useful to note that Nietzsche's use of the imagery of depth and of falling (motifs present in *The Abyss*, *Titanic* and *Avatar*) are taken up in the sonorous writing of French philosopher Gaston Bachelard. Admittedly, Bachelard was far, far removed from the place and moment of 'creation' of *The Abyss*. However, his words have use: 'Even before any reference to morality, metaphors of the fall are fixed, it would appear, by an undeniable psychological reality. These metaphors all produce a psychic impression that leaves indelible traces in our unconscious: the fear of falling is a primitive fear. We find it as one component of fears of many different kinds. It is what constitutes the dynamic element of the fear of the dark…' (2011: 91). This 'fear of the dark' will certainly drive a number of key sequences across Cameron's films, evidencing his awareness of primal motifs and themes. Indeed, in 1989 in an interview with *Movieline* magazine at the time of the release of *The Abyss* Cameron acknowledged the degree to which he was steeped in both science fiction and more ancient narratives: 'All those residual images from my childhood, when I read sci-fi voraciously, like Bradbury, Clark and Heinlein. It's such a visual form. I was always interested in the fantastic ... anything with spectacular mythological energy' (1989). With this broad frame of reference in mind, with this book the intention, in part, is to investigate how Cameron's films are invested with a sense of 'mythological energy' as they explore the concept of living, thinking and feeling with technology.

Cameron's body of work as a writer and director has been produced during the transition of narrative-fiction feature films from the era of the photographically recorded and photochemically-processed production to the evolution and metamorphosis of filmmaking into the digital pre- and post-production context where images are significantly computer-generated or 'captured' rather than 'filmed'. Indeed, this is where *Avatar* evidences such a powerful hybridisation of painting, performance, animation and photography (in the 'traditional' sense of proving an indexical recording of a world that any one of us could encounter). As such, filmmaking is now no longer *only* centred on photochemical processes used to record existing realities. To some degree, the digital process of 'painting' film, of not having to necessarily photograph in order to create an illusion, is seemingly a rendition of the kind of work that self-described experimental filmmakers like Norman McLaren, Len Lye and Stan Brakhage engaged with over many decades whereby they made marks directly onto film rather than using film to capture a reality at which the camera was directed (the pro-filmic event) with film running through the camera apparatus. The process and approaches of abstraction with which animation can render insights finds a ready-made home in the 'painting' of filmic illusions.

In seeking to further understand ways in which we engage with popular cinema we might first ask the question: what are some of the elements that characterise the processes of storytelling and the demands and consequences of human evolution on the role of creativity, in terms of the construction of stories and the generation of meanings? Is it not the case that storytelling and, more broadly, the making of art(ifice) is a luxury of sorts, at odds with the evolutionary fact that we, as animals, have lives founded fundamentally on acts of survival and the perpetuation of our gene pool. With this in mind, why, then, has human culture committed such energy across the millennia to the process of 'making things up', of diverting our attention from more vital pursuits in order to engage with the apparently frivolous endeavour of telling and receiving stories? This issue is mapped out by Brian Boyd in his book *On the Origin of Stories: Evolution, Cognition and Fiction* (2009); his concerns are useful and relevant in terms of how we might think about the role that cinema plays in cultures and also in terms of how we might consider the expressive qualities of filmmaking style in the production of narratives. By extension, we might arrive at some sense of 'meaning'. As David Bordwell has written, in a set of reflections online entitled 'All Play, No Work? Room 237': 'To be convincing, though, an interpretation can't merely take a one-off cue to make references or evoke themes. What really matters are patterns...' (2013a).

Regarding the profound enjoyment that we can take in a story and our commitment to the process of telling stories, Boyd asks: 'How did a behaviour so complex, often so costly in terms of time and even resources, and of so little apparent benefit in a competitive struggle for existence, ever become so established throughout human-kind?' (2009: 94). He goes on to observe that 'art as a kind of cognitive play stimulates our brains more than does routine processing of our environment' and then indicates that 'art, even if it diverts energy from immediate survival or reproductive needs, can improve cooperation within a group enough for the group to compete successfully against others with less inclination to art ... art also simply fosters more intense sociality within the group' (ibid.). Another issue that Boyd investigates is the need for a story to hold appeal before anything else occurs in the telling of a tale. How do you get the audience to pay attention before you begin giving them what you want them to pay attention to? There is a line of thought here that might alert us to the ways in which studio films are marketed. Certainly, Cameron's films have all been vividly and rigorously marketed, emphasising their genre-specific credentials.

Cameron's Background
First, then, a little of Cameron's biography. The personal life is not automatically, necessarily, or with any certainty, analogous with the creative endeavour and it is interesting how, in the construction of his filmmaking persona, Cameron's youth is a relatively modest element in the narrative. By contrast, consider the centrality of Spielberg's recollections of his youth to the construction of his filmmaker persona. In *Time* magazine's 15 July 1985 edition, Spielberg provided an essay entitled 'I Dream for a Living'; this has arguably become a fundamental text in understanding the public and media construction and perception of Spielberg as auteur with the autobiographical substantially informing the 'meaning' of the films he directs. Martin Scorsese, too, has developed a filmmaking persona that is partly constructed around the work as an expression of and connection back to his childhood.

James Cameron was born in 1954, in the town of Kapuskasing ('The Wilderness Destination – Naturally' as the town's website proudly states). We might comfortably claim, then, that Cameron's films as writer and director have long engaged with dramatising, and applying spectacularly scaled visuals, to the relationship between human endeavour and the threat, mystery and possibility residing in the wilderness as recreated and appropriated in *Aliens* (1986), *The Abyss*, *Titanic* and *Avatar*. Of *Titanic*, David M. Lubin has picked up on the wilderness resonance: 'While not by any means an intellectual film (and far less an intellectual's film), *Titanic* nevertheless prompts viewers to posit to themselves questions about our society's divide between rich and poor, the nature of love, the meaning of sacrifice, and modernity's faith in, even obsession with, technological prowess and mastery over nature' (1999: 12).

As a young man, Cameron developed a keen interest in both science and engineering and also in the reading of prose science fiction and fantasy. During these formative years, he also developed an interest in the natural world. In a number of promotional interviews and presentations ahead of, and during, *Avatar*'s original theatrical release in late 2009, Cameron recalled sitting on the school bus as a fourteen-year-old reading science fiction novels, which, in its own quiet way, has been attributed to the genesis for the *Avatar* project. Contrasting with this bucolic recollection has been a more recent, more complicated, and less naïve, relationship to the potential sources of inspiration for the film.

At the age of seventeen Cameron and his family moved from Canada to California; more specifically to the Los Angeles suburb of La Brea (home of the ancient tar-pits and the fossil record of animal life from 11,000 years ago). Critical to Cameron's narration of this period in his life has been his recollection of how Canada perceived America at the time. He has explained, in an extensive interview with Stephen Rebello for *Playboy* magazine about *Avatar* and the larger arc of his filmmaking career, that 'in Canada there was a general resentment against America. We lived in a border town, and America was this culture generator that constantly bathed us in its radiation. To move to LA was to go into the belly of the beast' (2009). Cameron's use of a mythical image in this recollection is a fleeting nod to his familiarity with the narrative world of mythology.

In engaging with Cameron's movies (in and of themselves, and as indices of other issues at large in some cultures) it might be pertinent to know that he grew up during the period in which the Vietnam War took place. As such, his films have often articulated an imagining and re-presentation of this subject. Indeed, his brother served in Vietnam. Furthermore, Cameron came to prominence in popular American cinema in 1984, the same year that Bruce Springsteen released his album *Born in the USA* in which the titular song evokes some sense of the plight of the American soldier going to war and then returning home as a veteran to a country that may have no place for him. It is a subject that was also articulated in *Born on the Fourth of July* (Oliver Stone, 1989) and *In Country* (Norman Jewison, 1989). This popular cinema engagement with the Vietnam War has been explored by Robert Hammond who has noted that the films made through the 1970s that responded to the war 'were on the one hand to retain a sceptical attitude to the model and to the war, while on the other seeking to find new ways of representing the war and the issues it raised' (2002: 64).

Critically, whereas a number of the generation of Hollywood-centric directors who preceded Cameron's 'arrival' in Hollywood had attended film school (with the notable exception of Steven Spielberg), Cameron had not. Instead, prior to securing his first work in the film industry he worked as a machinist, a lorry driver, a mechanic and a precision-tool engineer. Indeed, this influence has remained an important constant in the kinds of films he has made and, to a significant degree, the image that has built around his persona as a film director. Critically, Cameron has said of himself that 'I'm pretty blue collar' (2009a). It is a description that lends some sense of authenticity and autobiography, limiting though the idea of autobiographical 'content' can be in gauging the interest of a filmmaker's work to the kind of heroes who are the focus of his films. Typically, Hollywood heroes have arguably tended to be middle-class but Cameron's heroes are rarely so. Instead, his protagonists tend to emerge from a lower-middle- or working-class background.

Echoing the experience of British film director Ridley Scott, in 1977 Cameron saw, as a member of the paying public, the newly released movie *Star Wars*, which had been written and directed by George Lucas. Cameron has duly noted that this was the film that made him want to be a filmmaker, specialising in fantasy and science fiction genre movies. In the extensive interview with Playboy mentioned above, Cameron talked about his understanding of the popular audience, noting that 'for me this decade has been about retreating to the great fundamentals, things that aren't passing fads or subject to the whim of some idiot critic' (Rebello 2009).

Stirred by the example of Lucas's landmark film, Cameron engaged in a sustained process of auto-didacticism, fusing his engineering and illustration expertise with his interests in movies and storytelling. In a rather mundane, almost anomalous twist of fate, through a contact, he was introduced to a group of Mormon dentists who were keen to finance a film project. Cameron convinced these potential investors to fund his first short film production, a piece that he entitled *Xenogenesis* (1978); a film that he wrote, directed, produced *and* rendered the visual effects for. It was emphatically a science fiction piece and one which, more specifically, announced his interest in shape-shifting forms. *Xenogenesis* does in fact encapsulate dramatic situations, visual qualities and thematic elements that are sustained in Cameron's feature projects.

This short film was intended as Cameron's calling-card project with which to approach the Hollywood studios, both major and minor, and to this end the project served its purpose. He secured work within Hollywood's low-budget feature industry, working for Roger Corman's New World Pictures as an effects artist and art director. During his tenure at New World, Cameron worked on the feature films *Battle Beyond the Stars* (Jimmy T. Murikami, 1980) and *Galaxy of Terror* (Bruce D. Clark, 1981).

Corman's low-budget filmmaking style and production mode usefully impacted on Cameron's sense of a film director being an almost 'self-sustaining' unit who understands the demands and processes of the various departments that collaborate to realise a movie. Of his approach to the kinds of films that his studio produced across the decades, Corman has explained to British newspaper *The Daily Telegraph* as recently as 2013 that 'I developed a style. What I tried to do is make a film on two levels. On a surface level, it might be, say a gangster film. But on a subtextual level it might be about some thing or concept that was important to me. Maybe some people would understand the two levels, and maybe they wouldn't, but for me it was the way I preferred to work' (2013).

Certainly, Cameron's industry beginnings, which saw him working as a production designer and visual effects practitioner, are surely a motivating factor in the dominance of the visual in his work. Cinema is a visual medium and even directors who have not been production designers *et al* make 'visual' films. In due course, however, Cameron's movies also displayed a real facility for directing and eliciting believable performances from actors portraying characters in typically 'fantastical' scenarios.

Cameron's contemporaries, Joe Dante and John Sayles, also established their careers at Corman's studio at around the same time. Dante directed *Piranha* (1978), to which Cameron would then direct the sequel, *Piranha 2: The Spawning* (1981). He was commissioned to direct the film by an Italian producer who, like Cameron, had worked on *Galaxy of Terror* at Corman's studio. Whilst *Piranha 2* was a commercial and creative failure, it does tell a story in which humans are pitted against the menacing forces of the wilderness: the very subject that Cameron would go on to dramatise in several subsequent films. Indeed, *Piranha 2*'s longer-term value in aiding our consideration of Cameron's subsequent projects is to help keep in focus a kind of sincerely rendered B-movie sensibility. Of the B-movie mode, Xavier Mendik has parsed the form's various pleasures and notes that one of them is its capacity for allegory (see Mathijs & Mendik 2008: 9). The allegorical is certainly a mode that Cameron has adopted in a number of his films, notably in *The Terminator*, *Aliens* and *Avatar* in which not only the characters but the design of settings and place assume highly-charged emotional and conceptual resonance.

Cameron's trajectory, though, would stand in contrast to Dante's. The two film-makers have different formal and tonal approaches and certainly very different levels of wider, 'brand name' recognition. Dante's breakthrough into the commercial mainstream was prompted by *The Howling* (1981) and then built upon with *Gremlins* (1984), produced by Steven Spielberg and a commercial and critical success that, like his other movies, is characterised by an anarchic sensibility. Dante's films have assumed cult status: *The Howling*, *Gremlins*, *Gremlins 2: The New Batch* (1990) and *Matinee* (1993) all enjoy keen fan followings, and he continues to direct movies in the fantasy and horror genres, most recently with the film *The Hole* (2009). Like Lucas, Dante's films have resolutely remained committed to 'non-prestige' subjects, instead re-animating adventure, horror and fantasy genres. Even Lucas's underrated production *Red Tails* (Anthony Hemingway, 2012) invested its aesthetic (right down to font and colour for its opening titles) in a 1950s Hollywood World War II-movie sensibility. Both Cameron and Dante's film releases of 1984 evidenced a willingness to play with audience expectation. The latter's *Gremlins* spiked the image of suburbia as a place of comfort and calm, and in *The Terminator* Cameron spiked the image of the robot as a benign entity that had become so familiar in the form of C3P0 and R2D2 in the *Star Wars* movies. Dante, in relation to Cameron, is worthy of some consideration here in that where Cameron's films have always been characterised by a sombre tone, Dante's have relished the anarchic, playful and referential. That said, the latter's films have offered playful critiques of big business, the military, the idea of heroism and have also visualised the collision of suburban 'safety' with more primal forces.

Cameron's movies have shown how, in certain cases, the popular, mainstream movie format can revise the representation of heroism, of women, of technology and of nature. Additionally, his work has engaged intensively with the production processes and aesthetics of visual effects and, by extension, of animation, as an expressive tool. *Avatar* was certainly not Cameron's first engagement with extensive and 'envelope pushing' spectacle and his previous narrative fiction feature film, *Titanic*, housed some of its pleasures in this same spectacle of scope and detail.

In *Poetics of Cinema*, David Bordwell summarises a point made in the film writing of Vsevelod Pudovkin, who observed that 'The camera allowed the director to create not an actual observer, but an "ideal", omnipresent one' (2007c: 59). Bordwell proceeds to underpin this thinking by noting that Pudovkin was identifying the crux of our fascination with popular cinema's aesthetic and formal inventions. Of the contemporary mainstream cinema and its audiences Bordwell notes that 'although "style" as sensory bombast has become part of a movie's packaging and marketing, viewers remain almost completely unaware of style' (2007c: 262). Our consideration, then, is this: in what ways do James Cameron's films manifest a style (a set of patterns), and, by extension, how do these patterns communicate a set of meanings?

Assessing the impact on audiences of *Titanic*, Cameron commented, in an interview later anthologised by Brett Dunham, that 'I think the spectacle got people's attention, got them to the theaters, and then the emotional, cathartic experience of watching the film is what made the film work' (2012: 126). His observation goes some way, perhaps, to suggesting the hugely profitable (in every sense) relationship that exists between action cinema and visual effects. It also acknowledges the way in which an event-movie, with a mass-market commercial ambition, is produced with the expectation that it will be seen not only by regular theatrical audiences but by those audiences for whom a visit to the cinema is a very occasional experience and who will instead view it on a TV screen, or, increasingly, on a smartphone or tablet (to think that the 'latest' in technology is identified by a reference to the ancient world is amusing, surprising and accurate).

Cameron's place, not only as a director but also as an industrialist and entrepreneur, has created a context for him to publicly articulate a position about the evolution of twenty-first-century issues around cinema distribution and exhibition. He has invested (creatively and financially) in a cinema of spectacle and fantasy that, to some degree, stands in opposition to the thinking of film theorist Siegfried Kracauer who, during the earliest decades of film's evolution as practice, industry and cultural experience, asserted in his essay 'The Redemption of Reality' that 'the basic properties [of cinema] are identical with the properties of photography. Film, in other words, is uniquely equipped to record and reveal physical reality and, hence, gravitates toward it' (1997: 28). What Kracauer could not forsee was how cinema would eventually blend with painting and a kind of digitally-permitted form of sculpture and puppetry as evidenced in Cameron's *Terminator 2: Judgement Day* (1991) and *Avatar*, particularly. Kracauer's statement, then, is a warning, challenge and prophecy, and valuable in light of how we might want to think through the interest of the films and TV programming that Cameron has written, directed and produced. The 'James Cameron' brand now carries with it a number of assumptions and judgements (by both film industry and film audiences) in much the same way the names of Walt Disney, Steven Spielberg, Hayao Miyazaki and J. K. Rowling do. Like Disney and Spielberg, Cameron is an 'artist-industrialist', investing in developments in technology that can then feed back into his own production process. Indeed, in October 2013 Cameron announced that a major source of energy for the studio space in which he plans to film *Avatar 2, 3* and *4* will be derived from solar panels. The discourses around Cameron have increasingly, since the release of *Avatar*, emphasised comment about environment and ecological reference points.

Certainly, Cameron has been grouped with a number of other highly visible, much promoted and culturally constructed filmmakers who have produced visually arresting 'event movies' which, whilst popular, are typically considered to have little merit as quality films. Cameron's films are just instances of explosions and special effects, are they not? The kind of sensibility that his films manifest might also characterise the response to Peter Jackson and it was a mind-set that used to characterise many knee-jerk reactions to the films that Spielberg had directed before *Schindler's List* (1993). We might say, then, that this is akin to what might happen in movie musicals when the song-and-dance routines propel the action and enrich character. Indeed, David Bordwell has made the further point in his essay 'Anatomy of the Action Picture': 'When fans replay exciting escapes and fights, they're not escaping narrative; they're immersing themselves in it' (2007a). In developing our understanding of what the pleasures of action cinema, and the cinema of spectacle, are, we begin to consider points of interest beyond the cinema. Is there a connection to be made with the art history of 'spectacular' paintings that render the world in terms larger than itself?

Indeed, film critic Manohla Dargis has written that 'the movie industry has been in the business of big about as long as it's been a business ... film spectacle works more or less the same now as it did in 1912 ... spectacle didn't just enthral audiences; it was instrumental to the very development of feature filmmaking as directors learned how to make longer running entertainments' (2007). With this in mind we might want to look back to the work of filmmakers such as Abel Gance, most famous for *Napoleon* (1927) and *J'Accuse* (1938). In a piece for *Senses of Cinema*, Peter Hourigan cites a comment made by Gance about his own understanding of what might partly constitute the movie aesthetic: 'Is movement not, in fact, drama? Movement, in art, is rhythm. The possibility of inventing new rhythms, of encapsulating the rhythms of life, of intensifying them and varying them infinitely, becomes, at a given moment, the essential problem for cinematographic techniques. I think I resolved this by inventing what has since been called rapid montage...' (2009).

Being admittedly broad at this point, we can say that Cameron's movies construct meanings around representations of the human body; the appropriation of elements present in the narrative of the American frontier and the relationships between human-kind and technology. In her book *Screening Space: The American Science Fiction Film*, Vivian Sobchack writes that 'on the surface a case can certainly be made that the SF film developed out of the traditional horror film, that it *is* the horror film sufficiently "technologized" to suit the demands for "modern" horror from an increasingly pragmatic and materialistic audience' (2001: 29). Sobchack's clarification serves to furnish us with a way of approaching Cameron's work as a fusion of the genres of science fiction and horror.

Contextually, his production processes have increasingly moved away from being centred around film as photography to what we might think of more productively as 'screen media', in which the end product does not emphasise the authenticity of the photograph, an idea which has underpinned movies to date. With *Avatar*, Cameron has moved significantly into the fusion of photography and digital imaging that, we might propose, is akin to painting. You do not have to be 'in front' of a subject in order to paint it as you would do if you wished to photograph it. Certainly, though, even the integrity of the photographic image has been ameliorated over the last two decades. Photoshop software has contributed massively to 'our' sense of how a photographic image can be manipulated with increasing subtlety and more variety than traditional photographic processing would have allowed. That sense of the elasticity of image making is key to Cameron's film production processes and to some sense of him as an engineer of particularly vivid, intricate and spectacularly scaled illusions; given that all cinema is illusion.

Considering the Contemporary Blockbuster
As we have noted, 1984 was the year in which Cameron's second feature film, *The Terminator*, was released. At the risk of sounding facile it was the 'right' year for such a movie to have been released, as we will explore later. The film was a commercial and critical breakthrough for Cameron and initiated all ongoing considerations of him as an auteur. In terms of the emerging construction of a filmmaking identity, the popular press keenly latched onto the scale of his projects. This began to manifest itself with *The Abyss*. Here, though, is how the magazine *Entertainment Weekly*, in a piece by Anne Thompson entitled '5 True Lies About James Cameron', wrote about him at the time of the original release of his movie *True Lies* (1994):

> *True Lies* made $25.9 million on its opening weekend and should easily top the traditional golden box office mark of $100 million. But James Cameron has never been traditional, and after spending more than most movies ever hope to earn in order to create a fitting successor to 1991's *Terminator 2: Judgment Day*, he knows the stakes are higher for both his reputation and the film's profitability. *True Lies*, a 2-hour-and-21-minute, computer-enhanced action comedy, isn't just designed to wow viewers and thump the competition; it's also meant to cement Cameron's identity as a fearless and free-spending ultra-macho perfectionist. But if the film doesn't get close to the $200 million mark, his cover is blown. (1994)

With each film that Cameron has subsequently made, he has embellished his directorial and writing persona, presenting himself as a filmmaker committed to the fusion of traditional human-interest drama with the demands of creating visually spectacular illusions in the tradition of the event movie. Robert Zemeckis, a filmmaking contemporary of Cameron, has commented that *all* cinema is a special effect, noting that even the most unadorned close-up of a human face is a process of illusion-making.

But the event movie presents audiences with the most elaborate of artifices. In a piece originally published in *Sight and Sound*, Larry Gross discussed the event movie by explaining that 'the reason that a simple knee-jerk condemnation of the Big Loud Action Movie today is unsound is that some of the greatest films in cinema history – from *Napoleon* to *2001* – overlap and interweave in their aspirations and in their formal procedures with the Big Loud Action Movies – this corporatized crap – that Hollywood makes today' (2000: 3). Indeed, Gross has identified David Lean as an antecedent of the contemporary event movie and, appropriately, Cameron's *Avatar* would be discussed in terms of its scale and creative affinity with Lean's *Lawrence of Arabia* (1962). It is useful here to parse the history and aesthetic qualities of the form and to recognise how they relate to the increased globalisation of the Hollywood film through the facility of technology and distribution. Let us note, though, that the event movie is not a new kind of film. We have only to look back at *Intolerance* (1916) and *The Jazz Singer* (1927) to cite two examples of relatively early cinema that offered their audiences spectacle, both visually and sonically. In her essay 'The Masculine Subject of Science Fiction in the 1980s Blockbuster Era', Christine Cornea comments that the emerging popularity of event movies during the 1970s and early 1980s 'all led to an exponential growth in profit returns surrounding certain films, increasingly coming from beyond the home market' (2007: 13). As such, blockbuster films have increasingly became multi-media, cross-platform events, and Cornea notes that 'a blockbuster ... is intended to appeal to a diverse national and international market' (ibid.). It is also appropriate to make the point that visual spectacle is easier to understand than psychological drama and so a certain kind of science fiction and fantasy film has become perfectly placed for this. Of cinematic spectacle Jose Arroyo has sketched out the derisory attitude often adopted towards it, writing that 'Hollywood cinema as exemplified by the action/spectacle mode of the last two decades is widely seen as mass culture at its most crudely capitalistic: the selling of lowest-common-denominator highest-impact sensation with no other purpose than to facilitate the exchange of affect for cash' (2000: ix). Indeed, in her essay 'Size Does Matter' Alexandra Keller notes that 'What *Titanic* appears to put on offer for the spectator's consumption as image is a counterpoint version of history – history as spectacle' (1999: 143).

Noting the schism that now exists between 'event movies' and more modestly realised films (and connecting Cameron's past with his present), Mark Bould, in his book about the director's contemporary John Sayles, has noted that 'Cameron's films exemplify the tendency in American filmmaking in which originality and innovation have been relegated to the status of technical issues in the production of startling spectacle. In contrast, Sayles has produced a body of work in which character, dialogue and performance are central and special effects are as cheap as they are rare' (2009: 23). The films that Cameron has directed and written are blockbuster films with their own aesthetic and an emphasis on the 'pleasures' of kinetic and sensory qualities. As such, perhaps they are sometimes closer to ballet and dance than to 'traditional' drama; indeed, perhaps they are more inherently cinematic. Geoff King has noted that the blockbuster constructs an illusory world in which 'everything is larger than life; not real but hyper real' (2000: 1). It is a quality that we might also associate with the intense rush of physical sensation, pleasant or otherwise, to be found in taking a rollercoaster ride. We can reasonably say that many of the audiences for Cameron's films (whether going because it is one of 'his' films or otherwise) will be familiar with such fairground attractions. Certainly, there is an understanding that theme-park rides draw on particular conventions derived from the 'classical' construction of narratives. Janet Abrams has noted of the integration of theme-park ride experience and cinema as 'the Freudian dream of flight has been accomplished as a purely optical experience' (2000: 107). Abrams goes on to say that popularity of theme-park rides, rendered through cinematic devices (notably 'Back to the Future: The Ride') that 'the overwhelming popularity of this ride suggests an augmented public appetite for the experience of speed itself, as visceral commodity, and for thrill without threat of personal danger' (ibid.). Is it that our increasingly static working and domestic lives require a counterpoint: the experience of movement, perhaps prompting a reconnection to a 'fading' and ordinary inclusion of physical movement at speed in our lives. Have we dis-abled ourselves? Folding special effects guru Douglas Trumbull's work in 'ride-films' back into our sense of cinema, it is appropriate to refer to his understanding here. Trumbull has said that 'there's a tremendous appetite for altered states ... the potential [for filmmakers and theme-park rides] to offer profound transformational experiences ... to modify the way people feel and behave' (quoted in Abrams 2000: 110).

Narrative and spectacle, then, are not necessarily mutually exclusive, even in a blockbuster. Geoff King has observed that the mode of the blockbuster has *not* eliminated narrative as much mainstream film reviewing might wish to suggest, but instead that these films offer a 'new' kind of narrative experience that, whilst it might be less coherent than before, *does* invest the action sequences with the requirement to carry meaning (2000: 2). Developing this sense of spectacle and cinema, in his essay 'Art, Image and Spectacle in High Concept Cinema', Bruce Isaacs explains:

> There is for Cameron something elemental in cinema that engages with the first principle of the medium itself, the technological formulation of the image. It is perhaps why Cameron begins his auteurist romance with cinema via the medium of the science fiction genre, which, he appreciates, inscribes into its generic criteria a fascination with its promethean desire to makeover the visual (and aural) image. (2011: 92)

In relation to Cameron's cinema particularly, *Titanic* and *Avatar* work most rigorously to refashion the inherent qualities of cinema.

In an interview during promotional activity in 1986 for his third feature as writer-director, *Aliens*, Cameron commented to Randy L'Officier: 'Being a visual person, I work backwards from the imagery that I like. The logic of a scene, I believe, is secondary to the enjoyment of it' (1986). This emphasis that Cameron recognises as the sensory pleasures of film, or the event of watching, on what we might consider its graphic capacities rather than its dramatic potential, underscores each of Cameron's films and might prompt us to consider Tom Gunning's reflections on early cinema as a cinema of attractions:

> The early history of cinema, like the history of cinema generally, has been written about and theorized under the hegemony of narrative films... Although such approaches are not totally misguided, they are one-sided, and potentially distort both the work of filmmakers (like the Lumière Brothers, August and Louis, and Georges Méliès) and the actual forces shaping cinema before 1906 ... early cinema was not dominated by the narrative impulse that later exerted its sway over the medium... (1986a: 64)

Indeed, it is tempting to wonder what a silent film by Cameron would be like. Certainly, in each of the feature films he has written and directed there are traces of the silent film/action cinema aesthetic. It is the sensibility that defines what has been dubbed 'the cinema of attractions' that predates the realisation and experimentation with ways of integrating narrative structures that were partly rooted in the literary traditions of character-orientated plot and realistic, psychological motivation of main characters. As film evolved into narrative forms there was also the recognition of what a filmmaker could achieve in terms of manipulating time, notably in terms of structuring narratives around parallel action, implying two separate events occurring simultaneously.

Cameron's comment about his own aesthetic sensibility, then, perhaps prompts a connection with the 'graphic' non-narrative interests of the *Star Wars* filmmaker, George Lucas. Like Lucas, Cameron has significantly influenced what studios and audiences understand as cinema's potential in terms of mainstream science fiction and fantasy. Like Lucas, to some degree, Cameron has primarily made feature films from his own original screenplays; typically *not* adapting an existing novel or similar. When he *has* made sequels it has been to films that themselves were produced exclusively for the screen and that had not existed as novels or otherwise previously.

Whilst Cameron's movies tend towards the traditional generic ideological positions constructed by Hollywood cinema, several of his films do offer instances where the film text counterpoints dominant modes of representation of the female and of physical disability. Each of his films since *The Terminator* have all been debated in terms of their potentially encouraging, and potentially discouraging, representations of the female.

On the subject of *The Terminator*, Douglas Kellner and Michael Ryan have commented:

> The triumph of conservatism made itself particularly felt in the fantasy genre, in large part because the sorts of representational dynamics afforded by fantasy were peculiarly well suited to the psychological principles of the new conservatism... In such major fantasy genres of the period as technophobic films and dystopia, a struggle between right-wing and left-wing uses of the fantasy movie is evident... If conservative filmmakers used the motifs of technology and dystopia to project terrifying images of collectivization and modernity, liberals and radicals used them to launch covert attacks against the conservative ideals of capitalism and patriarchy... Fantasy films concerning fears of machines and of technology usually negatively affirm such social values as freedom, individualism and the family... Future films on the right dramatize contemporary conservative fears of 'terrorism' or 'socialism' or liberalism' (e.g. *Logan's Run* or *Escape from New York*) ... Left films (*Blade Runner*, *Outland*) take advantage of the rhetorical mode of temporal displacement to criticize the current inequalities of capitalism. (2004: 48, 53)

In terms of the context in which Cameron emerged as a writer and director within the Hollywood mode of production, it is useful to cite Robin Wood's influential criticism. Wood has said of the cinema of the late 1960s, which provided a context in which Hollywood cinema evolved (and to which Cameron was responding particularly), that 'the central theme of American cinema has been, increasingly, disintegration and breakdown' (1986: 28).

The action movie format in which Cameron has worked, and for which he has arguably enriched and developed the mass market reputation and recognition, holds a kinship with the silent film as described by David Bordwell in his comment that 'spatial configurations are motivated by realism ... the use of technique must be inimically motivated to the character's interactions' (1985: 19).

In Cameron's films we have a body of work that evolves and finds its place in the tradition of the *visual* where photography, optically-generated, and now digitally-generated, elements merge. In early twenty-first-century cinema images have the potential to almost 'seamlessly' fuse the photographed with the drawn or 'painted'. Jean-Pierre Geuens has noted that

> a scene that required an improbable camera position would also benefit from graphic action and various kinds of pyrotechnics, traditional or otherwise – all situations that incidentally also showed up best on the monitors. ... Whereas it is unlikely that the cinema of Bergman would have significantly benefited from the use of video assist, that of Cameron or Zemeckis makes little sense without it. In this type of filmmaking, in fact, the device itself is no more than an advanced representative of other, more intensive technologies that later on enhance the surface appeal of the film in postproduction. (1996)

This project of engaging with the potential in fusing 'old' and 'new' media, in order to construct an illusion, is key to Cameron's modus operandi. He is engineering images. In a touchstone essay, entitled 'True Lies' (after the Cameron film), and which was written at the time in which digital visual-effects and the enhancement of live-action photography by images rendered using computer software, Stephen Prince posed the fundamental question: 'What are the implications of computer generated imagery for representation in cinema?' (1996: 49). For Prince, the concept of 'perceptual realism' is key, that realism as a matter of perception is just as important as realism as a matter of reference. How interesting that Prince grapples with the impact of computer-generated images (characters, human and otherwise) and environments. To quote Cameron again, in December 2011 at a filmed interview at BAFTA in London: 'It's meaningless now' (2011). The 'it' that Cameron refers to was the established trust that filmmakers *and* audiences had in the reciprocity between realism (and its claim to truth) and photography, both still and moving. Cameron's sense of the direction of cinema extends Andre Bazin's 'What is Cinema?' interrogation. This performance-capture approach prompted questions about an actor's performance and how digital technology was a potential 'threat' to it. Cameron objected to the lack of recognition for *Avatar*'s actors (particularly at awards time). Responding to these performances, film historian Kristin Thompson wrote: 'In some sense it may be true that the performance is preserved, but once the film runs through the theatre projector, can the audience really tell what that "template" was like? I think not, and that's why there's a reluctance to nominate these actors... Take the widely circulated image of [actress] Saldana juxtaposed with Neytiri. There are numerous differences... The effectiveness of Neytiri's snarl (for example) has a lot to do with the fact that she has been given exaggeratedly canine teeth' (2010).

In December 2009, both Zemeckis and Cameron had their latest films on general cinema release: *A Christmas Carol* and *Avatar* respectively. Each secured significant media interest, typically centred around the qualities of visual spectacle that characterised each title, both of which extensively featured the motion-capture technique. Where *Avatar* was photoreal, Zemeckis's films opted for a more painterly visual design. At the time of the films' release, Rick Carter, production designer on *Avatar* (and who has worked extensively with Zemeckis since the late 1980s) noted in an interview with the *LA Times*, that the connection between Cameron and Zemeckis is on 'the Lennon-McCartney level. Look how healthy that competition was … there's a tremendous awareness of what the other is doing' (2009). The films of Cameron and Zemeckis, then, offer more than 'only' spectacle. If spectacle was the only reason people watched films then, to borrow from Bordwell's line of thinking, why not just delete the non-'action' sections and release them at probably around 45-minutes duration?

In describing and understanding Cameron as a director who actively and explicitly integrates visual effects into his actor-centred films, we can look to the examples of George Méliès and others as 'visual effects' filmmakers who form a tradition within which Cameron and his colleagues belong. When Martin Scorsese, a director of global recognition bolstered by the concept of the 'auteur', was promoting his Méliès-centric movie *Hugo* (2011), Cameron was involved in a conversation about the visual spectacle of 3D (he has become something of an advocate and validating voice for the use of 3D). Certainly, we might think of Méliès and others as being constructed as 'wizards' in their own terms and in terms of film and pop culture discourse around them, and it is interesting to remind ourselves that the term 'visual effects wizards' implies a number of values and relationships. In her study of visual effects production, aesthetics and culture, Michele Pierson has written of discourses around visual effects as being 'a culture of effects connoisseurship' (2002: 3).

Of Méliès's films, and by extension, the activity of producing visual effects, Linda Williams has suggested that 'his magic makes women disappear but that often in the process this image acts out as a drama of male envy of the female procreative power, "giving birth" to all manner of animals and objects' (1991: 65). Williams' analysis chimes somewhat with the tirade that Sarah Connor launches at Miles Dyson when she holds him hostage at his home in *Terminator 2: Judgement Day*.

Cameron and Genre
As a filmmaker working with the Hollywood studio system, through which he has asserted a significant degree of creative freedom, Cameron works within the limits and with the possibilities of genre and the expectations that come with those categorisations. These are expectations that function in terms of the audience but also in terms of the 'studios' themselves, by which we mean the executives who finance and commission projects. His work has been particularly synonymous with the genres of science fiction and the war film and within these classifications there is an almost inevitable 'bleeding' between forms. Hence, the science fiction of *Aliens* will integrate elements of the horror movie genre. *True Lies*, by contrast, allies a thriller template with the demands of a romantic comedy. In all cases, the engagement with genre, consciously or otherwise on the part of the filmmaker, is in part a process of navi-

gating ideological awareness and frames of reference across many of the 'big' narratives. Hence, the meaning of science, of true love, of civilisation, of nationhood all get a creative treatment in Cameron's films. Broadly speaking, his work can be engaged with as war movies, thrillers, science fiction, horror and romances, and, as such, they confidently assert the fluidity of genre. Of this fluidity, Rick Altman has said, 'that a new genre should be born in an expanding culture hardly provides cause for surprise' (1999: 5).

Cameron's films, then, are situated deep within the mode of the mainstream, narrative-fiction film, a form powerfully entwined with the broader range of American narratives, and the cyclical process of the cultural construction and national identity. Writing about national identity, Chris Barker has explained that 'nations are not just political formations. They are also systems of cultural representation' (2008: 252).

Perhaps one of, if not *the* most, surprising aspects of Cameron's films are partly characterised by their identity as stories about romantic love. In the context of the term 'romance' we can look also to the concept of romance inherited from literary tradition, moving from chivalric romance through to the romantic comedy of Shakespeare and on to the mode of the melodrama. Of the evolution of the love story genre in Hollywood cinema, much has been written about the romantic comedy. Surprisingly, perhaps, less energy has been devoted to the romantic drama. That said, we are not without a steer in terms of how the genre has developed. In her essay 'Depicting Love in Cinema', Erica Todd has noted that we read that the love story (about either romantic or companionate love) as in companionship, typically without a sexual element, can be distinctly considered in terms of narratives about passionate love and that such films connect to the more widely 'understood' modes of the romantic-comedy genre: 'Through the depiction of a romantic couple's passionate experiences, common traits like nostalgia, memory and the use of exotic locations recur. Successful films in this group often borrow elements from other genres, which can complicate the classification of the romantic drama genre' (2013: 12). Certainly, Cameron's films explore passionate love, most notably in the 'young love' of *Titanic* but also essential to *Avatar*, *The Abyss* and *The Terminator*.

As of this writing a deluge of Hollywood-studio produced science fiction films have recently been released: *Cloud Atlas* (Tom Tykwer, Andy Wachowski, Lana Wachowski, 2012), *Oblivion* (Joseph Kosinski, 2013), *Elysium* (Neil Blomkamp, 2013), *Gravity* (Alfonso Cuaron, 2013) and *Jupiter Ascending* (Andy and Lana Wachowski, 2015). To perhaps recognise the shift (driven by commercial inclination) one has only to look at the mainstream reception to the genre commercial hits in the 1970s and 1980s.

James Cameron can be situated alongside Tim Burton, Guillermo del Toro and Peter Jackson as the commercially popular fabulists of our current time. We might also include the writer-directors Alfonso Cuarón and Brad Bird in this grouping on account of the films *Gravity* and *The Incredibles* (2004), respectively. Steven Spielberg continues to feature prominently in this but belongs to an earlier generation. Significantly, though, Spielberg has continued to fascinate with the diversity of genres he has worked in; in 1993 he released *Jurassic Park* and *Schindler's List* and, more recently, in the space of twelve months released *The Adventures of Tintin: The Secret of the Unicorn*

(2011), *War Horse* (2011) and *Lincoln* (2012). Intriguingly, Cameron has spoken of how he might have adapted Michael Crichton's *Jurassic Park* novel (1990): 'But when I saw the film, I realized that I was not the right person to make the film, he was. Because he made a dinosaur movie for kids, and mine would have been *Aliens* with dinosaurs, and that wouldn't have been fair' (2012b).

Cameron, whilst part of the wave of filmmakers that followed Spielberg and Lucas and their early 1970s emergence, is often grouped with these two 'figureheads' of popular American fantasy filmmaking on account of all three men making films often set within overtly fantastical worlds and scenarios. However, there are two other directors who also established their respective identities in the early and mid-1970s and with whom we might propose Cameron has a particular alignment: John Carpenter and John Milius.

After his time working in visual effects production at New World Pictures, Cameron served as a visual effects supervisor on Carpenter's *Escape from New York* (1981) and it is this film that so potently informs the taut, urban thriller/science fiction form of *The Terminator*. *Escape from New York* was accordingly marketed on its original theatrical release with the proprietary credit 'John Carpenter's *Escape from New York*'. Carpenter had established a profile as a director whose earlier films – *Dark Star* (1974), *Halloween* (1978), *The Fog* (1980) – applied fantasy, science fiction and horror modes in hybrid forms to produce fantastical movies that were unsettling rather than comforting and pleasing. Of Carpenter's work, the film critic Kent Jones wrote that 'America doesn't have so many great directors to spare that it can afford to let John Carpenter fall through the cracks ... how did he come to be so marginalised?' (1999). In the *Wallflower Press Critical Guide to Contemporary North American Filmmakers* Hugh Perry describes Carpenter as having 'made his mark with a succession of horrors and thrillers that, while often breaking new ground, never stray from schlock value, camp and perhaps teenage-boy wish fulfilment' (2001: 71). Carpenter, then, serves as a useful reference point for the films that Cameron has written, directed and produced.

Ian Conrich and David Woods have written about the distinctions of Carpenter's movies and, to some degree, we can see the implicit connection here with what Cameron's films and their production contexts have been defined by: 'Of those North American filmmakers most associated with the horror new wave – David Cronenberg, Tobe Hooper, John Landis, Joe Dante, George A. Romero – Carpenter is arguably the one who has persisted most successfully in making mainstream horror or fantasy or science fiction films ... Carpenter uses genre to provide a kind of narrative "shorthand" that contributes to the impressive economy of his films' (2004: 3). Barry Keith Grant, in writing about Carpenter, implicitly suggests connections we could make with Cameron, saying that 'Carpenter has had a profound effect upon the genres from which he borrows. In the 1980s, along with Walter Hill, he was instrumental in the development of the new action film, as distinct from the traditional adventure of disaster film ... Like Hawks, Carpenter relies on action as a primary means of developing character and assessing moral worth' (2004: 11). Similarly, Cameron's protagonists are given expression, to some great degree, through action, from an athletic leap to a concerned glance.

Historically, Carpenter's challenge appears to have been finding a balance between satisfying a studio's commercial imperatives and needs with his own creative urges and this tension has been well documented, especially in a range of 1980s magazine publications. With just a couple of exceptions, Carpenter has remained committed to directing genre films rather than prestige subjects that might then be marketed as event movies. With the exception of *Titanic*, we might make the same claim for Cameron. Carpenter's budgets, though, have been notably smaller than those afforded to Cameron. For Carpenter, his commercial profile was waning and in crisis at the very moment that Cameron's was in the ascendant. By 1984 Carpenter had experienced the commercial failure of his remake of *The Thing* (1982) and then of the SF-romance *Starman* (1984). In 1986, in the same summer that Cameron's *Aliens* was released, Carpenter's *Big Trouble in Little China* was yet another commercial disappointment. Although the reputations of these Carpenter films has risen across the passing of time, each firmly rooted in generic tropes, forms and ideologies, at the moment of their original theatrical release they were commercially unpopular, perhaps too esoteric for the mainstream. Certainly these films did not conclude with a comforting sense of wellbeing or hopefulness.

Unlike Cameron, both Carpenter and John Milius were graduates of the USC film school, albeit graduating from different cohorts. A contemporary of Lucas and Spielberg, Milius's name remains much less widely recognised than that of his classmates. He contributed dialogue to the screenplay for *Dirty Harry* (Don Siegel, 1971), *The Life and Times of Judge Roy Bean* (John Huston, 1972), *Jeremiah Johnson* (Sydney Pollack, 1974) and *Apocalypse Now* (Francis Ford Coppola, 1979), amongst other commissions, and wrote and directed *Dillinger* (1973), *Big Wednesday* (1978) and *Conan the Barbarian* (1982). The narrative interests of Milius's work can be understood to have a connection with Cameron's in terms of the emphasis on men and women of action and the image of the wilderness as a crucible for drama. With the studio-financed productions *Big Wednesday* and *Conan the Barbarian*, Milius created sequences that delight in the human body in heroic motion. Where Milius's work is politically reactionary in its perspective on a subject and its modes of representation, Cameron's films combine the reactionary and the progressive. Staying momentarily with *Big Wednesday*, its focus on a surfing fraternity relates to the Cameron-produced thriller *Point Break* (Kathryn Bigelow, 1990).

Of his own working process, and his particularly vivid construction of a filmmaker persona, Milius has said 'I became a loner. I became a mountain man. A lot of those things are very good qualities and they help you do your work, help you be singular and keep the artistic integrity of your work intact, but they don't make it very easy to live your life' (quoted in Coehlho 2010). Milius has become the subject of a recent documentary film, *Milius* (Zak Knutson and Joey Figueroa, 2013), that explores his career trajectory and goes some way to suggesting how his reactionary politics were somewhat at odds with Hollywood's generally more liberal disposition.

It is for his films specifically, though, that Milius is a valid frame of reference in helping us understand the kind of sensibility that Cameron was 'inheriting' in terms of particular approaches to film genre in the 1970s and 1980s. His emphasis on the atavistic chimes with Cameron's creative sensibility. In Milius's cinema, as writer/director, we watch narratives focused on men of action who engage with the wild: in *The Wind and the Lion* (1975) we are offered representations of both the American and Middle Eastern wilderness; in *Big Wednesday*, a Vietnam-era movie in its setting, we see the wilderness of the Pacific Ocean as a place in which young men define themselves; in the later *Farewell to the King* (1989), we see the wilderness of a tropical jungle function as a place in which a white man tests his ego, just as it does in the Milius scripted *Apocalypse Now*. This wilderness/people relationship similarly informs most of Cameron's movies, notably *The Abyss*, *Titanic* and *Avatar*, and accentuates his self-aware, mythologically-informed poetics. Cameron's films thus offer an evolution of the kinds of themes that Milius explored around wilderness and identity: a set of concerns with a particularly American narrative tradition reaching back to sixteenth-century literature about contact with the native communities of what became named America (after Amerigo Vespucci). Cameron's films have refracted atavisitic concerns, expressed through the prism of science fiction and fantasy modes rather than the more specifically historical moments (with the exception of *Titanic*) that Milius's films adopt. His *The Wind and the Lion* dramatises President Teddy Roosevelt's engagement with the Middle East. Reflecting on this project, Milius has commented that 'the Marines like it a great deal and I like the scene where he [Roosevelt] talks about the bear' (2009). For Milius, his films have typically given expression to a conservative, ultra-traditional perspective, with an idolisation of the military presented in narratives about self-discipline, honouring lines of command (the status quo) and the expression of an atavistic sensibility. In *Conan the Barbarian*, Milius adapted Robert E. Howard's source material about the titular hero Conan who endures the archetypal challenges of body and soul in vanquishing an evil tyrant. In *Red Dawn* (1984), American teenagers respond in a violent and aggressive fashion to a Russian invasion of the American West and in *Farewell to the King*, adapted from the novel by Pierre Schoendoerffer, the drama centres around a white man, who, having established himself as the leader of a jungle tribe, does not want to return to the 'civilised' world of mainstream white culture. Of Milius's work for the film that became *Apocalypse Now*, Brooks Riley has noted that

> Milius seems to have had his own preoccupation with *Heart of Darkness*, which had more to do with his identification with and of Kurtz as a 'rotting god' and 'legend to a primitive culture'. Combining his own professed desire to 'lord it over the monkeys' with his apolitical obsession with war as the ultimate expression of 'man's inherent bestiality', Milius fashioned a script that structured itself in general terms after the Conrad work, but which incorporated many references to his own interests. These were represented most clearly by Kilgore (named Kharnage in the first draft), a surfing major whose own godlike resistance to fear is matched only by his Patton-like lust for napalm's 'smell of victory'. The Kilgore section of the original draft, though appropriately shortened by a few pages, stands otherwise untouched and remains the most recognizably Milius element in the final film. (2014)

Film Authorship and James Cameron
In 2009, whilst promoting his independently produced, and rather beautiful, feature film *Tetro*, the American writer/director Francis Ford Coppola spoke about the popular image of filmmaking that has been constructed, representing it as an experience centred around the image and activity of the romantic and independent artist struggling to create personal work that has the capacity to counterpoint the commercial imperatives of the major film studios who want some certainty in their financial gambles. Coppola, whose career narrative has been emblematic of the tensions and opportunities for 'artist filmmakers' within the mainstream film industry, observed: 'I think, yes, when you write something, especially something personal and something that you've actually experienced or been involved with characters or people who are people you love, when you write it you tend to be all the characters in it' (quoted in Bochenski 2010). In saying this, Coppola spotlighted the continuing allure and power of the concept of the film author as being able to assert an element of autobiography in a project. The tension between the demands of the mass-market film and the pursuit of the personal is especially interesting and, when achieved, can be startling: *The Conversation* (Francis Ford Coppola, 1972), *American Graffiti* (George Lucas, 1973) and *Taxi Driver* (Martin Scorsese, 1976) are just three cases in point that partly formed the tapestry of popular American filmmaking in the 1970s that Cameron would surely have recognised.

The concept of film authorship, then, has embedded itself in film culture as perhaps still the most prominent approach to adopt in the 'reading' of a film; in a reading of the interest of cinema as an expressive form. Cameron and Twentieth Century Fox, who have in part or wholly financed his movies (with the exception of *The Terminator* diptych), have embraced this concept for creative and commercial ends. However, authorship is a much-contested issue given, in significant part, the collaborative production processes of popular filmmaking. The concept of film authorship has come a long way since its second wave of formulation in the 1950s, having first found expression in Russia and Britain in the early twentieth century, morphing from being a relatively obscure scholarly term to now standing as a marketing device and branding tool. Hence, *James Cameron's Avatar* – a proprietary credit attributable to the commercial success of *Titanic*. The auteur term is complex as it forms a tension between the idea of the creative individual and the collaborative process of filmmaking. We might propose that in our current moment the presence of the director as 'author' is less important to the culture of film discourse, but the cult of recognising the director as progenitor of a film's meaning and value continues to hold allure as it humanises a very technical and industrial process.

Cameron has placed himself confidently within the auteurist frame, as we understand it, since his second feature film *The Terminator*. His directing and screenwriting career was established and developed within the era of the so-called 'high concept' film. This term is of contested origin; it may have been coined by the American TV executive Barry Diller in the early 1970s in response to network demands for TV spots that run no more than thirty seconds in duration so that a 'narrative' would have to be simplistic enough to be communicated and used across a range of marketing materials and outlets. Alternatively, according to Jeffrey Katzenberg (previously, head of Paramount, then Disney and now of DreamWorks Animation), and related by Justin Wyatt in his book *High Concept*, Michael Eisner coined the term during his tenure as CEO at Paramount during the early 1980s. Whoever we might attribute the origin of the term to, the concept remains the same: brevity of story description has established itself as central to the promotion and selling of the mass-market media product: 'The larger structural changes within the industry – such as conglomeration, the development of new technologies, and the rise in marketing and merchandising – operate to privilege films which can be sold and summarised in a single sentence' (Wyatt 1994: 18).

As writer, director and producer (sometimes taking all three roles on a project), Cameron fulfils the archetypal construction and image of a film author operating in the context of the 1980s popular American film, which partly inherited some of the tendencies of the New Wave of the 1970s. Of the Hollywood movies of the 1980s, Bordwell has observed in his essay 'It's the 80s, stupid' that

> You can make a good case that the 1980s gave America a burst of first-rate films and remarkable new talent. ... The era saw a revival of ambitious independent films, which played alongside program pictures, Oscar bait, and summer blockbusters. Romantic comedy, action movies, and science fiction enjoyed a strong run. ... The 1980s kept genres firmly at the center of Hollywood. Instead of working against genre conventions, as many Movie Brats had done (not all; remember Bogdanovich), many of the most talented 1980s directors found ways to do what they wanted in and through genres. In this sense, they were more like Hawks and Ford and other classical filmmakers. The 'personal' mainstream film wasn't a contradiction in terms. (2008)

The concept of authorship in relation to film producers in American popular cinema is reinforced by the example of Cameron's work and we might also look to the examples of also David O. Selznick, George Lucas, Julia Phillips, Jerry Bruckheimer and Roger Corman as reinforcing the producer's creative centrality to a project offering a signature style that becomes meaningful to the audience beyond the identity of the director. Consider the importance of Cameron's name as producer of *Strange Days* and his above-the-title credits as executive producer on the documentary *Exodus Decoded* (2006) for America's History Channel and for the action thriller *Sanctum* (Alister Grierson, 2011).

From the beginning of his work as a film director, Cameron, then, moved towards working in the popular, genre-based Hollywood film industry at a time when the generation of filmmakers who came to prominence in the early 1970s had moved to a position of commercial and critical viability. His contemporaries energised fantasy filmmaking in the early and mid-1980s: Robert Zemeckis directed *Romancing the Stone* (1984) and *Back to the Future* (1985); Tim Burton directed *Beetlejuice* (1988) and *Batman* (1989); Ron Howard directed *Splash* (1984) and *Cocoon* (1985); Kathryn Bigelow directed the stark vampire movie *Near Dark* (1987). Indeed, Bigelow's was the most non-mainstream title of this 'wave' and her breakthrough film perhaps had more in common with a title like *The Terminator*. Bigelow and Cameron (who were later married for a short period) would go on to collaborate on *Point Break* and *Strange Days*. This cluster of writer/directors had backgrounds in film school (Howard and Zemeckis both attending USC) and art college (Bigelow). Burton had trained at Disney's Cal Arts institution as an animator before working in the Disney animation studio. Cameron, then, was the anomaly, having not been formally educated in film-making practice.

Cameron's *The Abyss, Terminator 2: Judgement Day, Titanic* and *Avatar* all invested significant amounts of their pre-release publicity in the narrative and identity of Cameron as world-builder and inventor; as being someone involved in not 'only' telling a story but also, and maybe more importantly, developing and pushing the capacity of technology in service of film. Walt Disney and George Lucas serve as similar frames of reference here, being constructed as filmmakers who have 'needed' to develop increasingly sophisticated technology in order to serve the realisation of their 'visions'. The use here of the word *vision* is central as it evokes a sense of the unearthly (and spiritual perhaps) and of a kind of separateness from the ordinary person's perception of things, of something akin to the kind of sensibility William Blake embodied and which, even earlier, finds a formulation in Vasari's *Lives of the Artists*. In turn, the image and construction of the American inventors can be usefully applied too, by citing the particular example of the inventor and engineer Thomas Edison, popularly known as 'The Wizard of Menlo Park'. We can look, too, at the example of Pixar Animation studio in California and Peter Jackson's Weta visual effects studio in Wellington, New Zealand. Of Jackson, Kristin Thompson has written that

> the digital revolution occurred, and special effects technology reached a point where Jurassic dinosaurs or morphing Terminators could be convincingly portrayed on the screen. Sequels and series gave Hollywood some of its biggest hits as the age of the franchise film arrived. Peter Jackson, a New Zealand director known mainly to fans of low-budget splatter movies, decided that Tolkien's novel was the ideal way to indulge his passion for fantasy and special effects. (2007: 2)

In a neat full-circle, Cameron commissioned Weta to produce the performance capture and animation for *Avatar*.

A film such as *Terminator 2: Judgement Day* or *Avatar* involves hundreds of personnel hired across technical, administrative and 'creative' roles. In *Film as Film: Understanding and Judging Movies*, written long before the emerging confluence of moving photographs, illustration and painting, V. F. Perkins observes of the collaborative process of filmmaking that 'provided that a film has its own unity, it seems unimportant whether the unity was evolved through cooperation and compromise within the production team or conceived by one man and imposed on his collaborators' (1993: 173). The tension, then, partly resides in Hollywood's operation as an industrial, compartmentalised and departmentalised system of production comprised of crews led by a director (accountable to a producer) working towards what we might presume is a shared sense of what a given product needs to be in order for it to sell enough tickets/copies in order to return a profit on the original investment. Where does an individual sit within this as a writer/director/creative? In the early twenty-first century, this model is now being challenged by an alternative possibility of arrangement in which online distribution, dictated by the producer, is beginning to reconfigure the ways in which filmmakers as 'artists' reach their particular audiences.

Furthermore, the Romantic ideal of the questing individual seeking to present a view of the world remains alluring and entrenched in cultural discourse. Nigel Morris observes that the concept (and reality of) 'auteurism implies more than creative freedom' (2007: 101). Furthermore, we can connect this to Cameron's name having to some extent become synonymous with the evolution of digital visual effects and, more recently, 3D cinema. As such, his authorship is not only of 'meaning' but also of the integration of visual effects within the broader terrain of a given film: implying a distinction between photographed and optically- or digitally-generated elements. Michele Pierson notes that the way in which the pseudopod's 'creation' for *The Abyss* has been narrated in descriptions of the film's visual effects undertaking follows a well-established curve: 'Like all Hollywood creation stories, Cameron's is an adventure narrative' (2002: 48). This conception of the director as 'pioneering creative explorer' has a tradition. In cinema, D. W. Griffith, Abel Gance, David Lean, Jane Campion, Akira Kurosawa and Stanley Kubrick, amongst others, have all rendered themselves in the mode of film director as lone romantic, challenged by the commercial imperatives of mainstream filmmaking.

On 24 September 2010, the *Guardian* published a list of the 'most powerful' figures in commercial filmmaking and Cameron came in at number one. The list echoed the annual one published by now defunct magazine *Premiere*. In its listing, the *Guardian* emphasised the money that Cameron's films had made as justifying him as number one in the film industry. In *Titanic: Anatomy of a Blockbuster* the point is made by Justin Wyatt and Katherine Vlesmas that Cameron 'could be described as the fiscally responsible auteur. An auteur can exist inside the current studio system only by working within a commercially viable genre and a marketing-orientated project' (1999: 33).

Understanding Genre and the Hollywood Context of the 1970s and 1980s
In the Hollywood cinema of the 1980s (if defining film study within discrete 'decade' timeframes is of any value) genres that were of particular commercial appeal included urban comedies, fantasy and horror. Westerns and high fantasy movies – films set in entirely fictional, non-earthly worlds such as *Conan the Barbarian* and *The Dark Crystal* (Jim Henson, Frank Oz, 1982) – were relatively unpopular, although some of the generic structures of westerns found new voices in certain genres such as action/adventure. Fascinatingly, thirty years later, Zemeckis, Burton and Cameron are all entrenched as the popular filmmaking establishment and as proponents of the fusion of photographic live-action realism and the joys and pleasures of animation. These filmmakers are required to promote such films as 'revolutionary' in order to reinforce the sense of spectacle and Hollywood's long-held investment in novelty and showmanship. Ultimately, though, the fusion of forms is perhaps more *evolutionary* and the

combination of moving photographs with drawn and animated elements reaches back famously to *Gertie the Dinosaur* (Winsor McCay, 1914) and Walt Disney's own *Alice in Wonderland* short films (1923–27).

Furthermore, the action movie aesthetic and its foregrounding of male protagonists made a connection back to something longer-standing with regard to the construction of masculinity in fiction. Susan Hayward has written of the action movie:

> Let us pause on [the phrase] 'male swagger' for a moment. For, in this context, an action hero embodies the tradition of its earliest courtly meaning whereby it referred to the swank of knights and nobles who would carry this swagger into battle. For some of our modern action heroes the swagger begins in the verbal and ends in supremely cool action. (2012: 8)

That said, Cameron's films have both reinforced (*The Terminator*) and revised (*Titanic*) the image of the action hero and a sense of the masculine. This process has been bound up in the idea of the film star. Since *The Terminator*, Cameron's films have functioned as showcases for emerging film stars. Thomas Austin and Martin Barker have explored the 'phenomenon' of the director as film star and note that 'stars may resolve ideological tensions' (2003: 14) both within a film and outside of the film text. They make the further point that 'film stardom is intertextual: economic, technological, discursive' (2003: 25). In relation to *The Terminator* and *Titanic*, particularly, Austin and Barker observe that 'ideals of human attractiveness, grounded in the body and in particular the face that provides the referent for an indexical representation… are a common component of stardom' (2003: 27). In terms of Cameron's creative collaborations with two of the biggest stars he has worked with, namely Schwarzenegger and DiCaprio, both of these actors manifest very different, but very potent, kinds of physical attraction for audiences. Then, too, there is the often difficult to determine boundary between their star persona and the details of a characterisation that they bring to the screen.

In *Science Fiction Film,* J. P. Telotte makes the touchstone statement that one of the principal functions of science fiction is to 'remind' the audience, or indeed the reader, about what it is to be human (2001: 35) and certainly this fundamental preoccupation of the genre (be it in film, computer games, comic books or literature) plays out in Cameron's films. With a major and a minor exception (*Titanic* and *Piranha 2*), in doing so, his films have repeatedly dramatised and visualised our fascination with the capacity of technology to duplicate and elaborate on the human body and the concept of human life: from the avatar to the terminator. In her essay 'Human Cloning in Film: Horror, Ambivalence, Hope', Kate O'Riordan writes:

> Contemporary filmic images of cloning draw on the repertoires of hope established in factual genres. This naturalises the 'realism' of contemporary reporting on science establishing biomedical hope as the 'real' version of cloning. The discourse of biomedical health and regeneration that dominates figurings of human therapeutic cloning in other forms is reproduced in global media imaginaries through these films. (2009)

Cameron's films are all emphatically action movies. In part, action films function as constructions of masculinity presented within the context of tests of endurance and images of courage and the place of the body in action. This casts a light on Cameron as the writer of the initial drafts of *Rambo: First Blood Part II* (1982) that Sylvester Stallone then rewrote. Of Cameron's draft of the screenplay, Stallone observed in an interview with film fan-site Aint-It-Cool-News to promote his new movie, *The Expendables* (2010) that 'it took nearly 30 to 40 pages to have any action initiated and Rambo was partnered with a tech-y sidekick. So it was more than just politics that were put into the script. There was also a simpler storyline' (2010).

Above and beyond their delight in spectacle and bodies in motion, action movies sell us on the idea of the tenacious, courageous man and woman apparently unsuited to the challenge at hand. As such, the action movie genre is a vessel for ideological expression; for the arrangement of characterisations, images and situations that construct and reflect back cultural norms and generally agreed upon patterns of behaviour and response. With a film such as *Rambo: First Blood Part II*, it's an interesting case-study in terms of how a film can be received by the wider culture and discoursed about in terms of representation and engagement and issues of 'taste' and impact on viewers.

Genre, then, belongs to the broader human tradition and practice of classifying information, of managing knowledge, ideas and expression in narrative. The term is rooted in literary studies and has been long established as a point of cultural interest. Hence, horror films might, beyond the surface scares, dramatise fears around consumerism or guilt. Then, too, there is the relationship between horror and the return of the repressed (event, person, emotion, trauma) that informs so many horror films.

Genre is thus fluid and develops a range of identities through time. It is not a fixed entity and a self-conscious sense of generic tradition and history characterises many genre films, particularly in the later stages of a genre's lifespan, before becoming parodied. Audience knowledge of cinema brings another level of reference and meaning to the viewing of a film. Genres have life cycles, moving through popularity to extinction to the finding of a new lease of life. The western concerns itself with wilderness and civilisation and the role of violence and race. Hayward notes that 'the term genre, then, does not refer just to film type but also to spectator expectation and hypothesis. It refers also to the role of specific institutional discourses that feed into and form generic structures' (2012: 182). Given the centrality of science fiction to Cameron's feature film work it is appropriate to sketch out the sustained interest of the genre for producers and audiences. Richard Hodgens observes: 'Science fiction involves extrapolated or fictitious use of scientific possibilities, or it may be simply fiction that takes place in the future or introduces some radical assumption about the present or the past'; he goes on to say that science fiction explores 'the technological and its potential for reshaping the human' (1999: 191, 193). In doing so, he returns us to the fundamental humanist interest of science fiction.

The science fiction genre has threaded its way through the entire history of cinema. The writer Jules Verne was credited with creating the *voyages imaginaire* and in late-1920s America science fiction flourished via magazines such as *Amazing Stories* and *Science Wonder Stories*. Subsequently, a vast range of science fiction and fantasy novels were published by writers including Edgar Rice Burroughs, Philip K. Dick, Lester Del Rey, Ray Bradbury, Isaac Asimov and E. L. 'Doc' Smith. In turn, this prose material subsequently informed a range of cinema science fiction.

Cameron's films, like so many popular American movies, dramatise the concept of heroism, and in doing so attest to a particular dimension of American national identity and mythopoesis. In considering Cameron's work as a product of the industrially organised Hollywood filmmaking system, and with a commitment to a very specific range of narrative constructions and ideologies anchored in the organising principle of genre and the mode of realism, we can identify the representation of a particular kind of North American identity as key. While Hollywood movies can be regarded as some version of America's national cinema, Cameron is Canadian and, as noted earlier, he approaches the USA with a sense of cultural distance. In his book *Regeneration Through Violence: The Mythology of the American Frontier, 1600–1860,* Richard Slotkin writes that 'the mythology of a nation is the intelligible mash of that enigma called "the national character"' (2000a: 3). Slotkin goes on to explain how 'a mythology is a complex of narratives that dramatizes the world vision and historical sense of a people or culture, reducing centuries of experience into a constellation of compelling metaphors' (2000a: 6). What Slotkin begins to grapple with here is narrative as allegory. Certainly, Cameron's films might be constructed, read, reviewed and re-constructed as allegories. *Avatar* arguably demonstrates most keenly Cameron's interest in allegory and the commercial and cultural appeal of such an approach. *The Terminator* and *Aliens* also function in allegorical ways. How do we define allegory, then, in relation to cinema? Ismail Xavier sets up a useful understanding, saying that 'in allegory the narrative texture places the spectator in an analytical posture in which he or she is facing a coded message that is referred to as an "other scene" and not directly given on the diegetic level. The spectator's willingness to decode finds anchorage when this "other scene" is signalised as human experience "in time"' (1999: 16). We might suggest that Cameron does so with particular singularity. As such, it is useful to offer a sense of the several-thousand-year-old tradition of what constitutes heroism. Angie Hobbs has delineated the qualities of heroism as described in various ancient world texts, particularly of ancient Greece. She has provided a delineation of the fundamental concept at hand, and in so doing, suggests for us a way into understanding part of the allure of a 'James Cameron Film' for audiences: 'courage involves both emotional commitment and evaluative belief, an intellectual and emotional appreciation of what things are worth taking risks for, and in what circumstances' (2000: 22).

In the pages that follow, then, our ambition is to unpack the potential reasons for, and resonances of, the popularity of James Cameron's films. Where do they inventively and vividly find the powerful connection between the traditions and conventions of genre cinema and aspects of situation and thinking that characterise daily life for so many of us living in a world of digital technology? Furthermore, what does Cameron's body of work do to spark our creative thinking about our place in a potentially 'posthuman' world and, by extension, what do his movies show us about the idea of heroism?

CHAPTER ONE

Genesis: From Short Film Visions to Low-Budget Monster Movie

Cameron's first film as writer and director was a short project entitled *Xenogenesis*, produced independently. His intention was to show the film to Hollywood studios to demonstrate his capacities as writer, director and, indeed, as visual effects artist. Ultimately, it did fulfil its purpose, serving as Cameron's calling card for entry into the low-budget film industry. The film, additionally, is of value in terms of its connection to Cameron's subsequent films. Rather like another science fiction short film, *THX 1138: Electronic Labyrinth* (George Lucas, 1966), Cameron's *Xenogenesis* is embryonic in its expression of the themes, situations, images and tonal qualities that the writer/director would go on to manifest in major studio feature films, announcing, particularly, the preoccupation with the concept of the post-human condition.

With an eleven-minute running time and shot in colour, *Xenogenesis* begins with a series of title cards identifying the names of the film's key production personnel. This title sequence is consistent with the tone of the credits in the opening title sequence of *The Terminator* as the 'computer styled' font clicks into life across the screen, accompanied by what might be a telephone ringtone, a sound that implies the importance of the electronic and technological. The relationship between humans and technology and of our relationship to natural wilderness and the simulation of the biological are subjects that each find expression in *Xenogenesis*. The title cards cut to the following: a brief sequence comprised of vivid painted images, clearly indicating the science fiction genre, which are shown via a series of camera tilts and pans. The first such image shows a human head being interfaced with electronic circuitry; it is an image that is both horrific and compelling, and it encapsulates the cyborg and avatar themes of Cameron's later films. There follows an illustration of a futurescape and subsequently an image of a man and woman in this futurescape. We then hear a sombre female voice-over explaining that 'They made him a machine – trained to deliver humanity from the final cataclysm. She was raised by a machine that knew the power of love. They searched a wilderness of space.' In the world of the film, xenogenesis is explained as 'ultimate adventure'. This voice-over is redolent of the sombre tone of Sarah Connor's in *Terminator 2: Judgement Day* and Jake Sully in *Avatar*. The voice-over in *Xenogenesis* presents us with the human/artifice opposition and synthesis that will underpin most of Cameron's films. Certainly, the adventure genre sensibility that characterises so much of his cinema is evident as early as *Xenogenesis*.

After the prologue, comprising a sequence of pans and tilts across a number of painted images depicting a futurescape and integration of humans with technology, the film then cuts to live-action material. We see the man in a yellow jumpsuit and wearing a hi-tech backpack running through what looks like a 'digital' terrain that anticipates that of *Tron* (Steven Lisberger, 1982) and possesses a sense of the vertiginous that we might recall from a key action scene in the original *Star Wars* film. The image is comprised of both live action and matte-painting elements; in essence an example of the virtual filmmaking that Cameron would extend the detail and photorealism of with *Avatar*. As the man runs, an immense robot, moving along on tank-like tracks, emerges from a wall and engages the protagonist in a cat-and-mouse chase across the narrow walkways over the 'cityscape'. This simple premise anticipates the cat-and-mouse narrative structure of both *The Terminator* and *Aliens*. In *Xenogenesis*, Cameron's organisation of space is rendered with precision and clarity and there is a sense of tension and jeopardy in the scenario. As the man flees, seeking to escape capture, a smaller spider-like robot emerges and there is a cut that takes us inside the vessel to show that it is being piloted by the woman referenced in the prologue. She has come to rescue her partner and pilots the robot using a telemetry device (in a scene anticipating the climaxes of *Aliens* and *Avatar*). She confronts the larger robot eventually immobilising the enemy machine. At one point, its tank-track wheels are framed in a shot that Cameron will repeat when showing the tanks in motion in the future war of *The Terminator*.

In due course *Xenogenesis* would lead to Cameron's employment at Roger Corman's New World production house, working there as an art director, before going on to contribute visual effects for *Battle Beyond the Stars*, a pastiche of the western genre-inflected success of *Star Wars*. *Battle Beyond the Stars* had a screenplay written by John Sayles, a genre-savvy director who went on to work primarily as a writer and director within the context of American independent cinema. His science fiction film *The Brother From Another Planet* (1984) makes an interesting analogue with *The Terminator*. That film had no obvious visual effects and was a contemporary, urban-set drama about an alien in our world, making his way through New York City. Of the film, Mark Bould has commented that its

> retreat from special effects is accompanied by a rejection of the frequently unreflexive imagery of cinematic science fiction. As the title of this film, its opening Afro-Caribbean music and our first glimpse of the Brother tells you, race will not

be displaced onto the figure of the alien. Racial difference will not be imagined as species difference but rather species difference as racial difference. (2009: 77)

Intriguingly, given the tangible differences between *The Brother From Another Planet* and Spielberg's *ET: The Extra-Terrestrial* (1982), Sayles and Spielberg had collaborated on the abandoned *Night Skies* feature film project in the early 1980s, with Sayles scripting for Spielberg to direct. This concept morphed into what became *ET*. Cameron would eventually write and direct two 'culture-contact' movies, in *The Abyss* and *Avatar*.

Staying with Cameron's earliest experience of working within the Hollywood film industry, it is important to recognise his contribution as a visual effects artist (responsible for matte paintings and also as director of photography on the film's visual effects elements) on the Carpenter film *Escape from New York*. This dystopian science fiction thriller, set in 1997, tells the story of Snake Plissken and his mission to rescue the American President whose plane has crashed in a New York that has become a walled prison of three million criminals who have been at war with the United States Police Force. The film's narrative propulsion certainly has an echo in Cameron's first major film *The Terminator* and in terms of generic possibilities for social comment there is a shared sensibility about a future war and a pervasive sense of cultural apocalypse, centred on the city. We might say that *Blade Runner* (1982) manifested this anxiety, also. Snake Plissken's gun-wielding, eye-patched persona suggests the identity of an urban warrior. As such, it rather anticipates the visualisation of the character of the Terminator and, perhaps even, finds a thread through to *Strange Days*, co-written and produced by Cameron. Indeed, Snake Plissken arguably serves as an antecedent for Cameron's character type of the lone, armed, physically resilient hero and his black vested appearance is echoed in Sarah Connor's attire in *Terminator 2: Judgement Day*.

Piranha 2: The Spawning
A sequel in name only to the original *Piranha*, directed by Cameron's contemporary Joe Dante, *Piranha 2: The Spawning* is a slight movie and yet it contains a number of elements that are, in fact, essential Cameron. What we see and hear at points in *Piranha 2* are still part of the fabric of his storytelling in *Avatar*. Indeed, *Piranha 2* even includes a plot point that the military are doing experiments out in the ocean and in this way it anticipates later Cameron films with plots involving questionable military activity on varying scales.

The plot is simple (as is the case with each of Cameron's films), being a story of humans confronted by an inhuman force that needs to be either vanquished or assimilated. We can sum up *Piranha 2*'s story as follows: a school of flying piranha fish prove a threat to the safety of holidaymakers on a generic Caribbean holiday resort. The local police officer and his estranged wife find themselves attempting to annihilate the threat after a number of gruesome piranha attacks on holidaymakers.

The action begins and we are introduced to the teenager Chris (Ricky G. Paull) and other islanders, notably Steve, the local police officer. His brusque, aggressive manner and lean physique anticipate Quaritch in *Avatar* and Hicks in *Aliens*. Like

Lindsey and Bud in *The Abyss*, Steve (Lance Henriksen) is estranged from his wife Anne (Tricia O'Neil), and the marine terror will bring them back together. Of all the film's sketchily presented characters, it is Anne who is the most interesting and who offers the most useful anticipation of later Cameron female protagonists, notably in a scene towards the end of *Piranha 2*'s 'second act'. In the scene, Anne seeks to convince Raoul (Ted Richert), the local hotelier, of the threat of the piranha. He won't listen: he is only interested in business and this attitude will duly become his undoing, rather as it will for Selfridge in *Avatar* and Burke in *Aliens*. 'I'm not just being hysterical, I'm just doing the best I can to convince you these things exist,' Anne says, trying to explain to Raoul the perilous situation at hand. This brief scene has its corollary in *Aliens* when Ripley tries to convince Burke not to send troops to LV-426. Anne, then, is undoubtedly the hero of the film, combining intelligence with physicality (she can swim in the deep sea). Furthermore, she has the same kind of intensity, and wish to protect, that characterises Sarah Connor as she tries to explain what she knows to the authorities in *The Terminator* and *Terminator 2: Judgement Day*.

Piranha 2 is a film in which everyone but Anne and Steve are unaware of the power of the wilderness. Certainly, the film trades on the example of *Jaws* (Steven Spielberg, 1975), as a local policeman seeks to restore order in a coastal community. *Piranha 2* climaxes with an attack of flying fish on the holidaymakers and Anne and Tyler, with whom she has been having an affair, then swim to the wreck and plant an explosive. They are subsequently surrounded by piranha fish, Tyler is killed and Anne gets to safety (courtesy of a mechanical device) and returns to Steve. It is an ending that is akin to that in *The Abyss* with Bud and Lindsey separated as a mission is undertaken in the depths of the ocean.

Only in the final twenty minutes of *Piranha 2* is there a sense of energy in the storytelling and the motifs that Cameron will later render so much more potently, in *Aliens* particularly, are present. That said, its several moments of visceral shocks (such as a corpse's arm dropping into shot) anticipate much more elaborately realised moments in later Cameron films. In terms of the realisation of the deadly flying fish, their appearance is impressionistically rendered through quick cuts as they whip past camera. One shot of a school of them hurtling towards camera in the shipwreck during the film's climactic action is a particular moment that Cameron will revisit with far greater menace in *Aliens*. Indeed, *Aliens* is in a sense a lavish reworking of *Piranha 2*'s human/monster conflict. The character of Steve is sceptical about the menacing presence in the early phase of the film, just as crew members are sceptical about whatever it is that Lindsey has seen during her time outside Deepcore in *The Abyss*. More interestingly, though, is that Steve's physical presence and terse manner anticipate Hicks in *Aliens*. As such, Anne is not so far removed from Ripley. Intriguingly, Tyler (Anne's lover) calls Steve a 'robot'. Tyler, by contrast, is presented as more expressive and softer. When we first meet Steve his aggressive manner as an authority figure has something about it of Quaritch from *Avatar*.

Cameron's horror movie affinities, which we see displayed in *The Terminator* and *Aliens* most evidently, are briefly suggested in *Piranha 2* in the sequence when Anne and Tyler sneak in to the morgue to look over the attacked body before the coroner gets to it. With only torchlight to guide them as they move through a confined space the scene has the feel of a horror movie trope, something that Cameron will realise much more powerfully in *Aliens*. Whilst *Aliens* sits well as a very much more accomplished, creatively consistent and 'meaningful' movie than *Piranha 2*, it is appropriate to note here that before writing and directing his sequel to *Alien* (Ridley Scott, 1979), Cameron wrote and directed *The Terminator*; this would be the film that re-energised the American science fiction movie sensibility and it also marked Cameron's legitimate breakthrough into the world of mainstream feature filmmaking.

CHAPTER TWO

The Terminator (1984)

In *New Hollywood Violence: Inside Popular Film*, Thomas Schatz affirms that 'from the *Great Train Robbery* [1903] a century ago to the current spate of summer blockbusters, Hollywood movies have been fundamentally about violence' (2004: 1). It is an observation that sits well in the context of the longer-term view of the development of white American culture's development. According to Richard Slotkin,

> In American mythogenesis, the founding fathers were not those eighteenth-century gentlemen who composed a nation at Philadelphia. Rather, they were those who tore violently a nation from the implacable and opulent wilderness – the rogues, adventurers, and landboomers; the Indian fighters, traders, missionaries, explorers and hunters who killed and were killed until they had mastered the wilderness; the settlers who came after, suffering hardship and Indian warfare for the sake of a sacred mission or a simple desire for land; and the Indians themselves, both as they were and as they appeared to the settlers, for who they were the special demonic personification of the American wilderness. Their concerns, their hopes their terrors, their violence, and their justifications of themselves, as expressed in literature, are the foundation stories of the mythology that informs our history. (2000a: 4)

We might suggest that in the early 1980s an equation had been made by film studio executives and financiers in terms of the commercial success and popular possibilities of the fantasy and science fiction film genres as family- and youth-friendly formats. To apply these genres to expressions of more difficult, less comforting perspectives was not the remit of the major releases. These movies, often optimistically-flavoured, were largely influenced by the immense commercial success of the films that were written, directed or produced (sometimes all three) by George Lucas and Steven Spielberg. Both of these filmmakers had in common a post-World War II childhood. They were of the Baby Boomer generation, one exposed to the threats of a nuclear-powered world, to the Cold War and the expansion of pop culture, with television as the focal point of that particular watershed. More specifically, in terms of the science fiction cinema of the 1950s and 1960s, Christine Cornea, referring to the writing of Susan Sontag, explains that 'the dystopian leanings of the 1950s American science fiction film … ultimately connected with the historical and political context from which they arose' (2007: 32).

A case has been made for contextualising the popular success typified by Lucas and Spielberg within the mainstream cultural mood engendered by President Ronald Reagan who held office between 1981 and 1989. In an article entitled 'The Heirs of Reagan's Optimism' for *Time* magazine, Fareed Zakaria offers a useful, brief overview of the sensibility of the Reagan administration and begins by quoting American historian Daniel Boorstin: 'American civilization, from its beginnings had combined a dogmatic confidence in the future with a naïve puzzlement over what the future might bring' (2012). Zakaria writes that 'optimism in this sense is not a philosophy but more of a temperament, a comfort with the country's eternal potential and a faith in its virtues. Reagan was the quintessential optimist. He was an ardent conservative who wanted to turn away from the liberation of the 1960s and 1970s' (ibid.). One has only to watch an early scene in *Back to the Future Part II* (Robert Zemeckis, 1989) to see the Reagan-era spirit being satirised. In the film's earliest part, Marty McFly finds himself transported from 1985 to 2015, whereupon he ventures into the Café 80s where a puppet-mask face of Ronald Reagan appears on a screen as Marty orders a Pepsi. The ersatz Reagan uses the phrase 'It's always morning in America.' (Complicating that film trilogy's representation of these sensibilities, however, is the original film's very Reagan-era conclusion.) Reagan's construction of a new sense of an optimistic spirit, part of which saw America adventuring abroad once more and, indeed, across space, seemed to chime with the tone of the movies. Under Reagan, space exploration was re-energised, partly as a demonstration of the military-industrial complex, and his administration also developed, with a view to implementing, the Strategic Defence Initiative of the early 1980s. The mainstream media renamed the official moniker, referring to it as 'Star Wars'.

Released amidst the Reagan-era cultural landscape, *The Terminator* eschews the established popular tonal qualities of the Lucas and Spielberg 'fantasy film' format in favour of a starker, harsher sensibility in which technology's threat to humanity was very strong and tangible, and anticipates the online, interconnected world in which we now find ourselves. Indeed, some might call the approach taken by Cameron with *The Terminator* as being more 'adult' but that is too simplistic a term and suggests that if Spielberg's and Lucas's films were aimed at the family audience they are automatically less worthy of formal and thematic interest. In his book about *The Terminator*, Sean French writes that the film is 'the sort of project that seems to have been developed without even the intention of being any good' (1996: 6). Yet *The Terminator* is a film that was realised in an exemplary way.

Where Spielberg and Lucas elected to make the unearthly feel comfortable and knowable, for Cameron the non-human and the unearthly are a threatening and uneasy proposition. There is a sense of desperation and of nihilism that underpins *The Terminator*; it is not a 'fun loving' presentation of the future, and throughout the movie there is the evidence of the horror genre bleeding through and enriching its narrative effects. In his writing about the horror genre, Robin Wood engaged with the ways in which popular film has articulated the idea of the Other; which is to say an entity that exists and operates outside of the mainstream. As such, the mainstream culture will typically assimilate the Other so that the Other no longer exists. The Other becomes normalised. Wood writes that 'since the early 1960s, the central theme of the American cinema has been, increasingly … disintegration and breakdown…' (2003: 24). He notes that the 1970s was 'the period when the dominant ideology almost disintegrated' (ibid.) and his description of a failing cultural mindset attests to the overarching influence of the tragedy and trauma of the Vietnam War, civil unrest and the Nixon Presidency; events that starkly suggest that the institution of mainstream party politics was compromised and that everything was complicated and not easily defined. In the cinema of Spielberg and Lucas, we might say that comforting narratives that re-presented conflict as easily divided between 'good' and 'evil', between the heroic individual and the degenerate world of governments and corporate entities, were popular approaches.

Since its original release, *The Terminator* has rather transcended its filmic origin. Some of its images have separated out from the film itself and assumed an emblematic and iconic status in terms of a particular moment in Hollywood filmmaking and, more critically, in terms of the kinds of representations and themes that we might understand the film to express. Certain images from the film that have circulated with great frequency have typically been of the Terminator's glistening endoskeleton and of Schwarzenegger in leathers. To some degree, these images have encapsulated qualities of the popular American genre film of the 1980s: urban, aggressive, increasingly sexualised.

We might propose that with *The Terminator*, Cameron's conceptual approach was to offer a consciously starker and less hopeful vision of humans' integration with technology that counter-pointed the ideas dramatised and visualised in the 'first' *Star Wars* trilogy (1977–1983). With *The Terminator*, Cameron offered up the id to *ET*'s ego. That said we might also look to *The Terminator* as functioning as an iteration of the science fiction and horror films of the 1970s and early 1980s.

Cameron has often acknowledged that an early part of his thinking process in developing the story for *The Terminator* was to deconstruct the narrative forms and design of the films that, by the early 1980s, had proved so commercially popular, notably *Star Wars* and *ET*. These two films have been extensively written about elsewhere and one favoured approach in unpacking their respective stylistic patterns, meanings and intentions, has been to apply an understanding of mythologically-informed tropes and devices with which to direct the intellectual and emotional engagement with a film. Melissa Mathison, screenwriter of *ET*, has said of the script that 'Elliot [the child who befriends ET] had to have the power in the movie. If even for a moment an adult took away Elliot's power before it became a matter of life and death, then Elliott would have lost all of his magic' (2002:15). *The Terminator*, then, is a generic fusion of science fiction, thriller and horror movie. In his monograph on the film, Sean French describes Cameron as 'a semiotician of immense resource' (1996: 11). What French is acknowledging here is Cameron's authorial presence and film awareness, each a component of his 'visionary' approach, but less in terms of 'originality' and more in terms of being a synthesiser who through this process of recombination creates new work, fusing established narrative traditions with technology that allows for the 'new' to occur.

Since cinema's inception action and film have complemented one another. From the Lumière Brothers' silent short films, their 'cinema of attractions' through to Keaton's silent action epic *The General* (1927) and on to *Ben Hur* (William Wyler, 1959), *The Bridge on the River Kwai* (David Lean, 1957) and the gloriously precise and kinetic truck chase of *Raiders of the Lost Ark* (Steven Spielberg, 1981) action films have proved fascinating. Often overlooked as embodying what might be considered a paucity of intellectual stimulation, the action genre has provided its share of thoughtful and intelligent filmmaking and ideological interest. Cameron has emerged as a major purveyor of smart and stylish action cinema which, starting with *The Terminator*, reinforced the possibility that existed in fusing characterisation with action so that it served as vital a function, if not more so, alongside dialogue. Suddenly, all the sound and fury of the genre became anchored in something emotionally real.

Central to the believability of Cameron's fantasy cinema is the 'authenticity' of the creatures and other fantasy characters rendered for the films. As such, it is appropriate to identify the importance of the collaborative work between Cameron and designer Stan Winston. Winston had started out as an actor and then moved into make-up and creature design, construction and performance during the late-1970s and early-1980s, his work featuring in Joe Dante's *The Howling* and John Carpenter's *The Thing*. Winston's own acting background informed how he typically spoke of the fantasy characters he was commissioned to create. In *Sight and Sound*, Peter Wollen, writing about *Jurassic Park* on which Winston had also worked, made a connection between Winston and a non-filmic reference point: Benjamin Waterhouse Hawkins, fossil expert and sculptor of the dinosaur figures in Crystal Palace in south London: 'Hawkins is ... the direct ancestor of Stan Winston, whose studio built the models for *Jurassic Park*' (2000: 185). The cinema of spectacle that Cameron is understandably synonymous with typically plays to our sense of a fascination with the enormous: the larger than life on a purely physical scale rather than only in terms of situation and emotional 'intensity'.

Genesis of The Terminator

Narratively, *The Terminator* was designed as an evolution and homage to the science fiction sub-genre of the time-travel story. Of his screenplay for *The Terminator*, in a 1985 interview with *Cinefantastique* magazine, Cameron noted that *The Outer Limits* television show had been fundamental to his concept for the film's narrative and visual style. The particular episode of the series that had been influential on him was entitled *Soldier*, written by Harlan Ellison. Cameron explained that what he liked about *The*

Outer Limits series was its film noir-inflected visuals. This fusion of the genres of film noir and science fiction provides *The Terminator* with so much of its aesthetic distinction. The film has a visual style that is quite in contrast to the brightly-lit, high-key visual style of *Star Wars* and *Back to the Future*.

Offering some explanation for what became the genesis of *The Terminator*, Cameron has recounted an aspect of his youth:

> I would have to say that in my febrile youth I was an absolutely rabid science fiction fan. I recall the classics, all the old Ace paperback novels. When I went to college, I put the brakes on that reading and got into the 'real world' which made me realise that many science fiction writers have a much better perspective on life than those writers who are mired in the specifics of day to day life. (1984: 56)

Speaking similarly about his earliest days as an aspiring filmmaker, Cameron, in an extensive interview with Stephen Rebello in *Playboy*, commented: 'When most people saw *Star Wars* there was the shock of the new. For me there was the shock of recognition' (2009).

With only one feature film credit then to his name at the time of developing *The Terminator*, the screenplay was submitted to the Hollywood studios. It certainly generated interest with a number of studios that recognised that cheaply produced science fiction continued to be commercially viable. At around the same time that Cameron would have been seeking funding for *The Terminator*, John Carpenter was developing and preparing *Starman*, a delicately presented love story about an alien and a human. Carpenter's film suggested an 'adult' take on a similar narrative structure to *ET*. Columbia Pictures, who produced *Starman*, had passed on *ET* when Spielberg was looking to find a studio to finance the film in 1981. Like *The Terminator*, *Starman* was released in the autumn of 1984 but was a commercial failure. Of his film, Carpenter commented in an article by Janet Maslin entitled 'A Horror Director Creates a Magical Alien', 'I wanted to make a fairy tale rather than a sci-fi film' (1984). Intriguingly, in *Aliens*, Cameron would combine the fairy tale and the science fiction genres.

He developed the screenplay for *The Terminator* in the early 1980s and the resulting film is a drama built around concerns with identity, destiny and motherhood, the latter subject also being particularly central to *Aliens*. In turn, the concept of virtual and actual identity is all the more elaborately dramatised in *Avatar*, wherein the relationship between the authentic and the simulacra are key. As such, the latter film (a digitally-painted movie, we might say) reiterates and refashions some of the predilections of cyborg cinema that *The Terminator* explores. Indeed, Cameron's cinema directly engages with the concept of the simulacra. Jean Baudrillard's formulation of the simulacra in relation to cinema expressed thus:

> The cinema and its trajectory: from the most fantastic or mythical to the realistic and the hyperrealistic. The cinema in its current efforts is getting closer and closer, and with greater and greater perfection, to the absolute real, in its banality,

its veracity, in its naked obviousness, in its boredom, and at the same time in its presumption, in its pretension to being the real, the immediate, the unsignified, which is the craziest of undertakings (similarly, functionalism's pretension to designating – design – the greatest degree of correspondence between the object and its function, and its use value, is a truly absurd enterprise); no culture has ever had toward its signs this naïve and paranoid, puritan and terrorist vision. (1994: 46)

In terms of a science fiction subject concerned with the differences between authentic and manufactured experience, a film contemporaneous with *The Terminator* was *Blade Runner*, an adaptation of Philip K. Dick's novel *Do Androids Dream of Electric Sheep?* (1968). The writer had been a surviving twin, his sister having died not long after being born. That tragedy haunted Dick throughout his life and it might be reasonable to suggest that in that particular case the autobiographical informed and enriched the creative work. Dick's fascination with the image and reality of the double, or the copy, can be read as pertinent in terms of Cameron's use of performance capture in *Avatar* and the narrative interests of the authentic and the copy in that particular film. Much of *The Terminator*'s expressive possibilities, then, are to be found in its fusion of visceral horror and highly kinetic action. By extension, the interest in copies of the human form plays into the pre-cinema tradition of which *Frankenstein* is but one key text.

The Terminator's more graphically violent and grotesque moments echo the tone achieved earlier by Carpenter's *The Thing*. But unlike the Cameron film, despite the effectiveness with which *The Thing* was realised as a major, studio genre film, it did not enjoy commercial success; audiences perhaps just not wanting something as visually unsettling about an alien visitor. The summer of 1982 has since been reconstructed and imagined as a particularly fertile moment for science fiction and fantasy projects.

There is an oft-quoted observation, included by Paul Wells in his book *Understanding Animation*, that, whilst originally made in relation to animation, is pertinent to the conceptual effects of the science fiction film: 'To animate is to give life and soul to a design, not through copying but through the transformation of reality' (1998: 10). This mantra informs the realisation of the Terminator's endoskeleton in the film. The production's realisation of the endoskeleton employs an amount of economically staged, and convincingly rendered, stop-motion animation and miniature model work, intercut with shots of Stan Winston's full-scale make-up applications. The shots featuring stop-motion also engage us in a concern with how we view technology that mimics the human form. It is a sometimes unsettling aesthetic that has a history bound up with the human tradition of making copies of our essential likeness. Of automata, Wendy Beth Hyman notes that 'stories of enchantment, wonder, and, in thinly veiled allegory, the poetic triumph over the limits of material, the bringing of art to life. But others reveal something quite divergent: the devolution and disassembly of personhood, suggesting an identity comprised wheels and gears, an assemblage of "shreds and stuffe"' (2011: 4). Beyond *The Terminator* we can look to the film *AI: Artificial Intelligence* (Steven Spielberg, 2001) as a particularly rich set of ideas around the robot and the tensions between authentic and inauthentic experiences that define what it is to be 'human'. According to Spielberg, its writer/ director, *AI* is 'the story of a robot boy named David whose quest to become a real boy spoke to my own sensibilities of love and loss' (2009: 7). These tensions find a more recent presentation in the American television series *Almost Human* (2013), which dramatised a 'conventional' mismatched pairing of urban police in the USA but made one of them a human and one a cyborg. Whilst not a Cameron project, the series' thematic interest and sensibility brought to mind connections with the enduring influence of Cameron's movies.

Hard Body Masculinity
Initially, in Cameron's conception for *The Terminator* of the film, Arnold Schwarzenegger was to have portrayed the character of resistance fighter Kyle Reese, the man who comes back from the future to protect Sarah Connor from her fated nemesis the Terminator. Certainly, Schwarzenegger's almost entirely non-verbal performance maximises his physicality on screen and as the killer robot he offers a true performance (or presence) rather than merely a recitation of dialogue. He becomes a focal element of the film's *mise-en-scène*, his expression of character realised predominantly through movement, gesture and gaze. But he is also a vessel for ideology. Schwarzenegger had been a body builder and appeared in films such as *Hercules in New York* (Arthur A. Seidelman, 1969) and *Pumping Iron* (George Butler and Robert Fiore, 1977). His most significant starring role prior to *The Terminator* had been as the title character in *Conan the Barbarian*. Of the heavily-muscled body on film and in photography Niall Richardson has written about the Weider company, whose business was selling bodybuilding equipment, commenting that 'a key element in the Weider's forceful heterosexualisation of bodybuilding was the ambassador of the Weider empire, a man whose name would become synonymous with bodybuilding: the one and only Arnold Schwarzenegger' (2010: 27). Given the synonymous relationship between the agile, attuned, efficient body that is so central to the narrative and image of *The Terminator* (film and character) it is fascinating to consider the film in the context of Cameron's later *Avatar*, in which a physically disabled young man is the movie's hero. Of *Avatar's* representation of the disabled body Dana Fore notes:

> *Avatar* disrupts ableist voyeurism by 'handling' Sully in ways that maximize audience identification while working against the isolating imagery discussed by Norden. For instance, when Sully appears in his wheelchair, the camera alternates between close-ups of his face and medium shots of him moving in the lab or around the base. The close-ups establish both Sully's individuality and his masculinity by making his gaze central to the scene. In the words of E. Ann Kaplan, 'to own and activate the gaze' in film 'is to be in the masculine position'. If controlling the gaze does count as a performance of masculinity, then this cinematography also undermines the stereotype of the disabled man 'feminized' by his wound. The medium shots also underscore Sully's power and agency by allowing viewers to see the speed at which he moves and works. And these scenes are typically shot from *his* level, and not from the level of the

able-bodied characters looking down – a common way of presenting disabled characters that visually implies their inferiority. (2011)

The Terminator's integration of Schwarzenegger as a visual element in the film's design, rather than as an actor in the 'conventional' sense of reciting and interpreting bursts of dialogue, is consistent with Linda Williams' formulation about the role of the human body on screen:

> To a certain extent we know that the status of [the] body becomes as a relay to the body of the spectator within the already formulated institution of classical narrative films and their system of 'suture'. To a certain extent we also know how these films constitute the male viewer within the film as surrogate for the look of the male spectator and the female body as site of the spectacle. (1991: 509)

The exterior appearance of the Terminator itself, then, is a simulacrum.

To further develop our sense of how *The Terminator* places the male body, as well as Cameron's contribution to representations of masculininty, we can refer to *Hollywood: From Vietnam to Reagan and Beyond* by Robin Wood. He writes:

> The women's movement produced in Hollywood a backlash of hysterical masculinity of which the only surprise is that it did not happen sooner: the 'key' year is 1982, the year of the release of *Conan the Barbarian* and *First Blood* … With the collapse of radical feminism and the co-option of what was left of it into mainstream dominated culture, the hysteria died out but the over-emphasis on ultra-macho masculinity did not. (2003: xxxvi)

Conan the Barbarian, of course, starred Schwarzenegger who Cameron went on to cast in *The Terminator*, its sequel and *True Lies*, while Cameron also shares screenplay credit with Sylvester Stallone on *Rambo: First Blood Part II*.

In casting Schwarzenegger, Cameron traded, consciously or not, on an established aesthetic and cultural discourse around how the human body can be imagined and imaged. Susan Jeffords writes that it is

> one of the key images that came to embody the political, economic, and social philosophy of the 1980s – the hard body. The subtle mastery offered by Reaganism is never simply personal or national but a combination of both. It is for this reason that the hard body was able to function more effectively even than the American flag or individual wars to support Reaganism – because it served both forms of identification simultaneously. (1993: 28)

For Jeffords, Reagan's own body and physical presence and history on screen informed a strategy of the idea of the body informing and serving as a metaphor for Reagan's administration and by extension a sense of American national identity (Schwarzenegger would go on to be Governor of California, 2003–2011). The 1980s marked a moment of an emerging fascination with fitness and aerobic exercise and so Schwarzenegger's body-building history sat well within the popular cinema as evidenced by *Conan the Barbarian*, *Commando* (Mark L. Lester, 1985) and *Predator* (John McTiernan, 1987).

The relationship and tension between the technological and the biological and the possibilities for their fusion arises in each of Cameron's films. His interest in bodies and shape-shifting has continued to feature throughout his work and it is part of his recognition of interpreting the application of mythological tropes to popular movies. Those ancient stories often dwell on ways in which the human body has the capacity for transformation.

The film's showcasing of the hardness of Schwarzenegger's body is counterpointed by its inclusion of the scene in which Sarah and Kyle have sex. The scene shows us their fragile and delicate bodies, each so susceptible to the Terminator's force. The scene is a tactfully placed moment of calm and kindness amidst a film dominated by action in which aggression is key as bodies are pulverised and beaten.

Capturing The Terminator on Film

The Terminator screenplay began life as a first draft written by Cameron himself. Soon after, though, he involved Gale Ann Hurd, who he had met at New World Pictures (where she had been a production manager on *Battle Beyond the Stars)*, and she worked with him on it further. In revising the screenplay, now with some financier input, Cameron and Hurd were encouraged to develop and emphasise the suggestion of a romance between Kyle and Sarah and Cameron took to the suggestion. Arguably, the love story broadened the appeal of the science fiction film, which we might assume was the impulse behind the financier's direction. The script was completed in May 1982 and in November Orion agreed to distribute the film once it was completed. It took eighteen months to put the film's finance together with an eventual budget of $6 million.

With Schwarzenegger in place, Cameron then cast two 'unknown' actors for the two human protagonists: Linda Hamilton as Sarah Connor and Michael Biehn as Kyle Reese. Hamilton had appeared in TV movies but would be cast in a lead role in *Children of the Corn* (Fritz Kiersch, 1984), released just a few months before *The Terminator*. Biehn had appeared in a range of films, notably *The Lords of Discipline* (Franc Roddam, 1983).

The Terminator was initially to have gone into production in 1983 but when Schwarzenegger committed to starring in *Conan the Destroyer*, Cameron's film was delayed by several months. In the longer term, this was arguably fortuitous for Cameron's professional ambitions. His script for *The Terminator* went back out to agents as a writing sample and it was in this same period that Walter Hill (himself a highly regarded director of action movies and westerns), David Giler and Gordon Carroll read it and recognised that Cameron might be a suitable writer for a sequel to *Alien*. Producer Gale Anne Hurd noted, during interviews that she conducted during promotion for *Aliens*, that Hill, Giler and Carroll had met Cameron immediately during the period after *The Terminator*'s theatrical release success to discuss a possibile collaboration: 'They said "Well, there is the sequel to *Alien*" … No-one had come up with an approach that was satisfactory to all the various creative individuals involved' (1986: 12).

The Terminator: immortal body in the mortal world

The Terminator was filmed on location in and around Los Angeles between March and May 1984, with a November 1984 release already scheduled. Intriguingly, by the completion of production Cameron and Hurd also reached a point where they had worked out a sequel concept, which, if it came to pass, they planned to only produce and write but not direct. With the film edited to the filmmakers' satisfaction and that of Orion Pictures, the film's distributor, Cameron was confronted by an argument that ensued with writer Harlan Ellison who claimed that the premise of *The Terminator* was rather too close to his *The Soldier* (1964) episode for *The Outer Limits*. The matter was duly resolved with Ellison receiving a credit in the film's end-credit text that read 'acknowledgement to the work of'.

The Story
The Terminator begins with a prologue. We hear the sound of wind before we see an image. The black screen fades-in with an image that on-screen text informs us is Los Angeles, 2029 AD. It is an intensely apocalyptic scene and against the night sky a battle spaceship flies into view (its highly industrialised, almost ungainly looking appearance echoes Cameron's own design for the 'Mother' spaceship in *Battle Beyond the Stars*). The wide shot then cuts to a mid-close-up showing the metal wheels of a tank as they roll over human skulls. The image resounds with the compositional impact of comic-book panels, with their use of extreme close-ups in service of a sense of dynamic, kinetic motion. We then see soldiers and are soon able to identify that this is a battle of humans against machines. It is a brief sequence, offering just an unsettling hint of a nightmarish future, but one that is cinematically rendered, emphasising concision in laying out fundamental story information and providing an image that encapsulates the larger concern of the film. There is a bulky, bulbous, almost clumsy, form to the future technology in *The Terminator* that suggests an industrial reality and design aesthetic that we recognise in our own Western world of industrialised culture.

The realism underpins the design sensibility of a used future that has certainly become an established genre approach seen in films such as *Star Wars* and *Alien*, contrasting with the streamlined, commercial airline-influenced curvilinear forms of 1950s and 1960s science fiction. Certainly, the production design influences of *The Terminator* have been felt in a range of subsequent non-Cameron films.

The prologue then gives way to the film's terse and stark opening credit title-sequence, underscored by Brad Fiedel's austere and insistent, mono-rhythmic theme which suggests not the creation of a sense of spectacle or wonder but instead a sense of threat and menace. The relentlessly rhythmic pounding of the main theme cages a melancholy sub-theme that, later, will be an expression of the burgeoning romance between Sarah and Kyle. The title sequence itself is comprised of text that replicates the appearance of a computer font, right down to the inclusion of a flashing cursor. Indeed, 1984 was not only the year of *The Terminator*; it also saw the release of the first iteration of the Apple Mac computer, the moment in which the personal computer began to settle into the workplace and into the home. Indeed, this rapidly evolving and deepening relationship with the personal computer (with the digital as an extension of ourselves ... as an avatar) soon made its way into mainstream American TV: in 1985 a series aired that was entitled *Automan*. How appropriate, then, that *Alien* and *Blade Runner* director Ridley Scott directed the TV commercial that introduced the first Mac computer to consumers using images that evoked Fritz Lang's *Metropolis* (1927) and George Orwell's novel *1984* (1948). In Scott's commercial, a sportswoman, a physically dynamic and accomplished figure, disrupts the oppressive status quo. It is identifiably a Cameronesque trope.

The film then cuts to a shot of an alleyway at night as a garbage truck manoeuvres about. It is suddenly caged by electricity bolts and buffeted by a strong wind. We then see a naked and muscular figure (the Terminator of the film's title, portrayed by Arnold Schwarzenegger) crouching who then stands and walks to look over the city, Los Angeles, revealed beneath him – an echo of the shot at the start of *ET* when the titular hero approaches the edge of a hill to view suburbia at night.

Some in the audience for *The Terminator*, at the time of its original theatrical release in late 1984, might have immediately recognised this as the body of Arnold Schwarzenegger, the body builder from *Pumping Iron* and *Hercules in New York*. Others might instead have recognised him from *Conan the Barbarian* and its sequel, *Conan the Destroyer*, released just a few months before *The Terminator*. The importance of Schwarzenegger's body to the idea of a physically imposing character certainly manifested itself in the film's US release poster that centred entirely on the star baring his chest and bearing guns. (Interestingly, the British quad poster for the cinema release of *The Terminator* was not based around this image, but was instead a full-face illustration that rendered the face as part robot endoskull and part 'human' with the Terminator's gun rising up at the base line of the image, an image that spoke more of a horror film than of science fiction.) It is reasonable to assert that *The Terminator* plugged Schwarzenegger into increasingly popular material, marking his transition from a subculture into the mainstream. In the several years immediately following *The Terminator*, Schwarzenegger would star in the action movies *Raw Deal* (John Irvin, 1986),

Predator, *Red Dawn* (Walter Hill, 1988) and *Commando*; his starring roles functioning as something of an analogue to the performances of Stallone in films such as *Rambo: First Blood Part II*, *Cobra* (George Pan Cosmatos, 1986) and *Over the Top* (Menahem Golan, 1987). Of this mid- and late-1980s moment of the commercially popular action film (currently being 'resurrected' in Stallone's series of films, *The Expendables*), Jose Arroyo has noted that 'the spectacular was never restricted to action – stars were regularly presented as spectacle and narrative tended to linger on sensational sets and costumes ... As "only entertainment" ... they were regarded as the opposite of serious works of art designed to change perceptions, push aesthetic boundaries and challenge our views' (2000: vii).

In his nakedness, the figure is then shown approaching three punks. When they mock his appearance he kills one of them and takes their clothes. In this unfussy, explicit moment we recognise that this is something more physically powerful than any human could be and, in this moment, Cameron's affinity with the idea of the 'superman' announces itself: we have been introduced to the titular Terminator. Cameron's interest in the 'superman' trope, as an entity (human or otherwise) that is both physically and mentally resilient, constitutes both the capacity for benevolent and malevolent behaviour in the central characters of his films.

The film then cuts to a low camera position in the alleyway where the main action of the film began just a few minutes before and where, following another burst of lightning, another naked man appears. We will learn that his name is Kyle Reese (Michael Biehn). He is very much more physically fragile (read: human) than the previous stranger: Reese is effectively his antithesis, his body 'ordinary' (these things are relative) and scarred. Michael Biehn's nakedness is very different from Schwarzenegger's. Indeed, Reese's physical fragility anticipates (and echoes) the physical fragility of *Avatar*'s Jake Sully and this contrasts with his physical majesty in avatar form as a Na'vi.

Reese looks anxious and rightly so as moments later he is being chased by police, the action staged using a handheld camera that follows ahead and behind Reese. In his essay 'Machine as Messiah: Cyborgs, Morphs and the American Body Politic', Doran Larson writes: 'On grounds deeper than mere empathy, we see in Kyle a viable representation of the political body of the American 1980s. He is scarred in soul and body by a foreign war (if we read the future, like the past, as another country)' (2004: 193). Reese is chased by the authorities and flees, escaping through a clothes store, the camera tracking the action as he scurries just as it tracked the action of the scuttling soldiers in the future battle in the prologue. Everything in this film is about survival and, as such, the opening minutes of the movie in retrospect now stand as a microcosm of Cameron's overriding interest in the subject. As Reese scurries along like a rat on the run, he grabs a trench coat (which connotes a noir sensibility to this phase of the film), trousers and Nike trainers. He also grabs a rifle then emerges back out onto the streets.

It is appropriate to note here that Los Angeles and noir have a symbiotic relationship. Writer Raymond Chandler set his novel *The Big Sleep*, a modern American classic, in the city and Los Angeles has featured as the setting for a number of science fiction films; notably *Blade Runner* and the more recent *Elysium*; both films investing creatively in a sense of Los Angeles as a city of difficulty and overcrowding. In *Elysium*, there is a very acute sociological dynamic to the narrative whereas we might say that Scott's film touches more overtly on the concept of the identity of the individual. In both, however, the concept of the human/technology interface is central with *Elysium*'s protagonist Max Da Costa having his body enhanced by an exoskeleton of sorts. Chandler's acknowledgement of the fear that the urban space can conjure is picked up by Cameron not only in *The Terminator* but also, particularly, in *Strange Days* for which he served as producer and co-writer. In this later film the sense of a morally compromised urban world of crime that is centred around 'black market' digital technology is suffused with an acknowledgement of the 'tech-noir' sensibility that *The Terminator* more minimally presents. Critically, too, is that *Strange Days* takes the nihilism of *The Terminator* and amplifies it.

The film then establishes that both of these men (at this point we assume Schwarzenegger is a 'man') are searching for a particular woman and the action cuts from the low-key night-time city streets of LA to the high-key, sunny streets of the suburbs. We see a woman arrive late for work at a diner and when she punches in we see that her name is Sarah Connor (Linda Hamilton). Such economically presented details occur throughout the film, building tension and provoking the audience to piece together the larger fabric of the story rather than simply use dialogue for exposition. Certainly, the film is a highly effective example of how precisely a narrative fiction film organises dramatic information so as to create tension and sustain a sense of anticipation on the part of the viewer. Cameron's narrative maintains clarity, allowing the audience opportunities to develop their sense of the gist of a narrative based on audience familiarity with other, similar narratives. Of this essential function, David Bordwell has written that 'because the motifs or objects and persons can vary from tale to tale, only the actions ... can form the constants that trigger our intuition' (1988: 9). The film applies the suspense afforded by intercutting so that, having identified Sarah Connor, the action cuts to the Terminator all-too-easily procuring guns in an iconic scene that could be read as criticising the relative ease of doing so in the United States. There is a very dangerous tension here between story and reality. Other Cameron films also foreground the use of artillery, delighting in the engineering and aesthetic of them. There is a clear fetishisation of guns that plays out in each Cameron film, artillery becoming an extension and fusion of, rather than addition to, the human body. Of the difficult and tightly-knit relationship between gun culture and the broader American cultural landscape, within which a strain of national identity has crystallised around arms, Richard Slotkin has written that

> It is important to analyze turn-of-the-century vigilantism, because the anti-government rhetoric and fetishization of firepower of the contemporary gun-rights movement come from vigilante values. The gun lobby invokes the classic fears behind vigilantism: of a threat to personal safety by the lower orders or an assault on vital interests by government officials. It seeks to establish the right of a private individual to wage social war, at will, against 'government tyranny,'

the Bureau of Alcohol, Tobacco, and Firearms, or any class of people deemed 'dangerous' to public safety. In the words of the NRA spokesman Fred Romero, 'The Second Amendment is not there to protect the interests of hunters, sports shooters, and casual plinkers ... The Second Amendment is there as a balance of power. It is literally a loaded gun in the hands of the people held to the heads of government. (2000b)

Only in *Avatar* does the industrial and military complex find itself dramatically undone. Indeed, this later movie of Cameron's might be considered to have allowed him the chance to revisit aspects of his original screenplay that did not survive what eventually became *Rambo: First Blood Part II*.

In contrast to the scene that shows the ease with which the Terminator is able to arm itself, the action then cuts to an analogous scene showing Reese sawing off the shotgun that he has stolen. Emphasising the Terminator's efficiency, the action then cuts to a brief scene showing the robot looking in a phonebook for the name Sarah Connor and the corresponding address. When we see that there are several Connors listed, we begin to anticipate what may happen next, having witnessed the Terminator's earlier despatching of the youth for his clothes. Intercutting is the patterning effect deployed in the early part of *The Terminator* and Cameron will repeat this organising pattern very closely in *Terminator 2: Judgement Day*.

The film then cuts to an image of the wheels of a motorcycle crushing a toy truck lying on a suburban street, a darkly humorous reminder of the prologue that depicts tank tracks rolling over a human skull. We watch the Terminator approach the front door of the home on the suburban street and it kills the woman it has identified as 'Sarah Connor'. From a low camera position, the Terminator is shown invading the house, the camera ahead of the character as it walks forward aggressively, its menace emphasised by the use of slow-motion. Certainly, the moment has a visceral charge to it and there is nothing easy or escapist about watching it.

After this scene of visceral intensity, and of short-term suspense and release, the action then cuts to the diner where we met the first Sarah Connor, the TV news playing the story about another Sarah Connor being killed. 'Our' Sarah's circumstances are humble – appropriately so, for a future saviour of the world if we read the film in terms of a mythologically aware narrative. Such a narrative trope is consistent with Cameron's oeuvre, notably *Aliens*, *The Abyss* and *Avatar*. Sarah Connor, then, assumes a role akin to that of the Virgin Mary in that she is to be the mother of the 'saviour' of the world. Of the cultural resonance and longevity of Mary the Mother of Jesus, Marina Warner has explained that there is a cultural narrative that emphasises Mary as a submissive woman. In this context, Cameron's characterisation of Sarah counterpoints this in that she is neither submissive to the Terminator's threat nor to the broader institutional threats of *Terminator 2*. Considering the resonance of the Virgin Mary, Warner has noted that 'the doctrine that Mary is the Second Eve, who reversed the Fall, by accepting to become the mother of Saviour and thus help redeem the human race from the consequence of Adam's sin, was formulated as early as the second century' (1979: 31).

The film then cuts to a scene presumably set that night of Reese hotwiring a car. Critically, as he does so he looks at the working trucks and other machinery on a construction site; their bright lights shining, they trigger a memory for Reese of the industrial war machines of the future conflict, of which we have seen a glimpse in the film's prologue. There is then a flashback/forward in which we see Reese as a future soldier. There is a wideshot that shows tanks and soldiers in action and it pre-empts what will later characterise combat scenes in *Aliens* and *Avatar*.

Reese then awakes from his dream and the film cuts to a scene set in a Los Angeles police station where the death of 'Sarah Connor' is reported. The police are thus established as involved in the plot at this point but the film presents them as corporately inept. In Cameron's cinema the exceptional individual is typically more effective than the team, whatever their strengths and bonds, although his films also enjoy establishing a sense of a unit at work, notably in *The Abyss*.

The film cuts back to anodyne suburbia where Sarah and her buddy are preparing to go out for a Saturday night. Ironically, Sarah's friend says of them both that they are 'better than mortal man deserves'. In a suggestion that potentially even the most mundane moment can serve as a twist of fate, Sarah's date then cancels and, left at a loose end, Sarah goes out to see a film alone. We the audience know that she is now under threat, the imminence of danger accentuated by the apparently safe and anodyne quality of a suburban street. Indeed the suburban street had become so familiar to movie audiences in the 1970s and early 1980s on account of them being a setting that refrained in a range of Hollywood-produced movies, notably several directed and executive produced by Steven Spielberg and John Hughes. Of the image and concept of suburbia the sociologist Richard Sennett, in his book *The Uses of Disorder: Personal Identity and City Life*, states that

> this kind of family living in the suburbs surely is a little strange. Isn't this preference for suburbia as a setting for family life in reality an admission, tacit and unspoken to be sure, that the parents do not feel confident of their own human strengths to guide the child in the midst of an environment richer and more difficult than that of neat lawns and tidy supermarkets of the suburbs? (2008: 71)

Indeed, *The Terminator*'s use of suburbia as a counterpoint to the 'fantasy' of its premise intensifies the implication of suburbia harbouring potential menace that characterises *Halloween*, *ET* and *Poltergeist* (Tobe Hooper, 1982).

The action then cuts to an exterior scene and a close-up of Sarah's face as she walks through an underground car park. The action is accentuated by the film's synthesised music track that suggests the possibility of menace. We cut to a shot of Reese as he slowly drives after Sarah. Reese is introduced in the foreground of the shot as initially out of focus. The action then cuts back to the police department for a scene that, in part, gives the film an opportunity to satirise the forces of bureaucracy. How could these apparently rather inept men possibly stop the Terminator that we have seen in action? We cut momentarily to Sarah's apartment as the police try to contact her by phone, a brief moment that intensifies the overarching dramatic irony that drives the suspense in this phase of the film. The sequence then returns to Sarah, oblivious to what is unfolding, as she sits alone having a pizza and watching the story about the death of a woman named Sarah Connor on the TV news. Sarah is shown reacting anxiously in close-up. She goes through the phone book and sees that she is next in the listing of names. We then see her walking nervously along the street with Reese following her, looking threatening rather than protective towards her. Sarah knows she is being followed and she goes into the busy TechNoir club, all party-vibe chaos and neon glare. In the club she tries to phone the police. There is then a cut that shows the Terminator approaching Sarah's home. Intercutting the Terminator's approach is footage of Sarah's flatmate dancing in the kitchen, oblivious to the Terminator's arrival in the building. A handheld camera follows the flatmate into the kitchen, oblivious to the horror unfolding in the bedroom where the Terminator is killing her boyfriend. There is an authoritative use of a horror movie aesthetic here as we anticipate a young woman on the verge of peril. There is then a shot in slow-motion as the Terminator kills Sarah's friend. On the answerphone we hear the message: 'You're talking to a machine. Machines need love too.' It is not a subtle joke, but it is darkly comic, and also thematically appropriate; not only to this film but to almost all of Cameron's ensuing movies. The Terminator hears Sarah leaving a message and now knows where she is, and finds Sarah's ID card and so is now able to recognise her. Cameron's use of dramatic irony in these early stages of the film is thrillingly deployed. Indeed, the film exemplifies classical narrative structure; the deployment of narrative structure and shot composition is precise and clear.

The action then cuts back to show Sarah in TechNoir as the Terminator arrives. His blank stare is threatening. His eyes are the window to a 'vacuum', not to a soul. He does not blink. Indeed, the film editor and sound designer Walter Murch, in his book *In the Blink of an Eye* (2001), has talked about using actors' blinking patterns as a cue for making certain edits in order to build a rhythm for a scene; the blink of an actor's eyes potentially motivates the moment to cut from one shot to another in the composition of a scene during the editing process. Murch has discussed this subtlety in range of conversations. To quote him more fully, from an interview in *Paris Review*:

> Like most people, I was oblivious to blinking until *The Conversation*, which was the first feature that I edited. I had the repeated, uncanny experience of watching Gene Hackman's close-ups and deciding where to cut – *He put the tape down, and now he's thinking about what he's going to do with the tape and … cut*. Very frequently, more frequently than I would have thought, the point that I decided to cut was the point that Hackman blinked. I thought, 'That's peculiar.' (2012)

This subtle detail suggests a sense of Otherness. Indeed, the same detail of 'no-blinking' was adopted in the direction of Haley Joel Osment's performance in Spielberg's cyborg cinema movie *AI: Artificial Intelligence*, a text that can be profitably viewed alongside *The Terminator* as another contribution to 'cyborg cinema', to draw on the title of a study by Sue Short. On the differences between cinematic cyborgs, she writes:

> Cinematic cyborgs ... are diverse in the forms they take: presented either as former humans who have been physically modified in some way, as androids with organic components, or as machines that develop such a degree of sentience as to confound conventional distinctions between human and machine. Such figures typically combine advanced intelligence and strength with human values and vulnerabilities. If they fail to demonstrate due deference to these values, they are cast as villains: the enemy that humans must fight against. Yet what 'bad' cyborgs are essentially guilty of is emulating humanity's most negative traits, and their destruction therefore appears to be a means of denying and displacing this fact ... The fact that cyborg cinema emerged just as new electronic technologies were beginning to impact upon contemporary life is clearly no coincidence. (2011: 4)

Back at TechNoir, Cameron again uses slow-motion to intensify the movement of the Terminator through the dancers at the club as the robot closes in. We see Reese reflected in the mirror at the bar and the scene plays with our sense of spatial awareness to enhance the tension in this contemporary rendition of a classic western dramatic device: the shootout in the saloon. There is a cut to the Terminator turning and finally seeing Sarah, again rendered in slow-motion to attenuate the drama. We are then offered the Terminator's point of view as he approaches Sarah at her table. Reese turns and shoots, again in slow-motion. Sarah runs and there is repeated use of the camera tracking backwards in front of the characters as they walk towards 'us'.

Only now is the film ready to inform the audience of the bigger issues of plot and character motivation. Now, at last, we find out why Sarah is being hunted and we finally have confirmed that the Terminator is not a mortal man and we get to see the world (literally) through his eyes for the first time. The Terminator commandeers a police car in his unrelenting mission. A car chase ensues during which Reese explains to Sarah his identity and mission to protect Sarah. Reese describes to Sarah what a Terminator is, and that both he and it are from the future. The device of an explicitly action-orientated sequence that also allows for exposition and characterisation to be combined characterises a number of such moments across Cameron's movies.

The police are then shown searching for Reese and Sarah, who have now stolen a different car. They, and the audience, eventually discover some reprieve from the rapidly escalating intensity. Reese explains to Sarah the situation in the future and their exchange has a warmth to it, expressed in a series of close-up shots as he explains that artificial intelligence will become committed to enslaving and exterminate humans. Reese explains that he has returned from the future to protect her and he talks about the leader John Connor, explaining that he is Sarah's as yet-unborn son. The quiet is inevitably interrupted by the arrival of the Terminator. Now that we understand Sarah's destiny, everything that happens to her assumes all the more consequence. The story has now acquired a prophetic, Biblical resonance. The tension builds further as the police catch up to Reese and Sarah whilst the Terminator escapes.

The action then focuses on Sarah and Reese who have been taken to a police station for questioning. Sarah talks to a cynical and rather dismissive and patronising criminal psychologist about her situation. (Not being fully engaged in an experience is never a good thing in a Cameron movie.) There is then a cut to the film's most overtly visceral moment as we watch the title character performing auto-surgery on his synthetic skin and endoskeleton. The illusion is rendered realistically through the use of the increasingly convincing prosthetics technology that had been developed and showcased in the early 1980s, as advanced by the work of Rick Baker, Rob Bottin, Tom Savini and Stan Winston.

The action then cuts back to the police station to focus on Reese, who is handcuffed and struggling to explain his situation and the wider issues and ramifications at stake for the world as in the film. The logic of the time-travel story is addressed in this exchange and neatly 'tucked away' here whilst acknowledging that there is an inherent paradox in travelling back to the past to correct the future (indeed, 'Paradox' was the original subtitle for the film that eventually became titled *Back to the Future Part II*).

In her reflections on Cameron's film, Vivian Sobchack has noted that the Terminator is 'nearly impervious to that temporal bodily terminator: Death' (2001: 38). This sense of the immortal is refrained in the conclusion to *Avatar*, in terms of Jake Sully's consciousness (his soul) becoming truly unified with his Na'vi body. After Reese – all too human in his anxiety, anger and frustration – is shown pleading to be understood by the authorities, the film then cuts to the Terminator as it walks into the police station in pursuit of Sarah and starts shooting. Reese and Sarah escape after he finds her hiding under a desk. With Sarah in the foreground, her worried face clearly seen amidst low-key lighting, a silhouette approaches in the background. This composition is a horror movie trope: the monster approaching the helpless isolated woman. Indeed, the film adds to the sense of connection with the Terminator when we are at points offered its viewpoint as it sees the world through its electronic vision. The act of 'seeing' becomes a trope also in the climax of *The Abyss* and *Avatar*. In the latter film, the act of 'seeing' is an image that is fundamental to the premise of the movie as Jake must see as an avatar form.

The Terminator, then, functions from a plot narrative rooted in the chase. The film is a thriller (almost a cat-and-mouse scenario) blending science fiction and the Bible. In its midsection the film also becomes a 'lovers on the run' piece as Sarah and Reese hide out in a storm-drain in the woods on the edge of LA. Reese puts his arms around her to keep her warm and he tells her about her future son. He also explains that Sarah is a legend in the future. The blossoming romance between them is presented with a satisfying understatement. There is something darkly comic about Sarah and Reese recognising their attraction to each other as they sit at a table arming themselves for combat. In *Aliens*, there is an echo of this in the short scene in which Hicks instructs Ripley in how to use a firearm. Importantly, the device of the romantic subplot finds a place in each Cameron film from *The Terminator* onwards, the romance serving to amplify the issue of what makes and sustains our sense of humanity in our highly technologised, arguably post-human world.

If the film's accumulating mythic resonance sees Sarah Connor assume something of the quality of Mary the mother of Jesus, Reese becomes Sarah's Joseph. They talk

Sarah Connor and Kyle Reese: survival instinct nurturing romantic impulse

about 'being strong', physically, emotionally and intellectually and this resilience of mind and body is a critical character trait for protagonists in all of Cameron's later films. As Reese talks, the image of him dissolves and we again see the future battle scene with the action now focused on resistance fighters underground. We see a Terminator intrude and kill them. In a fleeting moment we see that Reese has a picture of Sarah in his jacket and the photo is then shown burning up. From this image of fragility the film segues to an image of the Terminator setting out to resume its hunt. Sarah and Reese hide out in a motel and have sex. It is a delicate scene, a pause before the protagonists return to the trauma of the chase. The motel setting reinforces the film's 'lovers on the run' sensibility, being a space that is somewhat apart from the ordinary social space. 'I came across time for you, Sarah. I love you. I always have', Reese explains to her and what follows is the film's most unadorned image: a close-up of their hands clasped together.

During their 'time out' Reese shows Sarah how to make bombs and Reese's loneliness is given expression as is his mantra: 'Pain can be controlled. You just disconnect it.' It is a statement that could be uttered by any of Cameron's heroes when under duress.

The film then moves into its final act with a major chase scene in which the Terminator appears to finally be destroyed, burning in the flames of an exploded oil tanker lorry. However, Reese and Sarah watch as the Terminator's 'immortal' endoskeleton rises from the flames. They run for cover into a factory where the final, primal showdown plays out. The setting is claustrophobic and conjures the horror movie staple of fragile women in confined spaces, a device Cameron would use again most powerfully in *Aliens*. With the Terminator finally destroyed the film's coda shows Sarah in the desert (again, a Biblically allusive image) recording tapes for her future son to listen to, just as in other Cameron films characters record their stories: Jake in *Avatar* and Rose in *Titanic*.

'There's a storm coming,' a little boy says to Sarah. He then takes her photo and she drives off towards a literal and metaphoric storm cloud, the desert an apocalyptic setting of particular resonance (an idea used to great visual effect in the earlier *Mad Max 2: The Road Warrior* (George Miller, 1982)).

Conclusion

The Terminator established something of a generic template for future-set horror-inflected science fiction features. We might cite Paul Verhoeven's unofficial science fiction 'trilogy' *RoboCop* (1987), *Total Recall* (1990) and *Starship Troopers* (1997) as major studio productions that evidenced the Cameron influence, though with far more of a satirical line. Drawing on Robin Wood's pithy description of the arc of *The Texas Chainsaw Massacre* (Tobe Hooper, 1974), the Terminator's relentless killing mission is an extension of the earlier film's view that the 'annihilation [of humanity] is inevitable' at the hands of an 'Other' force (2003: 88). Indeed, Wood identifies the Other as being other people, women, the proletariat, other cultures, ethnic groups, alternative ideologies, deviation from ideological sexual norms, children.

The character of the Terminator rapidly became iconic, its resonance quickly extending beyond the specific context of the film's narrative. In 2003, when Arnold Schwarzenegger was elected as Governor of California he was dubbed 'The Governator', a nickname trading on enough collective recognition of *The Terminator* and his performance of the titular character. The Terminator's terse statement 'I'll be back' became the most recognised line of speech from the film and the character's black leathers and shades immediately emblematic of a science fiction film that was not for kids. To some significant degree the film refreshed filmic science fiction after the genre's late-1970s 'renaissance' centred around optimistic movies, notably *Star Wars* and *Close Encounters of the Third Kind* (Steven Spielberg, 1977). As noted, *The Terminator*'s commercial success prompted a number of similarly-toned films to be made, notably *RoboCop*. Like *The Terminator*, Verhoeven's film was also produced by Orion. The very low budget *Trancers* (Charles Band, 1985) followed in the film's wake too. Of *Robocop*, director Verhoeven noted, some years after its release, that an aspect of its narrative was Biblically inflected: 'The point of *RoboCop*, of course, is it is a Christ story. It is about a guy that gets crucified after fifty minutes, then is resurrected in the next fifty minutes and then is like the super-cop of the world, but is also a Jesus figure as he walks over water at the end' (2010). TechNoir, the name of the nightclub in which the tense shoot out in the film occurs subsequently became a name that extended beyond the movie and informed the stylistic approach of a number of films thereafter. Arguably 'tech-noir' is Cameron's 'own' subgenre, a contribution to popular filmmaking that he would certainly return to in *Strange Days*, a fascinating hybrid of generic impulses and an interesting case study in authorship.

With *Blade Runner* and then *The Terminator* following a few years later, the idea of 'dark' science fiction expressed a level of pessimism and uncertainty about the relationships between humans and artificial intelligence. It was a frightening, rather than an exciting and positive, prospect. Upon its original theatrical release in North America in the autumn of 1984, *The Terminator* was received with enthusiasm both commercially and critically. This positive reception extended across the Atlantic, too, with the film recognised not only for its narrative allure but also an implicit and confidently articulated perspective on 'the world'. Chris Peachment, writing for *Time Out* at the time of the film's original release, commented that it had 'more than enough violence to make it a profoundly moral film' (1984).

With *The Terminator*, Cameron 'announced' an ongoing creative project for himself that would explore the ways in which humanity is revealed in conflict and in concert with technology. With its emphasis on the experience of female protagonists, the film offers a dramatisation and genre-specific setting for a cultural tendency of which Rosi Braidotti writes: 'It is significant that one of the most common images of the feminist debate over difference is the one about "mothers and daughters". Its recurrence expresses the political urgency of thinking about the formalization and the transmission of the feminist heritage' (2011: 128). Whilst *The Terminator* hints at the role of Sarah as a mother, who will, effectively, save the human race, Braidotti's concept is all the more potent when considered in connection with *The Terminator*'s sequel. To view both films as a diptych is useful in this context.

Whilst Schwarzenegger's body (in stasis and in motion) might be most central to the film's aspects of meaning, it is equally appropriate to cite the importance of Sarah Connor's physicality. In *The Terminator* she is ordinary, unassuming, mentally and physically unprepared for the experience that she will have to negotiate and survive. In the sequel, Sarah's body features prominently as an effective and dynamic presence. Our first encounter with her in the film shows her maintaining a strict physical regime. For Braidotti, in considering our post-human experience, the body assumes powerful metaphorical resonance. Of this, he writes: 'The body, or the embodiment of the subject, is a key term in the feminist struggle for the redefinition of subjectivity; it is to be understood as neither a biological nor a sociological category, but rather as a point of overlap between the physical, the symbolic and the sociological' (2011: 127). Cameron's imagining of the female body assumes further development in *Aliens* and *Avatar* and his long-in-development *Battle Angel Alita* project, adapting the manga title *Alita: Battle Angel*, might perhaps take this set of considerations to a 'limit' of sorts.

With *The Terminator* having received commercial and critical approval and success, widely considered a reinvigorated take on what the science fiction movie could accomplish as a low-budget endeavour, Cameron's film industry standing was rapidly raised and he found himself in a newly-minted position as a creative whom studios were keen to invest in. As such, Cameron began his longstanding relationship with Twentieth Century Fox and their debut collaboration remains, to this day, an American genre 'classic'. *Aliens* was a war movie that, in part, emerged as a worthy entry into Hollywood's emerging engagement with the Vietnam War.

CHAPTER THREE

Aliens (1986)

Ripley and Soldiers

On various occasions, whilst discussing *The Terminator* during promotional activity for its theatrical release across North America and Europe in late 1984 and early 1985, Cameron cited *The Driver* (Walter Hill, 1978) as key in his development process on the film. For him, Hill's film suggested a way to construct a sense of the forward propulsion necessary for the expression of *The Terminator*'s plot. This sense of propulsion also characterises the narrative dynamic of *Aliens*.

With *The Terminator* a proven commercial and critical success, Hill, in his capacity as producer rather than director, approached Cameron with an offer to direct a film that offered a futuristic setting in which to retell the story of Spartacus, the rebel slave who led an uprising in ancient Rome. Cameron resisted this particular offer but his newfound connection with Hill resulted in the offer to write and direct *Aliens*, the sequel to *Alien*, which Hill had co-produced with Gordon Carroll and David Giler as part of the company Brandywine. Hill's own directorial credits include the urban stories *The Warriors* (1979), *48 Hours* (1982) and the westerns *Geronimo* (1993) and *Wild Bill* (1995). Each of these movies is a vivid genre piece about men, violence and communities. With *Geronimo* there is a connection to be made with *Avatar* if both films are considered as films dramatising the genocide of a race.

For the sequel to *Alien*, Cameron developed a screenplay draft in response to a three-word brief from the film's producers that they wanted to produce a sequel that placed Ripley in the company of the military, that Cameron probably needed little encouragement to pursue. Indeed, it is essential to recognise the relationship between Cameron's conceptual work on *Aliens* and his effectively simultaneously work on the initial screenplay for *Rambo: First Blood Part II*, a film that pitted a one-man army against East Asian guerrillas.

Aliens pits a squad of Marines against a hive of aliens located in a human colony on LV-426 (the planet on which the Nostromo lands in *Alien*), far from Earth. In writing the screenplay Cameron was directed by the studio to focus the material around the return of Ripley. Of this arc, Cameron explained in an interview with Randy and Jean-Marc L'Officier for the now no-longer published *Starlog* magazine that

> they think she goes because she'll get her job back, but that's not the case. There's no amount of money that could do it. One of my biggest problems writing the film was coming up with a reason why she goes back. It had to be psychological. One of the things that interested me is that there are a lot of soldiers from Vietnam, who have been in intense combat situations, who re-enlisted to go back again. Because they had these psychological problems that they had to work out. It's like an inner demon to be exorcised. That was a good metaphor for her character. I did a bit of that in *Rambo* as well, but it didn't get used. (1986b)

That Cameron wrote *Aliens* and *Rambo: First Blood Part II* within a year of each other provides a useful corollary and enriches our understanding of how both films accomplish some of their effects.

Cameron's film is highly aware of its war movie antecedents and *Aliens* offers an expression of what Robert Hammond has referred to as Hollywood's articulation of responses to the Vietnam War particularly:

> In addition to being a part of the general stylistic trend of visceral cinema, this has a narrative function that is also reminiscent of the horror film in that it builds towards the moment of revenge. The narrative function of constructing a terrifying unseen enemy in *Platoon* [Oliver Stone, 1986], and in other Vietnam films, is to build towards a scene of atrocity. (2002: 66)

Hammond additionally notes that Sam Fuller, director of *The Big Red One* (1980) and himself a World War II veteran, noted that war and deceit go hand in hand (2002: 72). *Aliens*, like *Avatar*, provides several brief moments that attest to Fuller's perspective, in the relationship between Ripley and company man Burke. In particularly unsubtle terms *Rambo: First Blood Part II* includes a scene late in the film when John Rambo confronts his superior for his deceit.

Fairy Tales
In *The Uses of Enchantment*, Bruno Bettelheim writes that 'the deep inner conflicts originating in our primitive drives and our violent emotions are all denied in much of modern children's literature, and so the child is not helped in coping with them. But the child is subject to desperate feelings of loudness and isolation, and often experiences mortal anxiety' (1991: 10). These fundamental reactions to the big, bad world underpin key aspects of *Aliens*, a science fiction piece that is also a potent fairy tale movie.

Ripley and Newt make their stand against a bio-mech, futureworld fairy-tale monster

The film functions powerfully as a fairy tale about children and the protective role of the 'mother', as a primal, almost atavistic, figure. Additonally, this character configuration plays out in a war movie situation which we might propose is more 'traditionally' a male-focused narrative. Of the woman, and the reality and image (and, by extension, narrative element) of the mother, Joseph Campbell has noted that 'the male body lacks that recall to nature, to the female nature that there is automatically in the female body … yes, a woman can follow the hero journey, but there are other calls and there is another relationship asked of you, I would say, to the nature field of which you are the manifestation' (2004: 147–8). On the subject of the fairy tale tradition that *Aliens* inhabits, Jack Zipes has written:

> [Fairy tales] depict metaphorically the opportunities for human adaptation to our environment and reflect the conflicts that arise when we fail to establish civilizing codes commensurate with the self-interests of large groups within the human population. The more we give into base instincts – base in the sense of basic and depraved – the more criminal and destructive we become. The more we learn to relate to other groups of people and realize that their survival and the fulfillment of their interests is related to ours, the more we might construct social codes that guarantee humane relationships. Fairy tales are uncanny because they tell us what we need and they unsettle us by showing what we lack and how we might compensate for lack. (2011: 1)

With *Aliens*, Cameron offers the clearest example of his career in terms of how the fairy tale and the horror genre can enjoy a fruitful connection. Which is to say that the fairy tale explores the threat and horror of the unknown, of cruelty and of the terror of being separated from one's parents or parental figures. Of this dynamic, Bettelheim notes: 'In practically every fairy tale good and evil are given body in the form of some figures and their actions, as good and evil are omnipresent in life and the propensities for both are present in every man. It is this duality which poses the moral problem, and requires the struggle to solve it' (1991: 8–9). Indeed, Robin Wood has explored how we might consider horror films as being 'the actual dramatisation of the dual concept of the repressed/the Other, in the figure of the Monster, the true subject of the horror genre is the struggle for recognition of all that our civilisation represses or oppresses' (2002: 28).

Thematics aside, at the same time it is striking how structurally similar Cameron's screenplay is to that of Dan O'Bannon and Ronald Shussett for *Alien* over and above the conventions of traditional three-act structures. While Cameron and the producers may have been keen to take the sequel in a different direction, there was clearly an appreciation of what worked about the original. Both films spend a considerable amount of time establishing characters and building tension before dramatically shifting gears – if anything, *Aliens* is even more leisurely. In both we meet the iterations of alien in order of development: 'facehugger' first, then 'chestburster' and finally the mature alien. And the climax of each is a *mano-a-mano* between a costumed Ripley and an alien, the outcome of which is exactly the same down to the manner of the loser's dispatch.

In an interview published in *Starlog* magazine, Sigourney Weaver recalled working on *Alien* as that film's lead female and described the fully evolved alien as 'this huge, erotic creature, a wonderful exploitation of everybody's darkest fears' (1986: 40) For H. R. Giger, the original alien creature's conceptual designer, the design and realisation of the aliens and their world was an opportunity to explore the degree to which humans and their efforts are perishable. Giger's alien was not only frightening but it was also a believable new iteration of the 'bug-eyed' aliens of older science fiction literature and films. There was something truly primal about the alien; elemental and ancient, rather like a shark. The concept of the beast in the original *Alien* film was powerfully elevated by the sexual connotations of the design and this sensibility also informed the wider design of the original film and continued to influence aspects in the production design of the three subsequent films.

Alert to the foetal imagery employed in *Alien*, Cameron elaborated on this key element in the plot mechanics of *Aliens*, devising a conflict between Ripley as woman and her nemesis, the alien Queen. Christine Cornea has written how, 'where *Alien* destabilized both sex and gender norms, *Aliens* reinstated differences based upon sex, even as the boundaries of traditional gendered roles were extended' (2007: 152). The self, then, is human. The Other is non-human (form or behaviour). The alien, like the Terminator and an avatar, is the Other.

As a guiding principle in the construction of the screenplay, Cameron referred to the final twenty minutes of *Alien* in which Ripley engages in a cat-and-mouse pursuit with the alien. Critically, the film commits its first forty minutes to defining characters and establishing the dynamics of the group relationship, the characters in the language of war movie convention. Cameron applies a Steadicam in capturing much of the action, lending it an immediacy and nervous hesitancy that perhaps prompts some collective memory on the part of the audience of footage from combat zones. The war film aesthetic that characterises *Aliens* is allied with the tropes of the science fiction genre and so the film functions as an effective genre hybrid, and its commercial success would contribute, in part, to Hollywood's subsequent production of titles such as *Demolition Man* (Marco Brambilla, 1993) and *Starship Troopers*. Of this latter film its director Paul Verhoeven said 'although it was what appeared to be sort of "B" material, I wanted to bring it up to an "A" in a way, although it was clearly never going to be *Lawrence of Arabia*' (2010).

Like *The Terminator*, *Aliens* integrates visceral action and kinetics within a range of clearly delineated characters. Additionally, we should be mindful of the impact of the American comic book to the popular culture of the 1950s, 1960s and 1970s. Key within this mode was the work of Jack Kirby (1917–1994), widely considered one of the most significantly creative figures in the evolution of mainstream superhero comics, drawing, amongst others, the characters of Captain America, the Fantastic Four, the X-Men and the Hulk. Just as Cameron's staging captures the forceful physicality of his actors so, too, Kirby's comic illustration have been noted by Norris Burroughs of the Jack Kirby Museum's online archive and blog posts for their 'dynamic torque positioning' (2011) of bodies in motion. As such, Kirby and Cameron take emphatic delight in capturing the human body in motion. Tellingly, Kirby had worked at the Fleischer animation studio early in his working life but it was in comic book illustration that he excelled. Kirby's peak is widely understood to be the year 1972 and issues 6, 7 and 8 of the serial *New Gods*. His work is notable for having given expression to the 'fashion' for ideas about cosmic energy of the 1960s and we might propose that there is a connection here with the mental and emotional connections of characters across time and space that inform the drama of *The Abyss* and *Avatar*.

Aliens was filmed in West London in autumn 1985 at the decommissioned Acton Power Station and at Pinewood Studios, the location filming enhancing the believability of the fabricated sets. Key to the believability of the fantasy being constructed was the alien creature designs and their performance and the realisation of the alien Queen particularly. Cameron's regular collaborator Stan Winston (who also worked as Second Unit Director on the film) typically referred to 'characters' not 'monsters' throughout his work in genre movies. He led the work in realising the aliens, adapting and evolving Giger's original concept. Several years after work on *Aliens*, Winston and his studio would construct the dinosaurs for *Jurassic Park* and like *Aliens* here, too, was a film in which surrogate parents protected young people from the dangers of the world.

The Movie (note: this analysis is based on the 1986 released version of the film, although it refers in passing to the 'Special Edition', which restores some footage cut from the version released theatrically)
The film begins with a black screen and the sound of an ominous low-end hum. Slivers of metallic blue forms appear on screen and they gradually shift to become the letters comprising the film's title. Immediately, James Horner's discordant music establishes a sense of unease. The image then reveals, as the camera tilts down, the expanse of space and the miniscule form of a spaceship. The shot finds a more elaborately rendered echo during the opening moments of *Avatar*. For Vivian Sobchack this oft-used image of

planets, vessels and stars in concert can 'remove us from out of our limited physical selves and give us the visual scope of a god' (2001: 102).

The lonely ship approaches the foreground of the frame and Horner's score becomes more emphatic in expressing something bleak. There is a dissolve to the interior of the ship, the image echoing something of the tracking camera deployed at moments in *Alien*, the slow movement across the frame, a given space lit in a low-key way, with foreground silhouettes and dimly-lit mid- and background space, conjures a sense of unease and of a potentially unseen, unidentified menace. In the chamber we might recognise a space suit previously seen in *Alien* (but it is not essential if we do not) and everything is dusted with a layer of ice, almost like a fairy tale setting under the spell of a witch. Then a close-up on Ripley's (Sigourney Weaver) face. The action then cuts to show a small ship docking within the larger ship and there is then a cut to an image of the elemental: fire and light cutting through into the ice world of the chamber. The elemental image will be refrained later in the movie. An ominous robotic arm swings into view in the newly-made doorway and a light-beam emanates from it as the arm pushes forward into the chamber (this particular moment of action anticipates the pseudopod scene in *The Abyss*). We then see human beings silhouetted against the backlight as they enter with breathing masks and torches blazing to find Ripley asleep (like Snow White or Sleeping Beauty; an overt and slightly playful allusion to the film's fairy tale sensibilities) with Jones the cat. We do not know if these intruders are friend or foe. The scene is presented as a tonal extension of certain scenes in *Alien*, not indicative of the tone that the film will subsequently adopt. There is then a dissolve from a profile shot of Ripley to the curve of a planet in space: it is a visual match within the story but it also gives the nod to the Star Child of Stanley Kubrick's *2001: A Space Odyssey* (1968). Thematically, this visual flourish makes a connection between the image of woman and the life form of a planet. There is then a panning shot that reveals a large space station in orbit.

From the blacks, greys and blues of the opening moments of the film the action then cuts to a high-key, all white medical centre. A bureaucrat named Carter Burke (Paul Reiser) enters with the cat (a survivor of the trauma that unfolded in *Alien*) and approaches Ripley who is recuperating from her deep sleep. Burke informs Ripley: 'I work for the company. But don't let that fool you. I'm an OK guy…' But immediately our suspicions are piqued and the character of Burke as an administrator anticipates the character of Selfridge in *Avatar*. Burke will not enjoy a harmonious relationship with Ripley or her soldier crew. Such a class-based middle-management/worker dynamic will occur in other Cameron movies. We might wish to recall, too, his self-described 'blue collar' credentials. There is a hubris that these administrators embody in the face of nature's primal force, which finds an especially expansive realisation in the later *Titanic*.

As she acclimatises to a 'new world', Ripley does not yet know how long she has been asleep. When Burke tells her that it has been 57 years she looks shocked, perhaps even afraid. There is then a close-up on Ripley; we hear the amplified sound of her heartbeat; then an extreme close-up on Jones the cat hissing, open jawed, suddenly monstrous, a precursor of what Ripley will confront in due course. In slow-motion

Aliens as Vietnam allegory: soldiers fighting in a wilderness

we see Ripley become increasingly anxious as she envisions an alien within her and we see the flesh on her torso being pushed at from within; a glimmer of some of the more visceral, horror movie-inflected moments to come. The scene's emphasis on the animalistic miniaturises a broader aspect of Cameron's films in terms of the role of primal, atavistic sensibilities and the conflict between the wild and the civilised; a rendering, perhaps, of a deep-rooted narrative of American culture which historian of the American west, Frederick Jackson Turner, has simplistically described as 'the line between civilization and savagery' (1994: 116).

Ripley recovers from her panic attack, declines further medication ('I've slept enough'), and in the next scene she recaps, for the benefit of the Weyland Corporation board (owners of the Nostromo) and, by extension the audience unfamiliar with the events of *Alien*, what previously unfolded. Having established a colony of 'sixty or seventy' families on LV-426 subsequent to the events of *Alien* without encountering any evidence of hostile alien life, the board is sceptical of Ripley's story and her impassioned plea not to engage with the alien form again. Ripley's intense expression of concern and anger at the bureaucrats' unwillingness to hold any store in her story anticipates Sarah Connor's impassioned warning in *Terminator 2* and it also echoes Reese's explanations in *The Terminator*. Indeed, in *Avatar*, Weaver's character, Grace Augustine, is similarly imprisoned for objecting to an organisational strategy that she thinks is morally corrupt. Just as John Rambo finds himself being drawn back into a combat zone in the jungle in *Rambo: First Blood Part II*, so too, Ripley finds herself being co-opted into the fight against a largely 'invisible' enemy.

Ripley becomes the maverick that the establishment does not understand or does not want to make the effort to understand. Perhaps it is not too inventive to suggest that Ripley is also a metaphor for filmmakers working to present their project to a film industry with commercial imperatives and often committee-based decision making. The colonists on LV-426 anticipates *Avatar* and is an especially American frame of reference in terms of white European colonisers. Consider how the historical white colonisation of America was dramatised in Terrence Malick's *The New World* (2005). We can usefully refer here to Richard Slotkin's work (cited in the last chapter on *The Terminator*) on the subject of white colonisation of a cultural and geographic unknown in what we now name as America. As such, *Aliens*, like *Avatar*, builds its drama, in significant part, around images and a broader narrative that depict colonists entering into a wilderness for which they are unprepared.

We cut to an extreme close-up of a cigarette burning right down between Ripley's fingers. It suggests not only her shortening temper but the ash also evokes something of the apocalyptic as pictured in *Terminator 2: Judgement Day* in its prologue sequence when a nuclear fire rages across Los Angeles. Indeed, we might also note that in *Schindler's List*, perhaps the most affecting and chilling feature-film representation of the Holocaust, is encapsulated in the moment when Oskar Schindler notices flakes of ash landing on his car. Ripley's long fingers are also suggestive of the 'face hugger' stage of the alien life form. She is in her apartment with Jones and it appears an indeterminate amount of time has passed since her rescue. She is visited by Burke and Lt. Gorman (William Hope) of the Marine Corps. Burke informs Ripley that contact with the colony on LV-426 has been lost and they want her to travel there with a military detachment as adviser to the troops to ensure things are OK. She does not welcome this. She has accepted a job working on the cargo docks for the company and Burke tries to convince her that he can secure her reinstatement as a flight officer. Ripley, then, is a woman making her way in a highly masculine workplace and we might cite this as a critical theme of the film. In Cameron's next film, *The Abyss*, the experience of a professional woman in a largely all-male workplace can be seen as fundamental to the drama. *Aliens* and *The Abyss* both send 'Rosie the Riveter' to the stars and to the bottom of the ocean. Rosie the Riveter originated in 1942 in a song recorded by big-band leader Kay Kyser. Of the figure of Rosie the Riveter she is described as follows at the Rosie the Riveter Trust website:

> As the U.S. faced a new and daunting challenge of a global war in the 1940s, people on the home front came together as never before. The stories of their struggles, which broke barriers and shaped many of today's best social innovations, chart a path for new vision today.
>
> Rosie the Riveter is a reminder to all of us to try new things, test our limits, and believe in ourselves and others. (2014)

The action then cuts to Ripley as she wakes from a fever dream about the aliens. She rises up in her bed, moving into a foreground close-up. A handheld camera, lending the scene a *vérité* quality, follows her to a sink where she washes her tear-strewn face. There is an intimacy to the moment that a locked-down camera might not have been able to so easily express. Ripley then calls Burke to get his assurance that the mission is only to destroy and not bring back an alien for analysis before agreeing to accompany them – 'OK, I'm in.'

There follows a cut to a wide shot of the Sulaco in space and then a shot that dissolves, the sequence of shots taking us inside the Sulaco. We see a number of deep sleep chambers as the occupants begin to wake in a shot highly reminiscent of the awakening crew of the Nostromo in *Alien*. There is the sense in this moment, not so much of sleep, but of coffins being opened. The allusion to death is tangible.

Within moments the film's fairy tale reference point and resonance is again made when one of the soldiers, the masculine woman Vasquez (Jenette Goldstein), refers to Ripley as 'Snow White'. In the Marine cohort, Cameron offers an ensemble of characters who we will recognise in later Cameron films. Vasquez anticipates the character of Trudy Chacon in *Avatar*, and it is worth noting Cameron's representation of Latinas in his films. In both *Aliens* and *Avatar*, Latinas feature in key, action-orientated roles. In the context of the Hollywood feature-film mode the most recognised star is likely to be Jennifer Lopez. In an increasingly multicultural mass culture landscape the modes of representation of non-white cultures is swiftly assuming increasing relevance and resonance. Certainly, as Clara E. Rodriguez explores in her book *Latin Looks: Images of Latinas and Latinos in the U.S. Media*, we might broadly state that Latinos and Latinas are underepresented and misrepresented in mainstream media where their experiences are often narrated in terms of immigration, crime and welfare. In the figures of Trudy Chacon and Vasquez in *Avatar* and *Aliens* respectively, Cameron offers us images of Latinas who are motivated, self-actualising and hugely competent and confident in their abilities.

This scene begins to establish the character of each soldier, personalising them and defining their traits but also their separation from Ripley, Burke and their commanding officer Gorman. Ripley maintains a physical distance from the soldiers. The scene includes a long shot of the group eating and this presentation of a mundane, yet dramatically charged, moment encapsulates a sense of the class difference between Ripley and the soldiers. Ripley is now a middle-management figure, leading a team. In a film so loaded with an intensely rendered and meaningful sense of production design and creation of a fantasy landscape that functions metaphorically this scene is one of the film's only ones that is free of excessive artifice. That said, as Cameron's contemporary, Robert Zemeckis, has pithily noted: even a close-up is fake; a special effect, if you will.

We are introduced to Bishop (Lance Henriksen), the android accompanying the mission. Based on her previous experience of being in the company of an android (science officer Ash in *Alien*), Ripley insists that she is not happy that an android is working as part of the mission. But Bishop explains that he has an inbuilt behaviour programme, which forbids him to harm a human or even to engineer a situation in which a human might be at risk. This unease between human and cyborg plays out with similar intensity and perhaps greater prominence in Ridley Scott's addition to the *Alien* universe, *Prometheus* (2012), a film, according to Davina Quinlivan, that presents

> the new 'David 8' android [played by Michael Fassbender], marketed as if it were comparable with an iPad – a friendly yet meaningful gadget, a lifestyle accessory. While this dimension of Scott's new film seems little related to any critique of gender and sexuality, it is significant that androids have played pivotal roles in all of the *Alien* films and embody a hidden threat to everything that is natural and

suggestive of human life. The sterile androids are ultimately inhuman, but they also disrupt the logic of what it means to be sentient, to be real, filling the void between human heroine and matriarchal monster. (2012)

This idea is a very old one, going back in cinema at least as far as *Metropolis*. As in *The Terminator* and its sequel, the action of *Aliens* dramatises thinking around the degree to which a manufactured being can be invested with human traits. We can reach back to the example of E. T. A. Hoffman's story *Olympia* which was cinematically rendered in the 'Olympia' segment of *The Tales of Hoffman* (Michael Powell, 1951) and further back before that to the myth of Galataea.

The soldiers are then briefed by Lt. Gorman regarding the mission ahead of them and critically at this moment we see an apparently innocuous piece of technology in action (seemingly as a modest, background detail): the bright yellow load-lifter. We then see Ripley offering to use the load lifter in a brief scene that demonstrates the ease with which she handles the technology and that also introduces an element to which the film neatly returns at its climax. The load-lifter is a piece of technology that has its root in Cameron's short film *Xenogenesis* and we might also recognise how the load-lifter in part transforms into the robot suits seen in *Avatar*. By extension, there is a sense of telemetry at work in the load-lifter and robot-suits in *Avatar*. (There is an even more elaborate rendition of the image of the telemetry process in the (non-Cameron film) *Pacific Rim* (Guillermo del Toro, 2013).) *Aliens* thus visualises the industrial application of fusing the human body with the engineered and technological and gives it narrative purpose.

There is then a cut to the ship nearing the planet of LV-426 and the sequence then cuts to a scene in the drop ship which will take the team down. During the journey time, the scene functions as an opportunity to develop the war movie aesthetic and the militaristic drum snare heard on the music score foregrounds the allusion. We see the troops armouring up and a handheld shot follows them from the drop ship interior and out to the tank which will actually land on LV-426 (a similar moment occurs early in *Avatar* when Jake arrives on the planet of Pandora). There is then a close-up of Ripley looking anxious and this is followed by a cut to a concerned Corporal Hicks (Michael Biehn), watching her. Building on the earlier dinner scene, each soldier's personality is being further defined: the inexperienced and defensive Gorman, the posturing Vasquez and Drake (Mark Rolston), the loudmouth Hicks (Bill Paxton), the professional, competent Hicks (who falls asleep during the journey).

Picking up on Slotkin's thinking about American narratives of nationhood as explored in his essay 'Unit Pride: Ethnic Platoons and the Myths of American Nationality', we can propose that the film's military setting 'expresses a myth of American nationality that remains vital in our political and cultural life: the idealised self-image of a multi-ethnic, multi-racial democracy, hospitable to difference but united by a common sense of national belonging' (2001: 469).

Ripley looks at the screens and monitors as they approach the landing and the camera moves slowly over and towards the rooftops and exteriors of the colony buildings. We then see the buildings on the monitor screens. It is a minor observation but several of Cameron's films engage in presenting views of the world through screens and monitors. We do not necessarily see the world – we see it on screen and therefore inauthentically. *Avatar* elaborates the concept of the artificial and the authentic. Technology becomes an interface between us and the world around us. Technology and human experience are entwined rather than distinctly separate; increasingly so in the computer-generated-effects world which post-dates the production of *Aliens*.

Ripley and her crew land in the rain and the darkness and find themselves in terrain not dissimilar from the future wasteland shown in *The Terminator*. It is a world that is falling apart and without harmony, the inclement weather serving to emphasise this. A handheld camera then follows the soldiers as they move out from the tank and across the terrain to take their positions just outside an entrance to one of the buildings. Within the building await the claustrophobic spaces where the film's action will continue, very much in the spirit of the horror film. The claustrophobic in the horror film amplifies the desire for escape from trauma.

The crew use their motion trackers to identify where colonists might be located in the complex but none are found. By giving the soldiers their own viewfinders, the tension deepens as we are at one more remove from the action and so must see what they are seeing on their monitors. The corridors and rooms are bereft of people, and the abandoned coffee cups and food suggest something sudden and unexpected happened here. Ripley remains on the tank with Burke and Gorman and, via the helmet-cams of the soldiers, can see evidence of aliens, in particular holes in the floors and ceilings that may have been caused by their acidic blood. Importantly, the helmet-cams trade on a tradition of visualising war in movies and more significantly how the mass audience has encountered images of combat, particularly the Vietnam conflict. Gorman prematurely declares the site 'secure', and Ripley leaves the safety of the tank. As they explore the abandoned site, they come across a laboratory containing alien facehuggers in glass cylinders, one of which is still alive. This is the first clear evidence that the colonists have been in contact with the aliens.

The soldiers move on and are surprised to discover a little girl who tries to evade them. Ripley follows the terrified girl into her hideaway and amongst the detritus of her former life finds a photograph of her, revealing her name to be Rebecca. The infant is understandably uncommunicative but, as Ripley cleans her up back in the tank, asks to be called 'Newt', her family nickname, and reveals that her parents and brother are dead. This scene offers the kind of reprieve from kinetic intensity that is a necessary rhythmic shift and which worked so well in *The Terminator*. The film avoids making the relationship that develops around Newt and Ripley too sentimental. What is un-stated in the theatrically released version, but made explicit in a restored scene in the 'Special Edition' featuring material excised for initial release, is that Ripley actually had a daughter, who died during her 57 years of hypersleep; thus Newt becomes a substitute for the daughter Ripley never saw grow up. (Another restored scene shows that it is actually Newt's family who were responsible for bringing the alien life form into contact with the colonists; it is inferred that their encounter with the alien ship is engineered by the Weyland Corporation, just as the Nostromo's was.) Vicky Lebeau writes how

> Closer to the state of infancy, an infans (literally, without language) the small child tends to be discovered at the limit of what words can be called upon to tell, or to mean – a limit that then generates the questions of how to convey the child's experience in language, of what in that experience, of what in the image, falls outside of, and so resists, the world of words. By contrast, when it comes to the representative of the child, cinema, with its privileged access to the perceptual, its visual and aural richness, would seem to have the advantage: closer to perception, it can come closer to the child. (2008: 16)

This perceptual closeness to the child informs camera position at points in the action so that we are very subjectively given Newt's point of view. Furthermore, Newt initially interacts with Ripley without speaking.

In *Avatar*, the character of Grace Augustine echoes Ripley's maternal qualities combined with her professionalism and frustration and anger at the choices that the corporation are making in their engagement (or lack of engagement), with the 'realities' of the wilderness and the 'Other'. As such, Ripley and Grace, rather than any bureaucratic forces, become the moral compass of *Aliens* and *Avatar* respectively, functioning as the site of personal integrity in action rather than in bureaucratic effort or non-effort. In *The Terminator* and *The Abyss*, administrators are represented as ineffectual.

This quiet conversation is followed by a tense scene between the soldiers and the control unit, as the troops move deeper into the complex, whose environment has become increasingly 'alien-ised'. An increasingly nervous Gorman instructs the troops, from the safety of the tank, not to use live ammunition for fear of setting off a chain reaction of explosions, and they reluctantly accede – although Vasquez and Drake keep some back. The troops now come across their first colonists, trussed up like flies in a cobweb. We have an idea what is coming, but it is a shock for the troops when a conscious colonist screams to be killed just as an infant alien bloodily emerges from her chest. The troops duly incinerate this unwilling mother and vicious-looking offspring, but the noise only attracts the attention of the new residents of the colony, and from this point on the film shifts into a different register.

The alien ambush of the troops is visually chaotic, a mixture of brief shots from the scene interspersed with fuzzy helmet-cam combat being viewed by Ripley, Gorman and Blake from the tank, one camera after the other going blank as the soldiers are picked off. Paralysed with fear and uncertainty, the inexperienced Gorman is unable to offer coherent advice to his rapidly diminishing force, so Ripley now takes charge and drives the tank through the corridors to rescue the soldiers – only Hicks, Hudson and Vasquez make it out.

Having driven them to temporary safety outside the complex, Ripley argues strongly that the complex should be 'nuked' from space once they return to their ship, to the consternation of Blake, the company man, who remonstrates with her that the colony represents a 'significant dollar value' to the Corporation and he cannot sanction its destruction. Ripley reminds him that they are part of a military mission and, as such, Corporal Hicks is now the highest ranking available soldier, Gorman having been temporarily incapacitated during the rescue. Burke's corporate cynicism anticipates a similar attitude presented in both *Titanic* and *Avatar* in terms of the films' antagonists. Hicks agrees that the site should be destroyed and the landing craft that dropped them on LV-426 is recalled. However, this craft has inadvertently picked up an alien creature on its initial visit and the creature kills both pilots as it approaches the surface, crashing spectacularly. The mission is now marooned on the planet. Newt explains to Ripley that 'they mostly come at night' (a phrase redolent of a fairy tale text) and there is an image of Ripley, holding Newt, as she stands against the ominously stormy sky, an emblematic image of 'mother and child' confronting a harsh world, an example of what Jim Naureckas, in his essay '*Aliens*: Mother and the Teeming Hordes', describes as the film 'canonizing motherhood' (1987: 1).

Taking refuge back in the complex, Hudson loses his composure and it is Ripley who has to rally the surviving team through her action and intelligence, identifying how their area can be secured against the aliens. Her steadying function is echoed by Lindsay in *The Abyss* in the sequence in that film when the crew of the submarine oil rig begin to splinter under the pressures of an encounter with the unknown. The film then switches from war to horror genre for a scene in which Ripley and Newt sleep in the lab. Ripley awakes and sees that one of the face-huggers is no longer in its cylinder. Sure enough it attacks Ripley and Newt, attempting its sole purpose for living, to impregnate another organism.

The alien is a distillation of the horror-movie monster: organic and invasive. John Carpenter's *The Thing* (on which Stan Winston also worked) elaborately envisions this idea of the invasive alien violently taking over the human body, in the case of the titular alien by impregnation via a form of oral rape. In the extensive range of writing about the *Alien* series, the quartet of films (*Alien*, *Aliens*, *Alien 3* (David Fincher, 1992) and *Alien: Resurrection* (Jean-Pierre Jenet, 1997)) are often understood as dramatising the subjects of maternity, pregnancy, birth and death. In the discussions that have built around the quartet, but particularly the first two, Tom Shone has commented that the *Alien* world is 'a Freudian fever dream, with its crabby and post-coital atmosphere, its rebirthing imagery, its queasily gynecological production design, its night-sweat of male anxiety' (2012). Of the famous John Hurt birth scene in *Alien*, James Kavanagh, in his essay 'Son of a Bitch: Feminism, Humanism, and Science in *Alien*', has written that it is a 'particularly horrifying confusion of the sexual-gynaecological with the gastro-intestinal', the 'baby' alien 'a razor-toothed phallic monster [gnawing] its way through his stomach into the light – a kind of science fiction *phallus dentatus*' (1990: 76).

Surviving the encounter with the face-hugger, Ripley blames the conniving Burke for releasing it with a view to enabling him to smuggle an alien embryo or two back to the Weyland Corporation who appear to have ambitions to breed the species for their weapons division. The remaining troops intend to kill Burke for his treachery but before they can, there is another wave of alien attacks, during which the cowardly Burke meets his end, as do the considerably more honourable Gorman and Vasquez.

The last act of the film focuses on Ripley's mission to rescue Newt, from whom she becomes separated retreating from the aliens, a sequence akin to an elaborate revision of the ending of *The Terminator* with its industrial setting of machines, low-key lighting, chaos of machinery and the 'fusion' of human bodies with a 'heavy metal' setting. Leaving an injured Hicks in the care of Bishop, who has successfully remotely piloted another escape ship to the surface, a heavily-armoured Ripley returns to sub-level 3, the alien 'hive', to which she has traced Newt, who was wearing a tracking device. Ripley has approximately seventeen minutes to rescue Newt and escape to safety before the complex is destroyed and the following sequence plays out in close to 'real' time.

Ripley finds Newt cocooned and awaiting the imminent attentions of a face-hugger, and frees her. There is then a confrontation with the alien Queen, protecting her 'babies' just as Ripley is protecting hers. This entire sequence has its fairy tale corollary of an evil queen or witch holding an innocent child captive as in *Hansel and Gretel* or *Rapunzel*. The confrontation between Ripley and the alien Queen sustains the fairy tale motif that has been building throughout the movie. Of the confrontation with a mother figure in the fairy tale mode, Marina Warner has considered the shifting status of women:

> As individual women's voices have become absorbed into the corporate body of male-dominated decision-makers, the misogyny present in many fairy stories – the wicked stepmothers, bad fairies, ogresses, spoiled princesses, ugly sisters and so forth – has lost its connections to the particular web of tensions in which women were enmeshed and come to look dangerously like the way things are. The historical context of the stories has been sheared away, and figures like the wicked stepmother have grown into archetypes of the human psyche, hallowed, inevitable symbols, while figures like the Beast bridegroom have been granted ever more positive status. Generally speaking, the body of story has passed out of the mouth of the quiltmaker from Palermo, on to the lips of filmmakers – Steven Spielberg – or psychoanalysts – Bruno Bettelheim – or therapists – Robert Bly. The danger of women has become more and more part of the story, and correspondingly, the danger of men has receded: Cinderella's and Snow White's wicked stepmothers teach children to face life's little difficulties, it is argued, but films about a Bluebeard or a child murderer, as in *Tom Thumb*, are rated Adults Only. (1995: 417)

In his essay 'She's a goddamn liar: Perspectives on the Truth in *Aliens* and *Titanic*', Andrew B. Elliot suggests that 'without Ripley it might even be possible to imagine rooting for the Queen, such is the aversion we feel towards the Corporation and its "grunts" ... a deliberate attempt was made to render the aliens more like insects in the sequel, a strategy which – intentional or not – functions to negate any potential anthropomorphism, which means that as a non-human threat she must be destroyed' (2011: 78).

Ripley deploys a flamethrower against the Queen and the rows of alien eggs in images that evoke both the war film but also newsreel or photographs of real combat. Ripley and Newt escape the complex, meet the craft being piloted by Bishop, and narrowly escape LV-426 before the complex is engulfed by explosions.

The remains of the mission now arrive back at their mother ship, but there is no respite – the alien Queen has hitched a ride on the rescue craft and tears the android Bishop in two. With the injured Hicks of no use, Ripley uses the load-lifter exoskeleton to confront the Queen. The load-lifter becomes a future-world rendition of a suit of armour and Ripley an avatar of sorts, the limbs of the lifter moving in unison with her physical instructions. This costume is another echo of the climax of *Alien*, where Ripley climbs into a spacesuit (after stripping down to her underwear) to eject the alien from her escape pod. There is a close-up of the load-lifter's feet recalling the extreme close-up of robot feet slamming down on the ground at the beginning of *The Terminator*. After a tussle, Ripley dispatches the Queen (again from an airlock).

Of Cameron's foregrounding of female heroics and physicality, Peter Krämer in his essay 'Women First' has noted: 'The intended effect of this spectacle on audiences is amazement and excitement about the magical possibilities of the cinema and about the potential of the human body ... The film's iconography centres on weapons and the human body, indeed the human body as a weapon and the weapon as an extension of the human body' (1999: 111). Krämer goes on to identify how Cameron's cinema provided, in its earliest efforts, a notable contrast to the youth-orientated science fiction and fantasy movies of the 1980s: 'In sharp contrast to the family-adventure films, which are still almost exclusively focused on young males, the second main strategy for attracting women to action-adventure films is to provide a female character to the status of main protagonist. Arguably, it was the success of Cameron's *Aliens* ... which first signaled to the industry that female-centred big-budget action-adventure film were a viable option' (1999: 112).

Aliens now concludes very quickly, with Ripley, Newt, the injured Hicks and mutilated but functioning Bishop resting in hypersleep. Somewhat at odds with the preceding hour, the film ends on a peaceful note that borders on the melancholy, James Horner's plaintive whisper of musical accompaniment embellishing the visuals, which mirror both the end of *Alien* and also the introduction of Ripley at the start of *Aliens*.

Conclusion
Aliens, like its predecessor and successors, exploits humans' particular unease with insects and arthropods. Additionally, *Aliens* is suffused with images of congealed and viscous forms, and Cynthia A. Freeland has observed that the horror genre articulates notions about the clean and the defiled (1996: 475). Indeed, a key frame of reference for *Aliens* is not its progenitor but instead the cinema of David Cronenberg and, as Michael Grant has explored in *The Modern Fantastic: The Films of David Cronenberg*, his dramatisation of the fascination and revulsion with the body, particularly of its inner appearance and how we control, or do not control (2000: 2). (*Aliens* and Cronenberg's remake of *The Fly* were both released within months of each other, by the same studio, in 1986).

Other films released in the summer of 1986 by Twentieth Century Fox included *Big Trouble in Little China* (directed by John Carpenter) and *Space Camp* (directed by Harry Winer). Both were commercial failures and did not garner much widespread critical support (although, in common with some of Carpenter's other work from this period, *Big Trouble in Little China* has subsequently become something of a cult film). *Aliens*, however, was commercially and critically popular. Whereas sequels are often met with the knee-jerk response that the mode inevitably signals creative bankruptcy, Cameron's film indicates how sequels have the capacity to enrich the interests of the original title. David Bordwell has explored some of the fascinations of the movie sequel and observed that 'sequels offer the possibility of recognisable repetition with controlled, sometimes intriguing, variation' (2007b).

The gearshifts of the film were a particular focus of critical attention. In his review Roger Ebert wrote:

> The movie is so intense that it creates a problem for me as a reviewer: Do I praise its craftsmanship, or do I tell you it left me feeling wrung out and unhappy? It has been a week since I saw it, so the emotions have faded a little, leaving with me an appreciation of the movie's technical qualities. But when I walked out of the theater, there were knots in my stomach from the film's roller-coaster ride of violence. (1986)

In *Time Out*, Tom Charity noted that an appeal of this particular action movie was that it was 'confidently directed … this sequel dares to build slowly…' (1986).

Aliens' summer 1986 release was followed later in the year by Orion Pictures' release of Oliver Stone's Vietnam War movie, *Platoon*. That film, a dramatisation of Stone's own experiences as a young solider, was characterised by fidelity to realism and reportage. Of the film the director observed: 'It was not our intention to deal with the Vietnamese on the screen. First, as soldiers we had no contact with them … It was a fifteen-month-long game of hide and seek' (2001: 42). Certainly, at the time such a 'journalistic' approach to Vietnam was regarded as brave, within the context of a commercial mainstream film. However, Cameron's film arguably offers the more acute drama about the impact of an unseen enemy on a combat team and effectively splices together what Robin Wood understood to be the two defining developments in American cinema in the 1970s: 'the impingement of Vietnam on the national consciousness and the unconscious, and the astonishing evolution of the horror film' (2003: 49).

Aliens also works as a exemplary exercise in the melding of contemporary action movie tropes with the virtues of classical Hollywood cinema, with its internally coherent narrative and distinctive character types economically sketched. Larry Gross, in his essay 'Big and Loud', reflects on the history of the event movie action spectacular and its revision of established narrative structure. He notes that 'Both Jim Cameron's *Aliens* and Andrew Davis's *The Fugitive* [1993] take the relentless jeopardy structure and chase aspect of the spectacular scale imagery of the Big Loud Action Movie, and organise them with unusual coherence and an unusual component of emotional sincerity' (2000: 8).

With *Aliens*, then, Cameron asserted his facility in sythesising an elaborately staged 'fantasia' that utilised realistically presented, imaginary otherworldly spaces and places, with a dramatic core that remained true to the intimate scale of the central conflict at the centre of his previous film, *The Terminator*. The commercial success of

Aliens indicated the film's contribution, and Cameron's vital role, in the evolution of a 'new wave' in American fantasy and science fiction filmmaking within the major studio production context. His contemporaries in this were Robert Zemeckis who had directed *Romancing the Stone* and *Back to the Future*, Ron Howard who had directed *Cocoon* and Tim Burton, who would direct *Beetlejuice*. What *Aliens* additionally offers its audience is an elaboration of Cameron's commitment to rendering mythic tropes in such a way that they resonate with our creeping awareness that our bodies are not necessarily, entirely our own; that they can become sites for technological fusion and transformation.

CHAPTER FOUR
The Abyss (1989)

Writing about the ocean, Herman Melville noted in his novel *Moby Dick* (1851): 'Consider the subtleness of the sea; how its most dreaded creatures glide under water, unapparent for the most part, and treacherously hidden beneath the loveliest tints of azure' (1987: 380–1). Cameron's *The Abyss* takes the tradition of narratives of the sea and uses it as a setting for a drama that expresses the increasing human dependence on technology; a dependence that has benefits and deficits. Like the later film, *True Lies*, technology also serves a particular function in relation to the marriage depicted on screen. *The Abyss* is a film that celebrates technology and machines, of both human and non-human kinds. The fusion of nature and artifice showcased in the narrative of *The Abyss* provides it with a particular connection to *Avatar*.

In 1985, during production on *Aliens*, Cameron had commented to interviewer Adam Pirani, for an article that would be published in *Starlog* in 1986, that his next film would be the antithesis to the science fiction and 'hardware' setting of *Aliens* and *The Terminator*, but this prediction did not come true. Conceived and produced as a science fiction spectacle, with a marriage-in-crisis relationship forming the focal part of the protagonists' drama, *The Abyss* in fact deepened Cameron's association with the science fiction genre.

Nonetheless, with the film, one can sense an ambition on Cameron's part to make the visual effects and fantasy a backdrop to the domestic and workplace drama that unfolds. Furthermore, with this film Cameron's affinity for the format of the romantic love story is amplified (and both the romance story and the working-class protagonists of *The Abyss* are now familiar to us from *Aliens* and *Titanic*). It was produced at a time when director Steven Spielberg was synonymous with the making of a number of science fiction films that offered benign views of imagined encounters with nonhuman cultures, such as *ET* and *Close Encounters of the Third Kind*. Of the latter film, during its production phase, Spielberg said of its story of culture contact between humans and non-humans, that 'it's an adventure thriller, not science fiction but science speculation' (quoted in Ebert 1977).

Cameron's *Aliens* and *The Terminator* opposed the benevolent view of encounters with the non-human. With *The Abyss*, though, he adopts a more positive sensibility, moving away from something more nihilistic to a view that the Other can be embraced, a perspective that also informs the protagonist's experience in *Avatar*.

As part of the construction of his industry identity as a writer/director, Cameron has, on several occasions, stated the significance of Jacques Cousteau to his own sense of cinema and the application of filmmaking to submarine exploration and *The Abyss* could certainly be understood as a cinematic paean to Cousteau's oft-stated call for an increased human sensitivity to our interconnectedness with nature. In this film, as in *Avatar*, Cameron insists on recognising that human life does not exist in some separate sphere from the natural world. His film was not the first Hollywood production to centre on the spectacle of the sea, either above or below surface. Perhaps most famously, Spielberg had directed an adaptation of Peter Benchley's novel *Jaws* several years before *The Abyss*, and, most pertinently, Ron Howard had directed *Cocoon* in which an elderly retirement community encountered aliens who had returned to Earth to gather up some of their species who lay in the titular cocoons beneath the sea. As with Cameron's movie, the alien culture offers a positive experience for human beings. In both films, the alien culture provides a redemptive function for the human protagonists.

During a TED presentation in 2010, Cameron explained how he considered that 'there was an alien world right here on earth'; his reference points were the deep-sea environments. In his talk, Cameron also went on to discuss his interest in and permutations of having 'your consciousness injected' into technology, referring initially to deep-sea exploration but also offering a sense of what, as he called it, 'a posthuman' world might be like (2010). Certainly, this concept of the 'posthuman' is key to the sense we might have about the terrain of all of Cameron's films. Of the 'posthuman' condition, Rosi Braidotti writes:

> Not all of us can say with any degree of certainty, that we have always been human, or that we are only that ... While conservative, religious forces today often labour to reinscribe the human with a paradigm of natural law, the concept of the human has exploded under the double pressure of contemporary scientific advances and global economic concerns ... the posthuman condition introduces a qualitative shift in our thinking about what exactly is the basic unit of common reference for our species, our polity and our relationship to the other inhabitants of this planet. (2013: 1)

Popular cinema has always seen the mystery and essentially hidden world of the sea as a setting for genre stories, whether original to the cinema or adaptations of literary properties; perhaps most famously Melville's *Moby Dick*, rich with Biblical allusion. One of the most popular live-action films produced by Walt Disney was an adaptation of Jules Verne's *20,000 Leagues Under the Sea* (Richard Fleischer, 1954). Then, too, we can look at *Jaws*, *Cocoon* and *Waterworld* (Kevin Reynolds, 1995) as three major studio-released films that present the sea both as place of wonder and threat and separation from the rules that potentially govern *terra firma*. The sea is a wilderness, outside of the conscious forces of human culture. Suffice to say, the wilderness contains its own cultures, communities and interconnections.

In visualising the hidden world of the sea, its metaphoric possibilities quickly announce their variety. The tradition of paintings in which the sea is the subject is deep and wide. One has only to think of Winslow Homer's paintings such as *The Gulf Stream* (1899) that shows a black man adrift on a boat surrounded by sharks and a trail of blood already in the water. Certainly, the submarine settings of *The Abyss* contribute to the tradition of narratives about undersea environments. The interest of this film is enriched further if viewed alongside two documentaries that Cameron later produced: *Ghosts of the Abyss* (2003) and *Aliens of the Deep* (2005).

Cameron has had a longstanding affinity with the ocean and the starting point of *The Abyss* is to be found in a short story that he wrote as a teenager, following a science experiment (to explain liquid breathing) that was presented in a class at school. Cameron made much of a similar connection to boyhood reading in discussing the concept for *Avatar*. As recently as 2013, he featured as the subject of a *National Geographic* cover story that narrated his deep-sea exploration of 2012, extending Cameron's film industry persona as visionary and explorer.

For *The Abyss*, he exploits the otherness of the submarine world as a setting in which a fantasy can play out. In *Under Pressure* (2001), the retrospective documentary about the production of *The Abyss*, Cameron notes that he wanted the film to achieve some equivalence – by which we might assume translates as a 'grand statement about the state of things' – with Arthur C. Clarke and Kubrick's *2001: A Space Odyssey*. Of *2001*, Kubrick had explained that 'it's essentially a nonverbal experience ... I tried to create a visual experience ... it attempts to communicate more to the subconscious and to the feelings than to the intellect' (quoted in LoBrutto 1998: 277). Whereas Kubrick had once said that the universe was indifferent to human experience, Cameron's films suggests a great non-human interest in human experience.

The Abyss certainly pursues a line of optimism regarding its 'aliens' (NTIs – Non-Terrestrial Intelligences – rather than ETs) that is in contrast to the more nihilistic tone of his earlier work. Arguably, *The Abyss* also has a more overtly moralising tone than either *The Terminator* or *Aliens*. Where these two films both end with a sense of unease and melancholy, by contrast *The Abyss* seeks to arrive at a hopeful conclusion that emphasises connection and a recognition of the human interdependence with nature. Cameron's film evokes a similar sensibility to *Close Encounters of the Third Kind* with its benevolent view of alien life; but Cameron never suggests that the NTIs are *not* of planet earth.

The Abyss uses the established and well-recognised image and trope of apocalypse, and its connection with an alien Other, but deploys it in such a way as to ultimately contrast with the American science fiction film tradition of the 1950s and 1960s in which the movies were allegories of the perceived 'Red Menace' of communism. But it is worth recognising something of the mainstream global political landscape of the time in which the film was theatrically released. Cameron himself stated in an interview with Michael Dare for *Movieline* magazine during promotion for the film that 'there's still the paranoia of nuclear weapons, the potential for war, even though we're in a glasnost period. As long as the president of the US is the ex-head of the CIA, and the premiere of Russia is the ex-head of the KGB, there's a limit to how much you can really relax' (1989).

During the 1980s, US President Ronald Reagan, British Prime Minister Margaret Thatcher and Soviet President Mikhail Gorbachev moved through a series of nuclear armament negotiations and summits that, without fail, received major TV and press coverage. The Campaign for Nuclear Disarmament (CND) took on a particular presence. In 1983, British filmmaker Jane Jackson made a TV documentary as part of the ITV strand *World in Action* about CND entitled *A Common Cause*, focusing on women marching with their children from Chester in the north-west to the US cruise missile base at Greenham Common. The film was banned from being broadcast. BBC TV screened a drama series entitled *Threads* in 1984. With *The Abyss*, Cameron treats, with seriousness, the possibility of a nuclear threat, which further shows up the light-hearted treatment of the subject in his later *True Lies* as somewhat anomalous, both in his body of work and its treatment in the culture generally.

Conceptually, *The Abyss* fuses its science fiction-centred genre elements with a love story narrative more explicitly woven into the story than in *The Terminator* or *Aliens*. Indeed, this love story is set within a science fiction context in which the presence of otherworldly energy affects the mental 'stability' of the other human protagonists. It is a circumstance that also characterises the Cameron-produced adaptation of *Solaris* (Steven Soderbergh, 2002).

Gaston Bachelard has written of water imagery and the connection to Nietzsche's body of work, a point of relevance for us given the reference to the German writer that opens *The Abyss* and whose conception of the 'superman' finds a popular culture expression in Cameron's films. For Bachelard,

> Nietzsche is not a water poet. There are, of course, water images. No poet can do without liquid metaphors. But, with Nietzsche, these metaphors are ephemeral. They do not determine material reveries. Dynamically, it is the same with water which too easily becomes servile. It cannot be a true obstacle or a true adversary for a Nietzschean fighter. (2011: 129)

This quality of the 'Nietzschean fighter' characterises both Bud (Ed Harris) and Lyndsey (Mary Elizabeth Mastrantonio) at particular points in their submarine adventure.

As with the collaborative conceptual work undertaken for the productions of *The Terminator* and *Aliens*, Cameron and production designer Leslie Dilley created a production based in the realities of recognisable industrial design so that the events of the film would appear to be taking place in believable environments. Designers Ron Cobb and Jean 'Moebius' Giraud, both of whom had worked on the original *Alien*, provided conceptual art for the film, Cobb specialising in envisioning the industrial environments and Giraud developing the look of the NTIs. Giraud is a French illus-

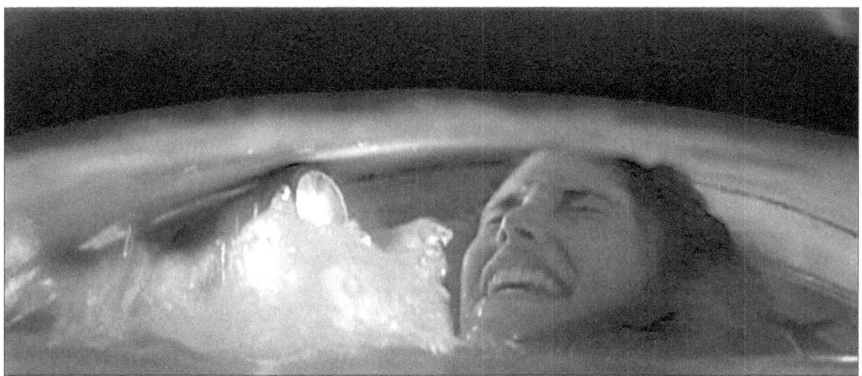

Survivors: the essential Cameron hero characteristic

trator known for his comic books such as *Arzach*, *The Airtight Garage of Jerry Cornelius*, *Blueberry* who established the magazine *Metal Hurlant* ('Heavy Metal') with several other illustrators in France in the mid-1970s to allow them a format in which to work more experimentally. Subsequently his work has been extremely influential on a generation of fantasy and science fiction filmmakers and audiences (as well as *Alien* and *The Abyss*, he produced conceptual art for such films as *Tron* and *Willow* (Ron Howard, 1988)). Giraud's often azure-tinged drawings of otherworldly humans and life-forms were distinctive with their strong lines and intricate detail. Paul Gravett has written about a particular project of the artist's which we could see as having a connection to the interests of *Avatar*: 'as part of his burgeoning personal mysticism, Moebius branched off in 1984 to devise a fresh series of his own cosmic reflections, *The Aedena Cycle* ... a sensitive eco-fable about two marooned explorers from an artificial world' (2010).

Giraud's NTIs in *The Abyss* resemble angels and Cameron brings to the film a specific Christian sensibility to aspects of the film, an extension of Sarah Connor's role and qualities in *The Terminator*. Of the expansive and extensive cultural tradition of imagining angels, Martin Palmer has explained that the term 'angel' comes from the word for 'messenger of god'. In a conversation for BBC Radio 4's programme *In Our Time*, Palmer noted that angels 'stop certain things happening. They warn people' (2009). With this description in mind, the angel reference embeds itself centrally to the larger narrative of the film, assisted by the musical choices of the film's composer, Alan Silvestri, including the employment of angelic-sounding choral music.

As with the films that were written and directed by Cameron after *The Abyss*, much was made at the time of the technological and illusion-engineering aspects key to generating audience interest in the film's story. Certainly, it fits into a longstanding Hollywood tradition of spending lavish resources to make a certain kind of film and Cameron became an exemplar of this with *The Abyss*; a narrative that continued in the promotion of his subsequent films, reaching its apogee with *Avatar* and its expensive technological innovations.

In promoting *The Abyss*, in a pre-online, pre-social media era, the studio and producers had only print media and TV available, with several extensive feature-length pieces running in magazines such as *Starlog* and *Premiere*. Uniformly, such coverage emphasised the engineering challenge of creating *The Abyss*. The set for the film's submarine mining rig was constructed in an unused nuclear reactor chamber in South Carolina. Submerged with water and then filled with floating beads and a tarpaulin cover in order to simulate the darkness of the deep sea, the location shoot was taxing. 'It wasn't difficult to be frightened because you *were* frightened', observed the actor John Bedford Lloyd in *Under Pressure*. This sense of the reality of the process of manufacturing an illusion in turn informing the on-screen text is familiar to us from other narratives about challenging film productions, such as *Heaven's Gate* (Michael Cimino, 1980) and *Fitzcarraldo* (Werner Herzog, 1982). It forges a connection between the manufacture of the illusion and the illusion's narrative.

Indeed, *The Abyss* marked a consciously engineered opportunity to evolve the application of computers to visual effects. Since the mid-1970s, the alliance between computer (digital) technology and the mechanical tradition has evolved with the digital now superseding mechanically- and photochemically-resourced effects processes. Film and photo-chemical image creation processes had been developed for *Star Wars* (in motion-control) to *Willow* and *Young Sherlock Holmes* (Barry Levinson, 1985). The move from optical to digital was one from a phenomenology anchored in photography to one increasingly informed by painting fused with the photographic. The pseudopod sequence in *The Abyss* occupied 75 seconds of screen time (seemingly fleeting now, but in 1988/89 it was a significant achievement) that took eight months to produce. Its integration of photographed and computer-generated images created what we might describe as a 'painted' image that, in turn, offers a deviation from André Bazin's expression of faith in cinema. As Colin McCabe has written, 'for Bazin, as for almost all realist theorists, what is in question is not just a rendering of reality but the rendering of reality made real by the use of aesthetic device' (1985: 60).

Key to the drama of *The Abyss* is its emphasis on the ways in which a group dynamic can fracture but also cohere under immense pressure. Placing working-class characters in extraordinary situations has been a defining quality of Cameron's films. In *The Abyss* the crew are again characterised by their blue-collar credentials. The film has a connection to the sense of claustrophobia generated in the World War II submarine drama *Das Boot* (Wolfgang Petersen, 1981). It also has a connection to the disaster movie subgenre overseen by producer Irwin Allen (*The Poseidon Adventure* (Ronald Neame, 1972), *The Towering Inferno* (John Guillermin, 1974)) and ahead, to Cameron's own disaster movie/romance fusion, *Titanic*. To echo the observation of Susan Sontag in her essay 'The Imagination of Disaster' (1965: 42), it was the disaster sensibility that characterised the American science fiction films of the 1950s as they dramatised how a culture responded to an overwhelming, destructive threat.

The Abyss is a pantheistic film that locates the typical *terra firma* context of pantheism to the wilderness of the sea. It is in the depths of the watery wild that characters' insights are realised. In film, the wilderness has a tradition of being constructed as the site of terror and fear and the Biblical allusion to Noah's Ark in Cameron's film is not lost. Indeed, in October 2013, the *Hollywood Reporter* ran a story about production on Darren Aronofsky's expensive, event-movie adaptation of the story of

Noah, and in the article the project is rather dismissively described as an eco-movie (see Masters 2013).

The Movie
The Abyss begins with the sound of sonar over an image of the Twentieth Century Fox studio logo. There is then is a title card with an excerpt from Friederich Nietzche's *Beyond Good and Evil* (1886) reading: 'When you look into an abyss, the abyss looks into you...' The preceding sentence from Nietzsche reads: 'He who fights monsters should look to it that he himself does not become a monster.' As such, we can make the connection with *Aliens*, in which Ripley fights the monster, as does Sarah in *The Terminator*. But to what degree do they become monstrous in their protective actions? Ripley fights to protect the little girl Newt. Sarah fights to protect her unborn child. (In this Nietzsche reference we see, too, an intimation of the character arc for Sarah Connor in *The Terminator* and *Terminator 2: Judgement Day*.) Immediately, *The Abyss*'s evocation of an explicitly literary reference suggests a different sensibility to that at work in *The Terminator* and *Aliens*.

We hear an angelic choir singing as the words '*The Abyss*' move towards the foreground and fill (or rather, consume) the frame. There is then a crescendo of music. The title segues to the film's opening image of a submarine, the USS Montana, moving through the deep-ocean murk. The action then cuts to inside the sub where the crew are picking up a signal pulse. The moment immediately announces yet another creative debt to the example of *Close Encounters of the Third Kind* – Spielberg's film includes an early scene set at an air traffic control desk as personnel track a UFO.

The submarine crew track the unidentified entity as it moves at 80 knots and then at 130 knots. There is a power cut on board and a shot from outside shows a bright light whipping at high speed across the exterior of the submarine. The light is not defined and passes out of frame. The submarine then slams into a rock face, takes on water, and sinks.

The action then cuts to a scene in which a helicopter lands on a sea-cruiser, emphatic martial music underscoring the moment. A unit of Navy SEALS jump down from the helicopter (a unit arriving in the wilderness, as they do at the beginning of *Avatar*). The last pair of legs that descend from the helicopter, behind a line of booted feet, are the high-heeled feet of Lindsey Brigman (Mary Elizabeth Mastrantonio). Like Sarah Connor in *The Terminator* and Ellen Ripley in *Aliens*, Brigman is a woman of intelligence and action. Like Ripley and Grace in *Avatar* she embodies professionalism; Lindsey observes at one point that 'luck is not a factor'. She is committed to professionalism and the pursuit of merit at work, regardless of one's gender. As such, she embodies an American democratic ideal of hard work superseding privilege.

We cut to a scene that introduces a team of miners at work deep below the ocean's surface and learn that Lindsey works as a technology designer for the company that own the Deepcore mining rig. The establishing shots of Deepcore have an immaculate and dreamlike quality about them. As such there is a certain similarity here with images of the exploration vehicles in the opening moments of *Titanic*. Images that rhapsodise points amidst the engulfing darkness have a fragile, vulnerable quality and run throughout *The Abyss*, and Cameron brings the same aestheticising of submarine nature to his later documentaries *Ghosts of the Abyss* and *Aliens of the Deep*.

Just as a large corporation mine the planet of Pandora for 'unobtanium' in *Avatar*, so, too, in *The Abyss* a corporation's employees mine nature only to be confronted by the power of a non-human intelligence and culture. Both *Avatar* and *The Abyss* centre on scenarios in which an 'abuse' of technology is eventually accounted for. Both are eco-movies that imply the damage done in considering nature as a resource to be mined and exploited and it is a scenario that in turn results in lessons learned for the humans, ultimately made insignificant by the immensity of the wild natural space.

The Abyss is replete with elegantly composed wide shots that remind us of the miniscule presence of humans and our technologies in the deep sea. Contrastingly, throughout the film a handheld camera is used to show the drama developing inside Deepcore, treating it with a documentary-styled sensibility; a certain kind of immediacy in a film so much invested in artifice. Leading the crew is Bud Brigman (Ed Harris), a man who describes himself as a 'calm person' – until we see him with his estranged wife, Lindsey. Across his films, Cameron excels at establishing a sense of the dynamic of the team at work. In this respect, his films are somehow in the spirit of Howard Hawks. *The Abyss* features one of the warmest scenes that he has delivered, with the crew working and bound together as they sing along to the country song, 'Willing'.

After their shift is over, Bud then informs the team that they have been charged with the work of moving Deepcore in order to use it as a base for an impromptu military exploration that forms part of an acute national security situation. The crew are briefed on the events that led to the sinking of the submarine shown in the film's prologue and Bud explains that he and his team are being tasked to attempt to recover any stranded crew. At this point, a plot detail is defined – a storm is building above the waves. It is an almost insignificant detail and yet we register it. The storm will duly endanger the rig, leading to increased peril and the opportunity for the drama to explore different ways in which characters cope with stress. At this point in the action, Lieutenant Coffey (Michael Biehn) is introduced, a character who will become consumed by paranoia and who functions with an unquestioning fidelity to military code in all of his decisions. Coffey embodies the inevitable pairing of ignorance with fear and is almost robotic in his application of logic when the film espouses the value of intuition and emotional connections, and he is placed in opposition to Bud. Whereas there is a shot soon after Coffey arrives on board Deepcore that shows his hand trembling, there is a similar shot that shows that Bud is still wearing his wedding ring which tells us enough about his attitude to the failing marriage. Bud's emotional awareness is his strength (rather than any physical or intellectual capacity) and he will reprimand Coffey, reminding him to be more 'people sensitive' on Deepcore. It will be this empathetic quality that makes Bud the candidate for the descent and revelation that comprises the final movement of the film.

At this point we might consider the relationship of *The Abyss* to a pioneering 'eco-film', *Silent Running* (1972). Written and directed by Douglas Trumbull (who had established himself as a visual effects practitioner in Hollywood), *Silent Running* is a film that Cameron has acknowledged an enthusiasm for. Charting the efforts of gardener Freeman Lowell (Bruce Dern) to maintain an 'Eden' on board a space station (a sort of greenhouse Noah's Ark) the film is a melancholy, naturalistically-presented work of science fiction exploring the human relationship (in terms of connection and disconnection) to the natural world. It also presents scenarios around the human engagement with technology in terms of Freeman's relationship with the robots on board the ship. Of *Silent Running*, Trumbull has explained that 'the main thing was just to make [a] science fiction film that would have some heart and soul to it rather than being a repellent science fiction movie with a lot of characters that are dehumanized' (2013). Trumbull's genre-aware comment returns us to the overarching concern across Cameron's films: what does technology, as a manifestation of science, mean for our human experience; particularly in taking the view that humans are part of nature rather than separate to it.

Key to the promotion of *The Abyss* was the now familiar emphasis on the fidelity to realism at work in the movie in terms of its recreation of an oil-rig and also a proposed scientific truth and the photorealistic rendering of its alien creatures. Certainly, throughout each of his feature films, Cameron has accented the importance of 'real world' research in the realisation of fantasy settings. As such, the film takes a moment to clearly define High Pressure Nervous Syndrome (HPNS) relatively early on, and in a rather modest way so as not to foreshadow too obviously the value of this information for the film's climax. As with *Aliens*, Cameron establishes the dynamics of the group before immersing them in the main narrative dilemma.

The predominantly blue lighting scheme of *The Abyss* is a colour that is emphatically used in Cameron's films. In Western culture, the colour blue has associations with the spiritual; this colour value logically extends to the film presentation of the NTIs being perceived as 'angels'. In writing about the NTIs, Roger Kaufman has commented that

> What appears to be a suicide mission [late in the film] becomes a rebirth, as Bud makes friends with a beautiful phosphorescent underwater alien creature … They are highly intelligent beings who have both 'masculine' and 'feminine' characteristics, much like many gay men and lesbians who comfortably straddle gender expressions. These entities are also evocative of the mythic fairies of Celtic folk heritage which homosexual people have long been associated with, often in a pejorative sense, but also in a reclaimed positive affinity with such creatures' enchanting attributes. (2011: 176)

Contrasting with the creation of a cruel world *The Abyss* dramatises a world where kindness and empathy are the basis for 'a happy ending'. Engaging with the Other has been a typical Cameron trope and in this film it is not in order to destroy it but rather to understand it.

The film then introduces the fluid breathing system that will become so critical later in the film. As per their orders the oil rig crew descend to explore the sunken submarine and the sequence assumes a retrospective interest in that we can read it as something of a precursor to Cameron's *Ghosts of the Abyss* documentary, in which he undertakes to explore and record on film an exploration of some of the wreck of the Titanic. As the crew explore, Jammer (John Bedford Lloyd) becomes terrified and extremely anxious and it is Bud who has to work to maintain Jammer's composure. Bud then explores further alone. We stay with Jammer who sees the glowing light of an NTI as it approaches him. Again, we do not see the creature fully but instead just the reflection in Jammer's helmet visor of the light that it emits. A distressed Jammer later explains that he thinks that he has seen an angel. This notion of the angelic allows for the film to function as a Romantic movie, notably in terms of its final act. Amidst the industry and engineering of the setting the film posits its faith in the numinous and the broader sense of 'extra-terrestrial' beings who are benign rather than malign.

As Lindsey returns to Deepcore she also briefly sees NTIs from the cockpit of the pod she is travelling in. She takes photographs but there is nothing to see in the images when she inspects them. Lindsey is certain that 'something' is out there but Bud is not convinced. This aspect of the film opens it out to a populist notion of the supernatural and the mystery of angels and the film here announces its interest in the science fiction/fantasy metaphor for spiritual faith. Coffey also reports back, believing the unknown entity must be the enemy. For audiences who had come to know Cameron's work through the stark tone of *The Terminator* and *Aliens*, the optimism and faith in the beneficence in the Other was something of a surprise.

Coffey and his troops go to the sunken sub from where they retrieve a warhead. Above the deep sea location a storm impacts on the beleaguered oil rig below, with the umbilical cable connecting Deepcore to the ship on the ocean surface becoming dislocated, sending the rig to the edge of the trench. They are disconnected and the moment is attenuated by the editing pattern of the sequence. Lindsey goes out to explore the damage and situation at hand, and, like *The Terminator*, *Aliens*, *Titanic* and *Avatar*, the film now becomes about surviving immensely traumatic events in which the human body's fraility, in the context of immensities of technology and of the wild, is tested. 'She didn't leave me, she just left me behind,' Bud says of Lindsey.

The action then cuts from inside Deepcore to a wide shot showing Lindsey at the edge of the drop-off close to which Deepcore teeters. The camera circles and then moves down towards her, offering the audience a believable sense of immersive space and scale and a sense of the fragility of her own human form amidst it. All power then abruptly closes down and Lindsey is cast into utter darkness outside Deepcore. The NTIs appear again and there is a wide shot of the NTI appearing behind Lindsey – a moment of dramatic irony, a wondrous variation of the image showing the alien tail rising up behind Newt in *Aliens*. This presaging of an encounter by energy being shut off (or on) evokes not only *Close Encounters of the Third Kind* and *Super 8* (JJ Abrams, 2011) but harks back, too, to Charles Dickens' novel *A Christmas Carol* (1843): in that real-world fantasy, at the moment just before Scrooge encounters the ghost of Jacob Marley, the bell in Scrooge's chamber rings of its own volition. There is then a moment of movie spectacle as an expansive wide shot shows the NTI form floating in the water in front of Lindsey, but when she soon returns to Deepcore and explains what she has seen Bud is not convinced, and Coffey thinks that she has encountered Russians. As

The kindness of strangers: non-terrestrial intelligence encounters blue collar workers

his suspicion grows, Coffey is then spied on priming the retrieved warhead and the tension rises, with Lindsey confronting Coffey.

We see that the crew are asleep and the silence and stillness of the human world allows for the NTI to return to Deepcore in a scene suffused with a sense of otherworldliness, enhanced by Alan Silvestri's choral music. The scene is a showcase event in the story where, we might say, the action stops in order to amplify a mesmerising new visual effect illusion. Cameron designed the scene so that, if it did not play believably on account of the visual effects that were being pioneered for the film, it could be cut and not affect the film as a whole. Of this scene's conceptual development, visual effects supervisor Dennis Muren led his team in creating a digitally-rendered aesthetic that was derived from a physical three-dimensional macquette design which allowed them to gauge the illusion of mass, volume and the play of light. The pseudopod finds the warhead but is attacked by a terrified Coffey.

Hippy (Todd Graff) discovers that the warhead has been primed for aggressive use on the NTIs and alerts his colleagues. Coffey attacks Hippy and then holds everyone at gunpoint, explaining that he is going to send the warhead to the bottom of the trench and destroy whatever is down there. Coffey locks the crew away and it is Jammer who rescues them and immediately after describes the NTIs that he encountered as angels. The dynamic of a microcosm of society contained with a submarine vessel extends the war movie scenario of *Das Boot* and also anticipates Cameron's dramatic concerns with *Titanic*. The scenario has a history, as Melville's *Moby Dick* and Joseph Conrad's *Heart of Darkness* (1899) both attest. In both Melville and Conrad, the boat or ship carry the 'civilised' world into a realm of the wilderness where accepted, broadly agreed codes of conduct and behaviour are challenged. In both Conrad and Melville's works, there is an unrelenting hunt that propels the narrative. Where Conrad's book articulates tensions around colonialism and white culture in Africa, Melville's Biblically-informed novel also charts the encounter between white America and Polynesian culture in the form of the relationship between Queequeg and Ishmael.

Cat (Leo Burmister) and Bud swim out to another part of Deepcore to stop Coffey. Cat saves Bud from Coffey's murderous intent just in time. Indeed, Coffey functions rather like both the Terminator and Quaritch (the antagonist of *Avatar*) in his relentless and unthinking action and his deep-seated antagonism towards the Other. The crew are certainly aware now that Coffey is experiencing a nervous breakdown of sorts. A tense scene then ensues in which Bud and Lindsey must pilot a sub in pursuit of Coffey as he steers another mini-sub towards the ocean floor in order to set a bomb that will detonate and destroy whatever the 'other' is that he believes they are threatened by. Coffey duly perishes and Bud and Lindsey then find themselves contending with their own larger problem as their sub begins to take on board water.

Bud and Lindsey begin to drown, a moment that anticipates Jack and Rose's dire situation in *Titanic*. Bud swims Lindsey back to Deepcore and revives her, shouting at her 'to fight!', to come back to life. This is a touchstone scene in the film and one that dramatises the imperative to survive. The scene is realised without recourse to any music score and with only minimal editing, conjuring a sense of real-time action.

Bud then undertakes the most dangerous mission, which constitutes the climax of the film, to drop to the bottom of the trench in order to disarm the bomb that Coffey had primed with about an hour to spare before it detonates. Bud must wear special fluid-breathing apparatus to do so. We have seen this apparatus already explained much earlier in the film. Rather in the way that the arrival of the extra-terrestrials at Devil's Tower in *Close Encounters of the Third Kind* becomes almost its own film, in *The Abyss* Bud's descent, and the revelation that he is then afforded transport to safety, gives the film a particularly positive tone quite in contrast with the endings of *Aliens* and *The Terminator*. Certainly, we might identify something symbolically appropriate in Bud's fall towards the bottom of the ocean. It is a mythic image of sorts (an echo of Cameron's acknowledged interest in mythic images) as Bud is removed from any connection with the human world. Indeed, of the image of falling, we can again invoke the writing of Gaston Bachelard here to articulate the relevance and resonance of images that depict falling. In his book *Air and Dreams*, we read: 'the change in the very substance of the one who is falling and who, as he falls, becomes one whose cause and responsibility we carry within us, in the complex psychology of the fallen creature … The fall must contain all meanings at once; it must be simulataneously metaphor and reality' (2011: 93).

Cameron's intercutting between Bud, as he drops away from human civilisation and almost consciousness, and Lindsey on board Deepcore, constructs a sense of tension. Bud descends and in his liquid-breathing apparatus he takes on a kind of avatar status, being able to exceed the natural limitations of the human respiratory system. The liquid allows him to breathe. Lindsey has to stop talking to him about science and instead talk openly to him: they have to 'see' each other just as Jake and Neytiri do in *Avatar*'s climax. Ordinary and virtual space combine in this climax and, in a way, Bud meets 'death'. He cuts the wire to defuse the stray bomb.

Bud thinks he will die in the utter darkness as he lies down on a ledge. At this point the film's *deux ex machina* device manifests itself as he is then approached by an NTI who takes Bud by the hand and flies him to their world. A series of point-of-view images from just above and behind Bud as he holds hands with the 'winged' NTI immerse us in the journey away from all that is known and tangible. Silvestri's score reinforces a sense of the spiritual and the angelic with its choir interwoven with orchestral performance. In their world Bud removes his breathing kit and sees news images on a waterwall. The NTIs know of the human world through TV images they can access and the scene plays as a more sombre version of the broad comedy *dénouement* of Joe Dante's *Explorers* (1985), in which three teenage boys pilot their home-made rocket ship, named Thunder Road in homage to the Bruce Springsteen song, into space and find themselves brought on board an alien spaceship. Unlike Cameron's alien encounter, Dante's film is pitched as a comedy. The NTIs explain to Bud that they have been watching human endeavour and it is here that the film's 'statement' is delivered. As in *Terminator 2*, the image of apocalypse is fundamental.

The message comes back: 'Online.' Bud and Lindsey are essentially text messaging each other, fifteen years before it became an ordinary part of our lives. Bud is brought back up to the ocean surface aboard the NTIs' structure and is reunited with Lindsey.

Reception

When *The Abyss* was released in North America in August 1989 it received a mixed reception in the mainstream press. Geoff Andrew of *Time Out* summed up the general response: 'James Cameron's follow up to *Aliens* abandons deep space for the spacey deep, and hits rock bottom … After a relatively gripping start, Cameron's *folie de grandeur* rapidly sinks into cliché' (1989).

Had *The Abyss* been a popular success upon theatrical release one wonders if *Terminator 2: Judgement Day* would have followed immediately, if at all. Certainly, the film provides an addition to Cameron's evolving visualisation of the idea of an avatar, and, ahead of *True Lies* and *Titanic*, the value of a romantic love story to carry so much of the expression of ideas around the experience of an authentic and inauthentic self. Furthermore, the film anticipates the 'green' sensibility of Cameron's later film, *Avatar*.

In retrospect the film's original reception suggested that the fim was too much at variance with the filmic identity that Cameron had established for himself as an 'auteur' with *The Terminator* and *Aliens*. *The Abyss* does not have the same sense of urgency to it, or the narrative pace that characterises the previous two movies. Perhaps most interesting about the reviews of the film at the time were their emphasis on the production circumstances of the film as an intensive logistical challenge. It was this same fascination that characterised many reviews of Cameron's later sea-set *Titanic* and, broadly speaking, echoes the kind of journalistic interest expressed in reviews and coverage of Coppola's *Apocalyspe Now*. In these terms, Cameron's identity and persona as a director were underscored by narratives about the film's production and the degree to which it tested a number of actors involved.

Upon its original release, *The Abyss* did not break-even but with Cameron's association and his own interest in the capacity of DVD to allow a filmmaker to revisit a theatrical release, he was able to re-present the film with its originally planned ending. Indeed, Cameron, like Ridley Scott, has recognised the commercial opportunity of revisiting a theatrical cut on DVD and, as such, was key to cultivating an interesting moment in the already fading DVD era.

As an aside, the place and prominence of the DVD 'director commentary' has, in audience's minds, eradicated the possibility of other meanings existing around a film beyond those offered by the director. Is the decline in sales of DVDs 'saving' us from the tyranny of the director commentary as the only means of understanding a film? Do audiences not consider their own critical sensibilities and imaginations powerful enough to crack the code of a text or apply various values to it? Of the 'culture' of the director's commentary Mark and Deborah Parker have explained:

> The questions of by whom and how the special features on a DVD are produced are important in understanding how such materials mediate the way we view and study film ... The DVD edition is essentially a re-orientation of the film ... The mode of inquiry encouraged by the special edition DVD combines a raw empiricism with a refined sense of craft and artistry ... The auteur almost inevitably re-emerges in director's commentaries, but the role is taken up with a self-consciousness and a circumspection that makes any programmatic rejection of the approach seem naïve. (2011: 15–16)

Intriguingly, the concept of the 'special edition' as ongoing revision to an already published, original text is not as new or recent as we might think. In the sixteenth century, Ariosto endlessly revised and re-edited his poem *Orlando Furioso*.

As a film, *The Abyss* now carries interest as antecedent of *Avatar* with its emphasis on a science fiction-inflected culture collision that provides the context within romantic love is tested and re-asserted. Looking back twenty-five years after its release, we might propose that the seriousness that characterised Cameron's film was just a little too sombre in the context of the typically more comedy-inflected releases of Hollywood studios. Whilst *Aliens* was certainly intense and sombre at points it was countered by the kinetic energy of its war film qualities. *The Abyss*, like *Aliens*, builds a sense of the characters at a rather deliberate pace but this does not then offer the audience a 'high energy' pay off; instead, it culminates with a rather attenuated sense of melancholy. With his subsequent film, Cameron would return to the creative victories of his second feature film and revisit the character of the Terminator, finding ways to infuse a non-human protagonist with human frailties.

CHAPTER FIVE
Terminator 2: Judgement Day (1991)

The Abyss was not quite the box office success that the studio had anticipated and with his next film Cameron returned to the story-world of *The Terminator*. With *Terminator 2: Judgement Day* (could a title any more overtly attest to a film's Biblical allusion?), Cameron explored the apocalyptic subject that has been key to his films in the most fully realised way. By the time of the release of *Terminator 2* (hereafter *T2*), Hollywood had released relatively few 'apocalyptically'-focused movies; although one might claim that the disaster movies produced by Irwin Allen all tapped into a shared fear. Since *T2*, however, that is not quite the case: *The Postman* (Kevin Costner, 1997), the Roland Emmerich-directed 'trilogy' of *Independence Day* (1996), *The Day After Tomorrow* (2004) and *2012* (2009), and *The Book of Eli* (Albert and Allen Hughes, 2010) have all followed. Japanese cinema has also continued to explore the subject, perhaps most potently through the *anime* form, in the likes of *Ghost in the Shell* (Mamoru Oshii, 1995), *Princess Mononoke* (Hayao Miyazaki, 1997) and *Akira* (Katsuhiro Otomo, 1998). Just a year before *T2*, *Akira Kurosawa's Dreams* (1990), a loose collection of stories inspired by the great director's own dreams, featured a chapter entitled 'Mount Fuji in Red' about nuclear destruction in Japan, and his subsequent film *Rhapsody in August* (1991) explored the subject of the atomic bomb falling on Nagasaki. Wheeler Winston Dixon has noted of popular cinema's engagement with apocalypse, around the world, that 'Japanese films of post-WW2 were more confrontational of apocalypse than British and American films had been eg: *The Last War* (Shuei Mastubayashi, 1961) in which we see Manhattan destroyed by a nuclear attack' (2003: 6). In Britain, it had been the animated feature *When the Wind Blows* (Jimmy T. Murikami, 1986), adapting the Raymond Briggs picture book, that had most powerfully visualised annihilation in this period (although the apogee of this mini-genre, in Britain at least, remains Peter Watkins' long-unseen *The War Game* (1965), made for the BBC but not shown by the corporation for another twenty years).

At what are, retrospectively at least, intervals, the subgenre of cyborg cinema defines the prevailing wind of Cameron's creative interests in commercial filmmaking. On the other side of *T2*'s release, by several years, a film adaptation of an Isaac Asimov story entitled *Bicentennial Man* (Chris Columbus, 1999), about a housekeeping android that becomes sentient, was released. In 2001, Spielberg's *AI: Artificial Intelligence* explored another rich layer in cyborg cinema in its depiction of an android child with emotional needs (and, co-incidentally, included an underwater, post-human episode that shares some elements with *The Abyss*).

Like *The Abyss*, *T2* assumes an overtly moral position. Pertinently, *T2* was one of a number of Hollywood films produced and released around 1991/92 which were considered to represent an image of the 'new man'; that is, a 'softer' more emotionally aware and openly expressive version of masculinity attuned, particularly, to the emotional and intellectual needs of children. In the same year that *T2* was released audiences might also choose to see *Regarding Henry* (Mike Nichols, 1991) and *Hook* (Steven Spielberg, 1991) (although, interestingly, relatively few of them actually did), both of which seemed to argue the link between what might be called 'emotional truth' and a child-like state.

It was Arnold Schwarzenegger who was initially the most vocal in urging a sequel to *The Terminator*. As his own film stardom continued to escalate through the mid- and late 1980s, he branched out from action genre movies and into comedy, notably with *Twins* (Ivan Reitman, 1988) and *Kindergarten Cop* (Ivan Reitman, 1990). In contrast with *The Terminator*, *Conan the Barbarian* and *Commando*, these were family-friendly movies and this newfound, more mainstream audience, can be considered to have impacted on the conception of the Terminator's persona in *T2*. Coming off *The Abyss*, for Cameron, the prospect of a sequel to *The Terminator* was not an immediate priority. However, the less-than-stellar performance of *The Abyss* appeared to give him pause for thought and by May 1990 Cameron had drafted a 140-page screenplay for what would become *T2*. As with *Aliens*, *T2*'s central conceit focused on an adult protecting a vulnerable child. The film shot from October 1990 until April 1991, a significantly longer production phase than for the original film.

T2 is not only a sequel, in that it furthers character dilemmas and ambitions raised in the original film, but it also refrains and embellishes images, scenes and editing patterns from the original. The film also resonates within a broader *anime* frame of reference. Cameron's interest in *manga* and *anime* have moved in and out of his filmmaking concerns and his name has been used as an approving source of recommendation for the *anime Ghost in the Shell*, a film adapted from the *manga* title of the same name. *Ghost in the Shell* had originally been a serial published every three months in the magazine *Pirate Edition* in 1989/90. We might propose that Cameron's engagement with aspects of *manga*, that may have been relatively unrecognised by a mainstream audience, played its part in the evolving opening out of *manga* and *anime* to a wider audience during the late 1990s/early 2000s, and consequently the number of *anime* released theatrically in the West, albeit on a relatively small scale, noticeably increased (and, indeed, a number of Hayao Miyazaki's *anime* projects have considered the subject of the human relationship to nature using the forms and tropes of fantasy and science fiction). Eventually the Walt Disney Company was prompted to recognise the audience demand for the format and have subsequently released dubbed versions of *Ponyo on the Cliff* (Hayao Miyazaki, 2009) and *The Secret World of Arietty* (Hiromasa Yonebayashi, 2010) to name just two. Indeed, as of this writing, Cameron continues to develop his own feature film project, *Battle Angel Alita* which adapts the *manga* title *Alita: Battle Angel*.

Critically, in the context of Cameron's work, *Ghost in the Shell* dramatised and visualised the theme of identity in the realm of human and cyborg/artificial intelligence relations. This Japanese expression of the relationship, in terms of both connections and disjunctions between the ancient (the human self) and the modern (technological development) functions as a useful counterpoint and analogue to the American narrative mode.

The other key thematic concern that canopies much of Japanese animation (and, by extension Japanese cinema), is the interplay between the ancient/traditonal and the modern/futuristic, between the 'real' and the 'fantastic'. This preoccupation was articulated with particular force during Japan's Edo period (1615–87) and is vivdly expressed in a number of *anime* contemporaneous with Cameron's films. In *Ghost in the Shell* human brains are fitted out with interfaces that allow them to hook up to and learn from computers. In the world of the film, the human soul is known as 'the ghost' and the most successful hackers are those who can hack into a ghost – but for doing this there is the severest penalty. *Ghost in the Shell* grapples, then, with what it is to be human in terms of the power and necesssity of memory (its exploration of memory and thought reverberates in Cameron's screenplay for *Strange Days*). The film's main character is a cyborg and throughout the film she ponders this with some intensity. Indeed, most of the characters are to some degree not completely human. The film presents a future in which human culture is even more profoundly immersed in computer and virtual technolgy than as we experience it in the early twenty-first century. The film is sceptical about this intensified process of humans 'living' technology. In a way that resembles *Akira*, *Ghost in the Shell* shows that technology can be harnessed for positive effect but it is when harnessed and exploited negatively that crises ensue. Of *Ghost in the Shell*, Cameron has described it as 'a stunning work of speculative fiction … the first to reach a level of literary excellence' (2009b).

Ghost in the Shell opens with a piece of text that reads: 'In the near future – corporate networks reach out to the stars, electrons and light flow throughout the universe. The advance of computerisation, however, has not yet wiped out nations and ethnic groups.' It is not such a stretch of imagination to make the connection between *Ghost in the Shell* to fundamental elements comprising *Avatar*. Further, one of the most emphatically engaged scenes of *Ghost in the Shell* centres on the characters of Motomo and Bateau talking on the boat about consciousness and memory (the 'ghost in the shell'). This identity confusion finds a corolloray in *Avatar*, and also evokes *Blade Runner* in which the synthetic humans are given false memories to enhance their sense of identity.

The connection between the Japanese *anime* form and the popular American film form find a connection between the subjects of nuclear war and the increasing promise and peril of ever-advancing technologies. Vivian Sobchack has commented that 'it must be remembered that although the sf film existed in isolated instances before World War Two it only emerged as a critically recognised genre after Hiroshima' (2001: 21).

With his *Terminator* diptych, Cameron offers us two vividly realised and connected movies that have significantly advanced the mode of 'cyborg cinema' as per Sue Short's considerations of the form. Short, in her study *Cyborg Cinema*, explains the ongoing allure of the cyborg, citing *Avatar*, *Iron Man* (Jon Favreau, 2009) and *TRON: Legacy* (Joseph Kosinki, 2010) each as potent instances (2011: ix). Indeed, looking back to the original *Terminator* film, it is useful to note that the audience for that film would have been very aware of the Disney Studio's family-orientated recently-released feature *Tron* which had elaborately fused the photographed, the animated and the digitally constructed. The previous year, a particularly unsuccessful cyborg science fiction comedy entitled *Heartbeeps* (Allan Arkush, 1981) had been released. The Hollywood studios, in the afterglow of C3P0's popularity in *Star Wars*, had struggled to furnish a new robot that could appeal to the general audience. The fact that it took Cameron to adopt an initially non-family-audience approach in showing what a cyborg could mean to humans is telling. In *T2*, though, that adult-orientated sensibility morphed (to use an appropriate term in relation to the visual effects utilised in the film) into something more sentimental and family friendly.

Short has also noted that in the cyborg we have an image of immortality (2011: 3) and in *T2* its titular character can only perish in the most elemental situation as he sacrifices himself and descends into molten lava. Indeed, in terms of the cyborg/immortal relationship, one has only to watch the adaptation of Asimov's story *Bicentennial Man* (another family-orientated science fiction film) to see this scenario play out. Short also observes that cyborgs articulate concerns around gender so that in terms of *T2* we have a movie that suggests that technology can liberate women rather than keep them subjected to patriarchy. For her, cyborg cinema allows for a 'rethinking identity' to happen. In *T2*, Sarah Connor reconfigures herself as a terrorist. Short has discussed Connor's and Ripley's relationships with the cyborg (the Terminator for Sarah, Ash for Ripley) suggesting it offers an analogue to representations of gender and a certain kind of transsexual identity (2011: 81). Indeed, in the Cameron-supervised TV series *The Sarah Connor Chronicles* its two female cyborgs are named Cameron and Weaver.

Building on the narrative device of *Aliens*, *T2* also expresses reservations about the activities of corporations, institutions and authorities, such as the police and the military, and their potential moral abdication of responsibility for the people they employ and the communities they engage with in pursuit of profit and advantage. This is expressed, too, in *Avatar*. The pervading sense throughout the film is that the world is not necessarily being protected and that, as a result, even the human body is increasingly open to transformation. In this way, Cameron's science fiction genre interests also touch on some of David Cronenberg's horror-science fiction movies, notably *eXistenZ* (1999).

The Movie

T2 begins with a title sequence that centres on what was, by 1991, a well-established emblem of the original film: the Terminator's silver robot skull composited against a wall of flames (indeed, a teaser trailer for the film simply showed multiple Terminators being produced on a factory production line). The first shot of this sequel is a long-lens image of Los Angeles churning with traffic and heat. There is then an image that speaks of human fragility: we see a child on a swing in a playground beyond the edge of the city centre in the apparently safe haven of suburbia. That this image plays in slow-motion immediately lends the action a certain menace and melancholy. The action then cuts to night and on-screen text informs us that we are seeing LA in the year 2029 AD. The now ravaged landscape returns to that we were presented with during the opening moments of *The Terminator*. A voice-over by the character of Sarah Connor (Linda Hamilton) talks about the 'nuclear fire'. A robot foot then slams down in close-up (echoing the original film's opening) and, as before, we are shown, albeit a little more extensively, but presented in a manner consistent with the original film, the battle of humans against robots. This prologue concludes with Sarah explaining in voice-over that the computer controlling the machines, called Skynet, sent two Terminators back in time to destroy the leader of the resistance, John Connor, the first being the one Sarah overcame in the original film.

The prologue then gives way to the opening credits presented as brushed steel text against a fiery backdrop of a playground in flames. This image of a furnace will bring the film full-circle by the time of the film's final act. There is then a cut to the blue light of night in a parking lot and we hear the sound of wind and see an image of lightning. In a nearly identical (and rightly so) composition to that in *The Terminator* we see the titular character (Schwarzenegger) arrive from the future, the robot's form identical to the previous film's robot. The cyborg walks naked into a biker bar and, again evoking the opening of the original, takes the clothes from a biker after a bar room rumble and rides away on his Harley Davidson motorcycle, soundtracked to 'Bad to the Bone' by George Thorogood.

We then cut to a shot announcing the arrival of T-1000 (Robert Patrick), who takes the uniform of an LAPD cop, along with his gun and patrol car, and immediately performs a computer search for John Connor. The action then cuts to the LA suburbs and we are introduced to the teenager John Connor (Edward Furlong) living in very ordinary surroundings just as his mother had done in *The Terminator*. Indeed, the intercutting pattern to establish the range of key characters rhymes with the approach taken in *The Terminator*. John is living with his adoptive parents, Todd (Xander Berkeley) and Janelle (Jenette Goldstein), in a lower-middle-class suburb of LA. Being adopted also lends John an immediately mythological situation – he is an orphan in the narrative tradition of many great hero archetypes. The film then cuts to Pescadero State Hospital and we are reunited with Sarah Connor. Our first sighting shows Sarah doing pull-ups from the leg of an upturned bed in a secure ward. It is an image in powerful contrast to the conditions in which we first meet Sarah in *The Terminator*. Her physical resilience, which became gradually apparent in the original, takes on something feral in this iteration. This detail of performance and behaviour, rather than anything said, immediately expresses her mindset. In the first close-up of her face we see this newfound survival instinct.

Psychiatrist Dr. Silberman (Earl Boen, playing another returning character from *The Terminator*) is recapping Sarah's history for the benefit of trainee doctors – and the audience – as he tours the facility. Sarah is then violently subdued by a couple of unpleasant hospital orderlies who forcibly ensure she takes her sedation drugs. Cameron has thus established virtually all of the major characters in an economical opening fifteen minutes, although their precise motivations are as yet unclear.

The film then cuts to the T-1000, now impersonating a police officer, hunting for John, who is out stealing from an ATM, displaying some of the resourcefulness of his mother. We learn that 'a big guy on a bike' has also visited the home looking for John, Cameron deliberately prompting us to question who the 'good guy' is in this scenario – the terminator who looks like the intended assassin of the first film or the one clad in a police offer's uniform. Back at the hospital Sarah has a dream vision of her former protector Kyle Reese (Michael Biehn) sitting with her, explaining: 'You're strong Sarah. Stronger than you ever thought you could be … Remember the message – the future is not set, there is no fate but what we make for ourselves.' This pro-individualism statement is highly characteristic of Cameron and finds expression in Rose's personal conflict in *Titanic* and in Jake's experiences on Pandora in *Avatar*. Like Sarah, Rose and Jake both find a strength of emotion and reason with which to move out of the confining circumstances in which they find themselves at the beginning of their stories. The dream vision ends with a premonition of a nuclear blast on the children's playground from the pre-credit sequence.

We then see Sarah with Dr. Silberman, both of them watching a recording of her hysterical 'monologue' about the forthcoming apocalypse. 'I'm much better now,' says Sarah (somewhat unconvincingly), who is now denying her story to try to get visitors' rights for John. Silberman, however, sees through her plans and Sarah violently assaults him, again resulting in her forced sedation.

We are then introduced to the character of Miles Dyson (Joe Morton, who had portrayed the title role in John Sayles' science fiction film *The Brother From Another Planet* from 1984), a scientist at Cyberdyne where, in an extremely secure facility they have the remains – a micro chip, an exoskeleton hand – of the original Terminator.

Out on the highway the Schwarzenegger Terminator traces John on his way to a shopping mall. At the same time, the T-1000 in the guise of a police officer is asking the public about John's whereabouts. The construction of the sequence that follows rhymes with the structure of the original film where the Terminator tracked down Sarah to the TechNoir club. We see John at the mall as both pursuing Terminators close in on him, and a friend tips him off that people are looking for him. The Schwarzenegger Terminator carries a gun inside a box of roses (perhaps a visual pun on the name of a popular band of the time, Guns n' Roses), and the climax echoes the nightclub shootout in the original film, not only in terms of dramatic pressures and tensions but also in terms of the staging of the action (the shootout and the tussle between Terminators).

Encountering the Schwarzenegger Terminator toting a shotgun, the terrified John, who has been primed by his mother to expect this meeting with a machine from the

Nothing is as it seems in a post-human world of copies and metamorphosis

future, cannot comprehend when it instead shoots at the T-1000 and shields him from the return fire. The Schwarzenegger Terminator is actually there to protect him. It is in this first encounter between the two Terminators that we first witness the particular breakthrough in special effects pioneered by *T2*. Improving on the 'morphing' effects of the aliens in *The Abyss*, the T-1000 is actually made of something akin to liquid metal, able to 'fill' bullet holes and indeed take on any shape of equal size that it so wishes, making it relentless in its pursuit.

Following an eventful chase sequence, which ends with our first 'full frontal' view of the T-1000 in liquid metal form, the Schwarzenegger Terminator explains to John that in the future he has been programmed to be his protector and that the T-1000 is a 'new model' (Schwarzenegger is a mere T-101). When John calls home, the 'Janelle' who answers the phone is actually the T-1000 in her form (we presume Janelle is dead) – while trying to ascertain John's whereabouts it casually kills Todd by turning its arm into a liquid metal sword and stabbing Todd through the skull. (It even kills the family dog.) John now realises that the stories his mother told him were true and learns that the T-101 has been pre-programmed to follow John's instructions and, presumably in a sop to Schwarzenegger's new-found family audience, John prevents him from killing a couple of interfering passers by saying: 'You just can't go around killing people.'

The action then moves back to the hospital where Sarah learns of the return of the T-101 and that her son is missing. As both Terminators descend on the facility (the T-1000 disguising itself variously as laminate flooring and an armed guard), Sarah breaks out of the hospital (viciously despatching the more obnoxious orderlies in the process) but, as with John, when first encountering the T-101 she initially assumes it means her harm, but John appears and they escape the pursuing T-1000 together. The Terminator asks a tearful John 'What's wrong with your eyes?' Just as the humanising of artificial beings was key to the action of *Aliens* in the relationship between Bishop and Ripley, Jose Arroyo notes that the film humanises Schwarzenegger but that 'because bodybuilding has connotations of gayness, Schwarzenegger's heterosexuality has to be continually asserted' (2000: 43).

In a scene that again then replays a moment from the original film, Sarah, John and the T-101 find a makeshift hideaway in a garage and whilst there Sarah repairs the

Terminator. However, where the scene now differs from its corollary is in being less horror-movie inflected.

The desert highway scenes that follow (another major Hollywood studio film of 1991, Ridley Scott's *Thelma & Louise*, also focused on outlaws in the American desert), which centre around the establishing of the nascent resistance against the machines, are to some extent played for laughs, as John schools the Terminator in slang ('Hasta la vista') and human interaction, but also have a certain melancholy about them, best captured in a briefly-held moment when John and the Terminator watch as two little boys play with toy guns. The Terminator explains that Miles Dyson of Cyberdyne is at root responsible for what will eventually become Skynet, the military process that will trigger the apocalypse. We learn how 'human decisions' have been 'removed' from the process, a comment that resonates in contemporary debates regarding the increasing concern about American and British deployment of drones – remote-controlled fighting machines – in combat zones.

Contemporaneous with *T2* was a fantasy comedy entitled *Toys* (Barry Levinson, 1992) about a toy company that converts to manufacturing war toys. A central image of that film is of children playing war games. Of *Toys*, at the time of its theatrical release, the *Los Angeles Times* wrote that '[20th Century] Fox, nervous about the seemingly "dark" cross-pollination between kids' videogames and military computer warfare, put the movie into turnaround in 1980' (Dutka 1992). The article also goes on to quote the film's director, Barry Levinson, noting that the film was not an anti-military statement but instead 'merely' a reflection on how 'unreal and amoral warfare has become' (ibid.).

In the desert Sarah and her party become reacquainted with Enrique (Castula Guerro) and his companions, modern-day outlaws known to Sarah from the years between the events of *The Terminator* and her incarceration. They have a hidden arsenal of weapons, which have been accrued in anticipation of the eventual apocalypse and therefore represent the first iteration of John Connor's resistance force. Sarah's terrifying dreams continue to haunt her and reach an apogee that motivates her to leave her companions to launch an assault on Dyson's family home to try and assassinate the scientist so as to eliminate the intelligence that will ultimately result in global annihilation: she has, to all intents and purposes become a terrorist, while the pursuing John instructs his Terminator-protector that killing others is fundamentally wrong. It is now Sarah, and not the cyborg, who is the relentless and violent threat.

Of the character of Sarah in the film Bruce Isaacs has commented that, 'as if to counteract Cornea's patriarchy claim, Connor slips towards the militant, anti-man tendencies that would later define the crudest copies of this female fighter' (2007: 90). Sarah confronts Dyson regarding the work of Cyberdyne: 'Fucking men like you built the hydrogen bomb. Men like you thought it up. You think you're so creative. You don't know what it's like to really create something, to create a life, to feel it growing inside you!' Sarah's statements evoke the central conceit of *The Terminator* around motherhood and protection, ideas that *Aliens* had visualised within the tropes of a fairy tale-inflected set of images. In a neatly fitting connection, Connor's critique of men rhymes, albeit much less politely, with Linda Williams' observations about why it is

Sarah has become the machine of vengeance

men who predominate as practitioners in the visual effects sector of the film industry (1991: 65).

T2 then moves towards its climax in which the 'rebels', with Dyson now on board, penetrate Cyberdyne's offices to destroy the threatening technology amidst an immense shootout (another example of the 'gun porn', to quote Cameron in his original context of discussing *Aliens*) between the Terminator and the police. John retrieves the microchip and exoskeleton sample but Dyson is killed. From here, Sarah, John and the Terminator take flight pursued by the T-1000, ending up in an industrial unit where the T-1000 is eventually destroyed, but not before the T-101 is seriously incapacitated and Sarah gravely wounded. The *mise-en-scène* of these scenes is highly reminiscent of the colony in *Aliens*. The T-1000 is eventually destroyed in an enormous smelting furnace; as it thrashes around it regresses through the various identities it has adopted in a way that brings to mind the grotesque array of forms that 'the Thing' takes in John Carpenter's 1982 film. Like many other scenes in the film, this sequence greatly expands the scale of one from *The Terminator*, in this case the factory showdown. Indeed, the factory furnace might suggest Hades, just as a similar lava flow setting did in George Lucas's *Revenge of the Sith* (2005). It is a space in which an elemental, natural force has a purging power.

After John throws the future artefacts of microchip and exoskeleton into the furnace, the T-101 is lowered into the furnace so as to eradicate all traces of the technology that could allow Skynet to exist and the film ends abruptly with a 'positive message' about the value of human life. In this, it resembles the climax of *Aliens*, which ends almost immediately after the defenestration of the alien Queen. *T2* was to have included an epilogue featuring an old Sarah Connor. Indeed, the material was scripted, filmed and even included in an initial edit of the film. However, it was poorly received at a test screening and was scrapped.

Reception

In reviewing *T2*, *Time Out* Geoff Andrew commented that 'the film is much the same as its predecessor, except that the effects are more spectacular, there's a lumbering anti-nuke subtext and the script's good natured wit is undercut by the sentimentalism of

Arnie's becoming a cyborg' (1991). In America, Roger Ebert noted that 'Schwarzenegger's genius as a movie star is to find roles that build on, rather than undermine, his physical and vocal characterisation' (1991).

In narrative terms, the film's cyborg cinema tropes continued to inform Hollywood science fiction and the film's production legacy resided in the ways in which it applied computer-generated characters to photographed images, contributing to the evolution of photorealistic, computer-generated effects work (in terms of characters and creatures) in such popular films as *Jurassic Park*, *Jumanji* (Joe Johnston, 1995) and *Star Wars: Episode 1: The Phantom Menace* (George Lucas, 1999); and they bring Cameron full circle to the large-scale realism of *Titanic* and also to *Avatar*. Critically, his keenly made point about the potential for a more poetic, and subtle, use of computer images (1998: 10) recognised the possibility of integrating visual effects more coherently and expressively into a film's *mise-en-scène*. In *Titanic*, Cameron would achieve this distinctively: one has only to watch the opening minutes of the film as elderly Rose begins narrating her story to Brock and his exploration crew.

T2's 'meaning' resides not only in what characters do and say but also in the more particular qualities of a visual effect. For Doran Larson, the presentation of the morphing T-1000 prompts a socio-political reading: 'The Liquid Metal Man of *Terminator 2* exposes ambiguities in the figure of the American body politic that have existed for over three hundred years; in contrast, the reprogrammed T-101 suggests a body politic as cyborg and offers false assurances of popular control over mass democracy in late capitalism' (2004: 191).

At the time of it's release, *T2*'s significant promotional energy centred on the evolution of computer-generated images or elements within images. These visual effects were notable for their believability, and they contributed to the development and refinement of digital characters over the next ten years. Digital characters, both fantastic and human, have now become an established creative choice, an instance of the technological advances in the cinema of spectacle that reverberates with Tom Gunning's description and analysis of early cinema experiences. Gunning couches his discussion of early cinema (most famously those of the Lumière Brothers and of George Méliès) as having their antecedents in live attractions. Indeed, Méliès had worked in theatre and live, staged illusions before moving into film production. Gunning writes that 'Méliès' theatre is inconceivable without a widespread decline in belief in the marvellous … The magic theatre laboured to make visual that which it was impossible to believe. Its visual power consisted of a *trompe l'oeil* play of give and take, an obsessive desire to test the limits of an intellectual disavowal – I know, but yet I see' (1986a: 117).

In a behind the scenes documentary, simply entitled *The Making of Terminator 2: Judgement Day* (1991), broadcast on American TV to promote *T2* at the time of its theatrical release, visual effects artist Mark Dippe at the visual effects studio ILM (Industrial Light and Magic) called Cameron the first 'digital filmmaker'. This term and reality, a quarter of a century later, has become a fundamental aspect of filmmaking and film culture more broadly. The construction of Cameron as a pioneer was critical to the discourse around the film and the subsequent discourse around Cameron's recognition as a director, as somebody marshalling a range of technological resources in pursuit of a creative endeavour. With *Terminator 2: Judgement Day* the shift in visual effects from an optical, photochemical tradition (that had been embedded in filmmaking since the earliest moment of cinema) to the digital form constituted a significant part of the audience fascination with the movie. The realisation, by ILM, of the metallic T-1000 cyborg (notably in the moment when it emerges from the flames after the exhausting truck and motorcycle chase through LA) can be regarded as a key moment in the refinement of the recently emerged technology that allowed characters to be realised by animators using a range of computer systems. The T-1000 evolved the example of the stained-glass knight in *Young Sherlock Holmes* and the morphing (as in 'metamorphosing') creatures seen in *Willow*. Cameron's engagement with this kind of virtual character creation would eventually manifest itself most fully in *Avatar*'s fusion of photographed performances combined with animation and what we might think of as digital costume and make-up. *T2*'s 'event movie' aesthetic initiated a run of such films in the 1990s that showcased digital character creation; notably *Jurassic Park*, *Jumanji* and the work of the Pixar Animation studio, starting with *Toy Story* (John Lasseter, 1995) which can be regarded as the summation of a twelve-year project that director John Lasseter had been engaged with since his work at Disney when, with animator Glenn Keane, he produced a short film (adapting an 'episode' from the children's book *Where the Wild Things Are*) to serve as a proof of concept for what computer-generated animation might achieve.

Outside of Cameron's involvement, further *Terminator*-focused feature films and other media have been produced. *Terminator 3: The Rise of the Machines* (Jonathan Mostow), again starring Schwarzenegger, was released in 2003; followed by *Terminator: Salvation* (McG, 2009), starring Christian Bale, who, as Christopher Nolan's Batman, brought an element of franchise cross-pollination to the role of John Conner. This third sequel also starred Sam Worthington, who in the same year of release was also the male lead in Cameron's *Avatar*. A franchise of comic-book novels were also published in the wake of the immense commercial success of *T2* in 1991 which initially grossed over $200 million in North America alone during its summertime release.

On DVD, *Terminator 2* exists in a bewildering range of versions: as original theatrical DVD, 'special edition' (with eleven minutes of additional footage) and the 'Ultimate Edition'. The DVD iterations of *T2* mark the moment Cameron recognised the scope to revisit his theatrical releases for creative and commercial interests. Directors Ridley Scott, George Lucas and Peter Jackson have adopted similar creative and commercial strategies in regard to certain films, to adjust and revise, to varying degrees, the original release of a film. At the moment of concluding work on this book, the DVD format is increasingly being considered as a waning profit centre for studios as the downloading or streaming of films becomes more the norm.

T2: 3D – Battle Across Time

In 2009, the promotion of *Avatar*, and the network of media discourses around it, would construct and encode James Cameron as a pioneer of the technology used to make films. He was swiftly enshrined as a filmmaker whose work and individual creative identity was synonymous with the 3D format. However, *Avatar* was *not* Cameron's first production to be shot using the 3D process. Between 1992 and 1995 he wrote, directed and produced a short film in 3D, designed expressly for exhibition at Universal Studios' theme park in Orlando, Florida and at Universal Studios, Hollywood. This project was entitled *T2: 3D – Battle Across Time* and it expanded the world of *The Terminator* films, and functioned as a quasi-sequel to *T2*. Critically, the short film was integrated with a live, stage presentation at Universal Studios. This was not the first time such a combination of film and live action had been presented in a theme park context. George Lucas and Francis Ford Coppola had produced and directed, respectively, a 3D short film entitled *Captain Eo* (1986) which in its powerhouse music video way promoted the transformative power of music and creativity with Michael Jackson (who always called them 'short films' rather than music videos) for exclusive exhibition at Disneyland, California and Florida and then at Disneyland Paris and Tokyo Disney. It is pertinent here, too, to acknowledge how 'event movies' have often been (pejoratively) described as being akin to theme park rides, where rich expressive narrative is sacrificed in service of set-piece spectacle.

Of the evolution of visual effects and their developing aesthetic relationship with the theme park attraction format, visual effects artist turned attraction designer Douglas Trumbull has observed that 'Kubrick was pushing into this new, nonverbal territory that took the audience on an adventure in space. It wasn't about the normal cinematic dynamics of close-ups and over the shoulder shots and reversals and conflicts and plot. He was trying to go with another world of first-person experience' (2012).

Upon its release in 1995, the *T2: 3D* attraction was heavily promoted and presented as the new James Cameron film. Unsurprisingly, the film was intensively marketed with stories about its production, in *Cinefex* magazine (always carrying a Cameron endorsement) and in a television special focusing on the 3D film element of the project and the labour intensive, two-week-long night shoot at an abandoned factory near Los Angeles. *T2: 3D* was entirely digitally processed.

Essentially, *T2: 3D* is a twelve-minute chase and shootout film that is the centrepiece of a twenty-minute theme park attraction. It had a budget of $60 million and starts in the present day before seeing John and the Terminator going forward to 2029 and being pursued by the T-1000. John and the Terminator are on their way to Cyberdyne to destroy it and are chased by flying Terminator discs (eerily anticipating military drone technology of the early twenty-first century and also serving as amped-up variations on those piranha from Cameron's debut feature film). There is a lot of point-of-view used in the film, in order to meet the aesthetic imperative of theme park rides, but the action is as fully staged as in a feature and the film occurs in a wasteland, its aesthetic really consistent with the feature film's future-world battles. It ends with them entering the core of Cyberdyne; then the live show continues with film footage integrated showing an immense six-legged poly alloy 'creature', evoking memories of the insect-like robot in Cameron's pre-industry short film, *Xenogenesis*, like a spider/scorpion protecting the core which is ultimately destroyed.

T2: 3D sits as a footnote to Cameron's feature work and yet it has importance in that it anticipates the 3D work of *Avatar* and, indeed, the conversion of *Titanic* for 3D presentation in 2012.

Cameron's 3D exploration with *T2: 3D* would anticipate a later feature project (*Avatar*) but in the wake of *Terminator 2*'s commercial success, he moved onto another project (*True Lies*) that tonally stands as a true anomaly in his body of work. It also seems difficult to deny its quality as a somewhat retrograde creative undertaking. Certainly, the passing of time has only accentuated a sense of unease that some might well have experienced upon the film's original release twenty years ago.

CHAPTER SIX
True Lies (1994)

Film scholar Robin Wood noted in his study of American genre cinema that 'the fear of nuclear war is certainly one of the main sources of our desire to be constructed as children, to be reassured, to evade responsibility and thought' (2003: 168). Wood's comment, whilst originally published at a time predating the release of *True Lies*, succeeds in sketching out the sensibilities that Cameron's film manipulates and derives its overarching dramatic effect from.

As in the postwar cinema of Japan, the force and threat of nuclear weapons has informed so much American science fiction, horror, thriller and war film productions and Cameron has acknowledged that he grew up in an era marked by a tangible hesitancy and implicit fear of 'the bomb'. This unease with the capacities of science and technology informs the drama and spectacle of each Cameron film. Indeed, *True Lies* takes the fears of how digital and information technology can be abused, that inform parts of the premise of *Terminator 2: Judgement Day*, and works through them on a smaller scale. Technology's allure, then, as both object of wonder and of peril is central to the drama of *True Lies* as it is in all of Cameron's films across the span of which the technological is largely affiliated with a sense of the masculine and the feminine made analogous with the natural. This latter correspondence is a motif that he revisits on a particularly elaborate scale in his later film, *Avatar*. In *True Lies* a significant part of the drama is derived from the ease with which a camera can so readily satisfy our voyeuristic impulse, and is crucial to the development of the plot and the film's presentation of a recurrent motif that is centred on the 'screening' and 'filtering' of reality through a captured image; which is, of course, the essence of cinema.

Two years before Cameron's film was released another high-profile Hollywood production, also with a spy-orientated narrative, entitled *Sneakers* (Phil Alden Robinson, 1992), combined comedy and drama in a piece about the burgeoning presence of digital technology in mainstream society and how this data could increasingly influence international power relations. Where *True Lies* focuses on a government agent *Sneakers'* protagonists function way outside the establishment, overtly dramatising the conceit that data was a near all-powerful currency in the late twentieth century. Appropriately, one of the producers of *Sneakers*, Walter F. Parkes, had also been a co-writer on the feature film *War Games* (John Badham, 1983) which explored the interface of combat and emerging digital technology.

It is fair to suggest, then, that *True Lies* is a film that we might now approach with a certain caution in our post-9/11 world. Writing these words, almost twenty years since the film's original release, it is somewhat astonishing to be confronted by a film that is, arguably, content to paint geopolitical complexities that have so characterised late twentieth- and early twenty-first-century culture and history with a very broad brush. As such, the film is problematic for any viewer who is even just a little sensitive to representation of non-white, non-Western culture. Additionally, the film's tendency towards stereotypes extends to its gender representation; a point that we might be surprised by given the interest of Cameron's other films with their physically, emotionally and intellectually resilient female protagonists. *True Lies*, then, is anomalous in Cameron's body of work; an oeuvre that has typically been marked by a certain thoughtfulness; it is perhaps just that bit too much an 'escapist' piece. Indeed, we might propose that Cameron's later film *Avatar* offers a much more thoughtful dramatisation of culture conflict, in doing so offering a corrective of sorts to the writer-director's seemingly misguided action-comedy.

In terms of its conception, *True Lies* marks what remains the only instance, to date, that James Cameron has adapted an existing work, although he may yet adapt the manga title *Alita: Battle Angel*. *True Lies* was developed concurrently with an eventually abandoned adaptation of the Marvel Comics character *Spider-Man*. As an aside, how fascinating it would be to see Cameron's realisation of his mythically aware concept for Stan Lee's most famous character. Certainly, by the early 1990s, Cameron had established and defined himself as a director able, like Spielberg, to satisfy genre expectations with stories about ordinary protagonists and with the immense commercial success of *Terminator 2: Judgement Day*, he was able to secure evermore extensive financial and logistical resources with which to produce his film projects.

By the time of work beginning on *True Lies*, its star Arnold Schwarzenegger was at the pinnacle of his commercial popularity, having starred most recently in *Terminator 2: Judgement Day* but also in films such as *Conan the Barbarian*, *The Terminator*, *Commando*, *Predator* and the comedies *Twins* (Ivan Reitman, 1988) and *Kindergarten Cop* (Ivan Reitman, 1990). Indeed, to some degree, and perhaps surprisingly, given the timbre of earlier Cameron films, *Terminator 2* had attested to Schwarzenegger's appeal for an audience seeking a combination of action *and* comedy and *True Lies* exerts itself in playing to this sensibility.

Schwarzenegger brought the concept for the production to Cameron in the form of an existing French film entitled *La Totale* (Claude Zidi, 1991). In promoting his eventual remake of the French original, upon the theatrical release of *True Lies*, Cameron would explain that he recognised in the source material a way to adapt it for an American audience. Certainly, the resulting film is dangerously blunt in its engagement with a potential threat to the USA and the American protagonists emerge as accomplished and good-natured (towards each other). Indeed, Matthew Willhelm Kapell and Stephen McVeigh note in their essay 'Surveying James Cameron's Reluctant Political Commentaries' that *True Lies* is 'a film that understands the minds of its American audience and their need for an enemy' (2011: 30). Indeed, we might say that this observation speaks to a longstanding tradition of American genre filmmaking that is especially acute in the genres of the western and the war movie.

Certainly, *True Lies* was not the first, and it will not be the last, Hollywood film to dramatise the subject of terrorism and the subject has a history of creative treatment in films such as *Black Sunday* (John Frankenheimer, 1977), *Patriot Games* (Philip Noyce, 1992), *In the Name of the Father* (Jim Sheridan, 1993) and the more recent *Munich* (Steven Spielberg, 2005). Like these films, *True Lies* can be considered to make the political personal, filtering a complex, intricate and subtle real-world tension or subject through a charismatic individual who functions as the film's protagonist. Staying with the relevance of a real-world tension, in viewing the film it is appropriate to recognise that in 1993, twelve months before the film's release, but concurrent with its production schedule, a terrorist attack had been made on the World Trade Center in Manhattan. With *True Lies*, then, Cameron has appropriated the ballistics of *Terminator 2* but applied them to a story set in a recognisably 'real' world. In doing so, the film reads as insensitive to the ongoing and complex and delicate evolving relationship between east and west.

To understand something of the context in which *True Lies* was produced, we might reference the work of Stephen Prince. In *Firestorm: American Film in the Age of Terrorism* he writes that 'in the second half of the 1980s, terrorism crossed over from exploitation pictures of the Golan-Globus variety and became an item in numerous big-budget, high-profile Hollywood movies' (2009: 33). In identifying the film's lack of subtle dramatic negotiation of its subject, Prince has written of the film that

> Many of these blockbusters did not deal with Middle Eastern terrorism at all. Recent events established a kind of cognitive priming for the culture, establishing terrorism as a label and a prism through which to view not just modern political violence but crime itself. Thus, some films, like *True Lies*, might portray Arab terrorists while many others avoided the Middle East entirely and used terrorism as a convenient generic prop for mounting high-octane action thrillers. (Ibid.)

It is certainly the case that in the more immediate timeframe after the film's commercially successful release, Cameron had considered a sequel to the film. However, this plan was abandoned post-9/11.

The subject that *True Lies* treats could not be more complex and sombre in its resonance but the deployment of an action-comedy approach arguably makes the film something of an ethical test in terms of our consideration of it as 'entertainment'. This predominant reservation aside, though, the film can still be read as a text of some interest in terms of how it offers the view of a critique of American imperialism. In going a little way to connect with a particular geopolitical context *True Lies* arguably also critiques the surveillance culture that has become increasingly embedded in the material culture of so many peoples' daily lives.

The Movie
The film begins with the Twentieth Century Fox logo which is then followed by the logo for Cameron's then, newly-minted production company, Lightstorm; the logo is a chrome-surfaced form suggesting the mythological image of Diana the Huntress; a significant image in the context of Cameron's films and their commitment to representing strong women. The title credit sequence begins with Schwarzenegger's and Curtis's names appear on screen before the film's title eventually appears, rendered with a graphic that riffs on the idea of a secret revealed. As the letters turn to show themselves accompanied by a martial fanfare (composed by Brad Fiedel who had also worked with Cameron on *The Terminator* films), this conjures up a quasi-war film sensibility that the movie hews to.

The first image of *True Lies* shows a snowy forest and a chateau on Lake Tahoe in Nevada at night. We are immediately introduced to Harry Tasker (Schwarzenegger) embarking on a mission overseen by his agency colleague Albert 'Gib' Gibson (Tom Arnold). What is made clear in these opening moments is the bonhomie of their working friendship. Harry even uses the phrase 'Honey, I'm home' to let Gib and their younger colleague Faisal (Grant Heslov) know that he has successfully breached security at the chateau. Indeed, as the film develops, we understand that the warmth Harry enjoys in his relationships at work is not echoed at home, and in that dilemma unfolds the film's romantic-comedy narrative.

Whilst offering a very different treatment of surveillance culture as dramatised in *The Conversation* (Francis Coppola, 1974), *True Lies* does share one trait with that earlier film in that it captures the *esprit de corps* within the surveillance team. As the early part of the film develops Gib is presented more like Harry's wife. In Cameron's earlier film *The Abyss* we see an echo of this sense of the social aspect of the workplace. To some degree, then, *True Lies* is a film about men at work, just as *Aliens* and *The Abyss* are workplace dramas set against particularly extraordinary situations.

As Harry's mission at the chateau continues, Gib and Faisal watch and listen to him using a panoply of technology housed on board their van. We see Harry successfully infiltrate the plush banquet and he finds the object of his mission: a woman named Juno Skinner (Tia Carrere) who he immediately dances and flirts with in a scene that partly functions as a pastiche of the kind of scene we might typically see in James Bond movies with their emphasis (at least in their earliest iterations) on a sexually confident male spy. Again, it is film scholar Robin Wood who pointedly explains the ways that film resonates, making a point of comparison between James Bond movies and the thrillers of Alfred Hitchcock; both of which inform qualities of *True Lies*. Discussing *North by Northwest* (1959) specifically, Wood writes that 'a light entertainment can have depth, subtlety, finesse, it can embody mature moral values ... If I fail to be entertained by *Goldfinger*, it is because there is nothing there to engage or retain the attention; the result is a nonentity, consequently tedious' (1989: 131). In considering the ways in which *True Lies* serves as a revisitation of the mode of the James Bond film Larry Gross has noted that

> in the Bond series, from *Goldfinger* onwards, espionage and plot mechanics disappear almost entirely. Pure-action set pieces, large in scale, take over, moving the series ever more towards science fiction without claiming to go forward in time (not literally, anyway) … The Bond films were very important for other reasons. Technology, not only behind the screen, but as subject matter, as object of pleasurable consumption, becomes central. (2000: 5)

Indeed, might we suggest that the commercial success of *True Lies* partly influenced the 'return' of the James Bond movie franchise that commenced with *Goldeneye* (Martin Campbell, 1995), in much the same way that the success of the Jason Bourne franchise is clearly an influence on the more recent iterations in the series: *Casino Royale* (Martin Campbell, 2006), *Quantum of Solace* (Marc Forster, 2008) and *Skyfall* (Sam Mendes, 2012).

The action of the opening sequence of *True Lies* then cuts to the buddy movie banter of Gib and Faisal, as they bring up Juno's details in a quick moment of necessary character and plot exposition. The action then cuts back to the spectacle of showing Harry escape the chateau before he is caught. The tension of the sequence builds, partly deriving its humour and interest from a sense of dramatic irony. This chase is the first of three increasingly elaborately-staged chase sequences in the film. With Harry safely back in the company of Gil and Faisal, the action cuts to Gib dropping Harry off at home in suburbia. It is as though the chateau encounter had never occurred. Gib hands back Harry's wedding ring to put back on. 'What a team,' Harry says. We then see Harry getting into bed where Helen (Jamie Lee Curtis) is sleeping. We will soon recognise that the in-sync teamwork sensibility Harry experiences at work does not characterise his marriage at this point in the film. There is a fleeting, tender moment as Harry embraces Helen but then he lies there looking unsettled. For all of his macho derring-do at the chateau, Harry is quickly sketched as being less than secure once back at home. In their essay 'Something and Someone Else: The Mind, the Body and Sexuality in Titanic', Peter Lehman and Susan Hunt write that, in its representation of masculinity, '*True Lies*, like *Titanic*, is caught within an unresolved contradiction about masculinity: on the one hand, it wants to affirm a powerfully phallic masculinity; on the other, it implies that such masculinity is not what it is cracked up to be' (1999: 101). Of interest, too, is how *True Lies* builds on the comedy-derived action of *Lethal Weapon 2* (Richard Donner, 1989) in which the home life of Roger Murtaugh collides with his profession as a policeman in a film that emphasises the verbal and physical comedy of a 'buddy movie' police procedural.

The film's comedy, then, largely centres around Harry needing to connect with a sense of the domestic and a more overt display of commitment to Helen. This need to reconfigure and reassert the romantic love in a marriage also characterises the relationship at the centre of Cameron's earlier film *The Abyss*. Helen embarks on a fling with a physically unimposing car salesman named Simon (Bill Paxton) who is depicted as a parody of attempted masculinity. Unbeknownst to Helen, Harry has set up the affair in order to monitor Helen.

As the film establishes its alternating plot structure, dividing between Harry undertaking the mission to confront a terrorist threat and save American, and, by implication, 'world' interests, and Harry's mission to save his marriage, we are introduced to where Harry and Gib work: the government's intelligence and security agency, Omega Sector. A scene occurs in which they meet with their boss, Spencer Trilby (Charlton Heston); the inclusion here of a cameo by Heston as Tasker's boss adds a strain of ideological interest to the proceedings. At the time of Heston's appearance in the movie he was serving as President of the National Rifle Association (NRA). Given the film's emphasis on guns and artillery the connection is not too far-fetched. Indeed, *True Lies* only makes more acute Cameron's conception for *The Abyss* in which an alien threat to North American (and global security) was engaged with peacefully by the film's protagonists. In that film, the antagonist embarked on a mission to meet an 'other' culture with aggression. Certainly, *True Lies* evokes the unsettling but astutely critical comedy of the scene in *The Terminator* when the titular character is shown all too easily purchasing a weapon. In *True Lies*, though, no such critique of gun culture is alluded to; instead, guns become extensions of the human arm in an almost cyborg-like way. In effect they 'cyborg' the humans turning into killing machines and certainly Harry's entire physical sensory system is augmented by artificial sound and vision enhancers. It is useful to quote Alexandra Keller here as she parses the importance to the *mise-en-scène* of these kind of augmentations:

> The extent to which Cameron frequently sees representation as more real than the real is the extent to which he often refers (somewhat obliquely) to history and politics as accessories rather than central ideological discourses. Image in Cameron's films is more real – or more revealing – than reality. This, of course, is a sleight of hand symptomatic of a TV-era director, three of whose films have been serials. If image says more about reality than reality, then Cameron has it both ways – his meta-images supersede the reality of the film, and yet it is clear that the film as a whole is itself a chain of images that supersedes the reality of the film audience. (1999: 15)

This is taken to a disturbing extreme later in the film. Indeed, the film's action conclusion sees Harry piloting a jet fighter and it becomes something of a suit of armour for him just as the load-lifter does in *Aliens* and just as the amp suits, worn by Quaritch and his soldiers in *Avatar*, do.

At the briefing with Trilby, Harry's young colleague, Faisal, talks through the intelligence that they have gathered about the Middle Eastern, anti-American terrorist activity that they are confident is in process. It is then clarified that four nuclear warheads have been smuggled out of Kazakhstan. Compounding the unease generated by the film is a scene in which Jihad leader Aziz (Art Malik) addresses a video camera about his mission as a response to American imperialism. Given the film's uncomfortable caricature of the Arab culture it is of note, as other commentators have also observed, that the character of Faisal, Harry's colleague, is perhaps an attempt on the filmmaker's part to offer some sense of balance in its representation of a non-white American culture. In their writing about the film, Kapell and McVeigh note that whilst Faisal works for the American government the action of the film never allows him an opportunity to behave heroically in the way that Harry and Gib do.

Instructed to gather more information on Aziz, Harry, Gib and Faisal learn that Juno Skinner has received money from a terrorist's account and so must be understood to be involved with their project. Harry, using his pseudonym of Harry Renquist, goes to Skinner's offices where he is identified by Aziz, the leader of the terrorist cell with whom Skinner is working. Aziz, leader of Crimson Jihad, confronts Juno, in a moment of verbal and physical aggression, and insists that she must find out about 'Renquist'.

From this moment of drama and conflict, the film then cuts to the ultra-ordinary and modest setting of a suburban kitchen as we see Helen, at home, telephoning Harry at work. Helen gets patched through and we see Harry pretending to her that he is doing his sales job. Helen explains that she is making a birthday dinner for him. In Cameron's earlier film *The Terminator*, suburbia is also a place into which threatening forces can very easily invade. The action then cuts to a sequence set at night and the beginning of the film's second elaborately-staged chase sequence: Harry and Gib realise they are being trailed as they drive across Washington and there is the growing sense of a 'hunter and hunted' scenario that offers a comically-inflected variation on a key sequence in the opening act of *The Terminator*. The sequence unfolds with Harry confronting Aziz, a prelude to an extensive chase through a shopping mall and a park. As Aziz walks along with his gun he is framed rather like the Terminator when he breaks into the wrong Sarah Connor's home. The elaborate and silly (a tonal anomaly in Cameron's cinema) chase that then ensues between Aziz (on a motorcycle) and Harry (on a stolen police-horse) is organised so as to imply the iconography of the western genre, not only visually but also in terms of the music score that we hear as Harry is carried by a galloping horse in pursuit of Aziz. The chase effectively constructs Harry as a cowboy of sorts: a chivalrous gunslinger embodying the image of the cowboy as noble hero as defined in the Owen Wister novel *The Virginian* (1902). The chase, whilst a showcase of the filmmakers' resources to engineer kinetic spectacle, does not see Harry succeeding in his mission to capture Aziz. Having failed to do so Harry returns home to find Helen asleep, his own birthday party missed. He apologises to her and their understated exchange is consistent with similar scenes that occurred in other films contemporaneous with *True Lies*, such as the family drama *Regarding Henry* and the fantasy *Hook*. Indeed, might we propose that the film's plot development involving the kidnapping of Harry's daughter can arguably be considered revenge for Harry's working-life lie. In Spielberg's *Hook*, the titular Captain does just that, taking an adult Peter Pan's own children away and back into Neverland.

With Aziz having escaped from the chase through Washington DC Harry continues to gather more intelligence on his adversary. With these narrative requirements satisfied the film then segues from its thriller scenario to further develop its domestic-centred comedy of remarriage storyline.

His suspicions about Helen growing, Harry makes a surprise visit to Helen at her workplace and he overhears her chatting with a man on the phone called Simon who she is arranging to meet. Harry is upset by the revelation and returns to work where he tells Gib of Helen's apparent infidelity. Gib carelessly retorts: 'What do you expect, Harry? Helen's a flesh and blood woman and you're never there.' Gib explains to the emotionally wounded Harry (Schwarzengger's performance ably physicalising Harry's slump in self-esteem) that work is what gets him through personal problems. Indeed, this suggestion of salvation being offered by work ('the mission') also characterises Ripley's experience in *Aliens* and Bud and Lindsey's drama in *The Abyss*. With Harry's concern for national and international security suddenly sidelined the action takes us to the Tasker's home where a degree of tension is apparent as Harry, Helen and their daughter, Dana (Eliza Dushku) share a meal. Cameron counterpoints the tension with a moment of visual humour as Harry listens intently as Helen speaks, the camera pushing in on a close-up, his head cocked, his eyes narrowing almost like the Terminator processing information.

It is as this point that Harry then decides to undertake his own 'homefront' mission and spy on Helen. He is a man who likes being in control and his mission to restore his marriage. It emerges that Simon has told Helen that he is a spy. He is not. Harry, deploying his immense intel technology, is able to determine that Simon is in fact a used-car salesman. Harry sets about asserting his masculinity as superior to Simon's. Harry's mission culminates with him executing a raid on a hideaway that Helen and Simon have gone to. Harry kidnaps Helen and during this true 'homefront' mission Harry momentarily confronts Simon, asking him what it is that women want; Simon explains that 'they want the promise of adventure, the hint of danger'. Whilst this reply is delivered comically it alludes to the larger story arc for Helen and acts as a 'prelude' to the scene that follows which functions as the film's most sombre and resonant. Critically, the scene is about an abuse of technology. It is a subject that Hollywood genre films remain attuned to; in spring 2014, in the context of what was 'just' a comic book movie, the Marvel Studios comic adaptation *Captain America: The Winter Soldier* (Anthony and Joe Russo) dramatised something of a preoccupation with the idea of surveillance.

By the time of *True Lies*, Cameron had established himself as a writer-director committed to collaborating with lead actresses to create female protagonists who are competent, assured and resilient. As such, the conception and presentation of Helen Tasker appears crude and limited. Intriguingly, and perhaps serving as an index to the enduring importance of Cameron's background as a production designer, film scholars Kapell and McVeigh have noted that 'Helen is supported by none of the visual motifs and metaphors – the dark, semi-dystopian, technological images – that carry Connor, Ripley and Brigman through their respective narratives … Whatever its [Helen's striptease] motivation, the trend [in Cameron's films] does point to a growing attention to the feminine which will pervade [*Titanic* and *Avatar*]' (2011: 137). Helen is a conventional, suburban wife and mother who, like Sarah Connor in *The Terminator* films, has her unassuming life exploded by a larger, apocalyptic threat. Broad though the comedy of *True Lies* is, the character of Helen Tasker can be situated as a less intense and stark variation on the protagonists Sarah Connor and Ellen Ripley.

With Harry having kidnapped Helen, the film's most emotionally true and realistically scaled scene develops. It is a scene that achieves real dramatic weight and which has very little to do with the established scale of jeopardy and tension that has characterised the film until this point. Instead, the scene relates entirely to the marriage aspect of the story. In this interrogation scene, Helen sheds all of her suburban gentility and becomes momentarily primal as Harry, unbeknownst to her, interrogates her. Just as in *The Abyss*, when distance and technology combine to bring Lindsey and Bud together more honestly, so it is with this scene, which offers a sense of the power of specularity as Harry watches Helen 'break'. Helen explains to the 'interrogator' that what she wants is an authentic life. Her life as wife and office worker is, to some degree, a cocoon that she needs to break out of. It is not enough for her. Just as Jake becomes an avatar to realise his true self in *Avatar*, Helen is living an unreal life as an avatar of her authentic self. Indeed, Helen also anticipates Rose Butaker, the female protagonist of *Titanic*, who is similarly desperate to move beyond the confines of her cultural milieu and more specifically the confines of a domesticated life. In this scene, the the plot device and motif of surveillance which stands at the thematic centre of *True Lies*, anticipates the drama of the Cameron co-scripted science fiction film *Strange Days* and also echoes scenes of Sarah's interrogation in *Terminator 2: Judgement Day*. Indeed, we might say that the film's interest in the abuses of technology in relation to privacy perhaps resonates all the more now than it did twenty years ago as another marker of our increasingly, arguably, 'posthuman' world.

In the interrogation scene, Helen explains that her embryonic affair came about because 'I needed to feel alive. I just wanted to do something outrageous. And it felt good.' She says 'There's so much I wanted to do with this life and I haven't done any of it.' Her marriage and life as a mum has been 'fake'. Understandably, she loses her composure under the pressure of the situation and it is in doing so that she emerges as a Cameron heroine, shedding her suburban composure and 'good manners'. Helen goes primal, suddenly having much more in common with Sarah Connor and Ellen Ripley.

With Harry finally understanding Helen's emotional situation he then arranges an 'adventure' for her, albeit one that makes for a scene that affirms the power of the male gaze and painfully objectificaties the female body as Helen dances for Harry, initially not realising that it is him. The scene certainly became the most discussed of the film upon its release. Indeed, two other high-profile early 1990s Hollywood studio films became the subject of wider cultural discourse in the mainstream press in terms of their representation of female protagonists: *Thelma & Louise* and *The Silence of the Lambs* (Jonathan Demme, 1991). In terms of these two earlier films they both foregrounded female protagonists within genre modes and moments of action that might typically, within the Hollywood aesthetic, be expected to centre around male characters. More specifically, mainstream debates about *Thelma & Louise* seemed to struggle in some instances to reconcile the image of women reacting with some violence towards aggressive males.

Harry's crude attempt to reconnect with Helen in the hotel room is interrupted by Aziz's henchmen who kidnap the couple. The film moves into its final act as the terrorist plotline refocuses the narrative. Finally, Helen comes to learn what Harry's job actually is. The couple are taken to Aziz's camp where he has a nuclear warhead ready to prime and deploy. Helen and Harry are tied up and amidst the tension and jeopardy still find time to chat like any couple would do in more mundane circumstances. 'You ever killed anyone?' Helen asks Harry nonchalantly. 'Yeah, but they were all bad,' Harry replies. It's a 'knowing' joke that refers to both Harry's character and also Schwarzenegger's established screen identity as an action movie star. However, the quip, in our post-9/11 world, cannot help but seem crass. Indeed, Harry's reply attests to the truth of the sensibility that the Robin Wood observation, with which this chapter opens, attests. Indeed, when Steven Spielberg's adaptation of H. G. Wells' novel *War of the Worlds* (2005) was released it was overtly a post-9/11 movie and it was a paternal hero at the centre of the story who was called on to protect his children.

Harry and Helen escape their captors and she is separated from him and taken prisoner by Juno. Helen comments: 'I married Rambo.' It is a throwaway line that wittily references Cameron's earlier writing career when he worked on *Rambo*, but it is one loaded with an uncomfortable ideological resonance in its comparison of Harry with a one-man army facing down a foreign 'other'. Having worked through accentuating the fractured marital relationship and bringing it to a crisis point (still to be resolved at this point in the film's running time) the plot then reverts to its action-thriller mode as the final act commences, incited by the acute sense of Harry embarking on a 'race against time' scenario as Harry must prevent a nuclear bomb being set off. This structuring device characterises *The Terminator*, *The Abyss* and *Titanic* particularly. As Harry races to 'global' rescue he must also retrieve Helen from jeopardy at the hands of Juno Skinner. With Helen rescued and reunited with her husband, the film's narrative moves towards its final act, in which the personal and the political will combine to satisfy both the demands of an audience seeking Cameron's established deployment of visual spectacle and with an interest in seeing how Harry responds (filtered through the Schwarzenegger star persona) to maximum jeopardy. Indeed, re-viewing the film in 2014 there is an interesting exercise to be undertaken in comparing it with another film that constituted a major studio summertime 'blockbuster': *Clear and Present Danger* (Philip Noyce, 1994). Like that film's predecessor *Patriot Games* it also dramatises the American military-political relationship with an enemy, refracting aspects of its protagonist's motivations through the imperiled lives of family and friends.

After a highly kinetic car chase, a nuclear bomb detonates. Where in *Terminator 2* the image of the moment of apocalypse is all-consuming, entirely filling the screen, in this film it is a detail in the background of a shot that foregrounds the reawakened romance of Harry and Helen. The couple embrace, framed on screen just off-centre, whilst in the remaining part of the frame a visual effect shows a nuclear blast mushroom-clouding on the horizon. In *True Lies*, the romantic aspect offers reassurance. Aziz is defeated by Harry and marital harmony for Harry and Helen restored. The politically-informed dramatic stakes become ever more personal when Harry's

The comedy of remarriage finds expression amidst an apocalyptic conflict

daughter Dana is kidnapped by Aziz. Having rescued his wife, Harry then goes to rescue his daughter in an elaborately staged and balletic action climax.

For Helen and Harry, then, the adventure that they eventually share resolves the problems of a marriage in crisis. As such this narrative echoes the romantic drama of *The Abyss*. One might suggest that *True Lies* could be read as a comedy of remarriage, *à la* two other Hollywood studio movies: *Twister* (Jan de Bont, 1996) and *Mr and Mrs Smith* (Doug Liman, 2005). Stanley Cavell has written extensively about the comedy of remarriage and, appropriately, given the thriller roots of *True Lies*, Cavell has said of Hitchcock's *North by Northwest* that it is 'from the genre of remarriage or rather from whatever it is that that genre is derived, which means to me that its subject is the legitimacy of marriage, as if the pair's adventures are trials of their suitability for that condition' (1988: 154).

Outside of its textual interest, *True Lies* also served the mainstream media as a catalsyt for their ongoing construction of Cameron not only as 'storyteller' but also as a resource-intensive filmmaker, a narrative that develops further in coverage of Cameron's subsequent film *Titanic*; and, as someone who was an inventor and engineer of movies in the tradition of filmmakers such as Thomas Edison, Walt Disney, Cecil B. DeMille and perhaps even Terry Gilliam. In this sense, he satisfied a particular American trope. For the American movie magazine, *Premiere* (August 1994), *True Lies* was the cover story (although Schwarzenegger, not Cameron made the cover); the feature article, written by John Richardson, was entitled 'Iron Jim' and it explored the making of the movie and also aspects of Cameron's career trajectory to that time. The hyperbole surrounding *True Lies*' production process characterised the magazine's article which somewhat enshrined Cameron as a macho engineer and pioneer: the subtitle for the piece is 'This time he wasn't just pushing the envelope – he was ripping it to shreds'. Richardson comments that '*Aliens* and *The Abyss* established his reputation as both a brilliant world class director and a potentially out of control visionary crackpot' (2012: 63), the kind of clichéd description that might also have been used to characterise other American filmmakers such as Coppola and De Mille.

Indeed, the title of Richardson's article is interesting as it riffs on a book title that was in the early 1990s familiar to many readers. In the summer of 1994, Robert Bly's

Iron John: A Book About Men (originally published in 1990 and reissued since) was still fresh in the culture as an examination of how modern men could investigate their masculinity. In the Preface to the book Bly writes:

> The dark side of men is clear. Their mad exploitation of earth resources, devaluation and humiliation of women, and obsession with tribal warfare are undeniable. Genetic inheritance contributes to those obsessions, but also culture and environment. We have defective mythologies that ignore masculine depth of feeling, assign men a place in the sky instead of earth, teach obedience to the wrong powers, work to keep men boys, and entangle both men and women in systems of industrial domination that exclude matriarchy and patriarchy. (2001: ix).

These dark sides are very much consistent with the often crude modes of Cameron's film.

On its theatrical release *True Lies* proved commercially successful, grossing over $145 million in North America alone, but reviews of the film were dismissive and considered the film a retrograde step for Cameron. Geoff Andrew, in *Time Out*, commented that 'half the time, this hi-tech action movie delivers, in a mindless kind of way: it's fast, crude and has enough explosions and cartoon-style violence to satisfy our baser instincts' (1994).

True Lies is certainly usefully viewed within the context of other films of this time such as *Executive Decision* (Stuart Baird, 1996), *The Peacemaker* (Mimi Leder, 1997) and *The Siege* (Edward Zwick, 1998), each of which were predicated upon a menace from the East. All of these films adopt the thriller, rather than the romantic-comedy/thriller fusion of *True Lies*, as the generic 'default position' with which to articulate fears and engage with the subject. We might say that, like so many war films, these 'terrorism-thrillers' focus on the spectacle of 'battle' rather than on any more subtle and muted sites on which such events inevitably impact.

In significant contrast to *True Lies*, Cameron's next film would be a melodrama and historical epic but one that shared with it a dramatic core centred around a quickly failing romantic relationship in which a woman strives to have her own authentic life in the midst of an impending apocalypse. Undoubtedly, *Titanic* would restore Cameron's standing as a great manipulator of cinematic spectacle that was anchored in a thoughtful engagement with the representation of gender and of the wilderness.

CHAPTER SEVEN
Titanic (1997)

In an interview with his occasional collaborator Randall Frakes, James Cameron noted that 'I've based my cinematic career on creating a sense of unity between the audience and the characters on the screen, through whatever means necessary. I wanted to try the same stylistic approach with an historical event and see if I could create that unity through recognisable emotions and situations' (1999: ix). This emphasis on the dovetailing of artifice and authenticity reaches its near-apogee in *Titanic*.

In terms of its dramatic conceit, particularly in relation to the earlier *The Abyss*, *Titanic* characterises the sea as a wilderness where both the masculine and the feminine are set in opposition to each other and where the unconscious forces of nature challenge the conscious forces of civilisation, gender and class.

The film can be identified as a key entry in a run of large-scale historical dramas (offering the visual spectacle of period costume and setting) that the Hollywood studios had financed after the immense commercial and critical success of *Dances With Wolves* (Kevin Costner, 1990). Other such titles included *The Last of the Mohicans* (Michael Mann, 1992) and *Braveheart* (Mel Gibson, 1995). Narrating its challenging production history is not the concern here; that process has been retold several times elsewhere, most notably in *Titanic and the Making of James Cameron* (1998) by Paula Parisi.

Critically, *Titanic* furthered Cameron's project of evolving digital visual effects not only for the purposes of spectacle, which is so important to his cinema, but also in terms of more subtle applications of the available technology. In his interview with Frakes, Cameron comments: 'I think the moment when Jack and Rose fade as the ship transforms into the wreck turned out to be a kind of effects epiphany because it shows the power visual effects can have to merge concepts in poetic ways' (1999: x).

This followed in a tradition pioneered by Ken Ralston and his visual effects team on Robert Zemeckis's *Forrest Gump* (1994). Zemeckis's movie provided a striking example of computer-generated effects being used not only for 'obvious' effects (notably, Forrest Gump meeting JFK) but also in terms of achieving a range of 'low-key' illusions and adjustments to initially photographed images, such as modifying the colour of the sky in an establishing shot or the process of placing leaves on a tree that may have been bare during the principal photography phase. Of most significance narratively was the digital removal of actor Gary Sinise's legs as his character, Lt. Dan, is a mutilated war veteran. Indeed, since *Forrest Gump*, Zemeckis has increasingly deployed the 'painterly' capacities of CGI within the photographic tradition of cinema. Zemeckis's performance-capture films all apply animation and digital painting to original moving-photographed footage of performers. Increasingly, the temporal distinctions between pre-production, production and post-production processes for a feature film schedule have become blurred and continue to be rapidly collapsed.

Cameron's interest in *Titanic* was initially prompted during research work for *The Abyss*. He had visited the Woods Hole Oceanographic Institution in Massachusetts as part of this phase and had also watched an earlier dramatic interpretation of the Titanic's voyage, *A Night to Remember* (Roy Ward Baker, 1958). This combination of empirical research and imaginative interpretation fused to foster the genesis of what would become *Titanic*.

Of his evolving approach to the subject of how the Titanic, in terms of its voyage and its voyagers, could become the basis for a movie, Cameron commented in *Cinefex* magazine that 'I started thinking that a pretty amazing film could be done by juxtaposing images of the wreck as it sits today with images of what happened on that night long ago, sort of collapsing time in a way that only cinema can do – like the Paleolithic bone thrown in the air in *2001*, turning into the spaceship, editing out, literally in a single cut, three million years of human evolution' (1997: 16). He also stated: 'I figured the best way to get in touch with the emotion of the event would be to take one set of characters and tell the story as a love story – because only by telling it as a love story can you appreciate the loss of separation and the loss caused by death' (1999: 116). Cameron's emphasis on death continues a preoccupation present in his previous films, embodied by the moment of apocalyptically-scaled destruction of the human race. As such, his work shares a motif with the popular Japanese cinema in the post-World War II era when a wide range of films, famously including *Gojira* (Ishirô Honda, 1954) explored the implications of nuclear power as a military presence.

We might say that *Titanic* looks the *least* like a Cameron film, with its largely high-key lighting and refined, historical setting. Only in its final hour does the film shift into action movie territory, familiar to us from *Aliens* and *The Terminator* particularly, the film having centred its attention up until then on defining character and conflicts. The film is predominantly characterised by a golden light that feels emblematic of the age in which the action is set. It sits interestingly alongside the historical romance *Far and Away* (Ron Howard, 1992), a movie that also centred on upper- and lower-class characters falling in love against a specific 'historical' backdrop. As such, is *Titanic* also to be read as an example of heritage cinema and presumed notions of good taste?

Like other Cameron heroines, Rose is looking to control her destiny in a world dominated by men

In the film, music assumes a particularly powerful role, primarily the nondiegetic score by James Horner but also, at moments, the diegetic music that reinforces class distinctions: the 'polite' music of the upper-class spaces and the fiddle and accordion music of the working-class space. In both cases, the diegetic music supports the melodramatic qualities of the movie. *Titanic* is certainly a melodrama as much as it is a disaster movie. Of the genre of melodrama, Christine Gledhill's research into the melodrama has been usefully surveyed in *The Cinema Book* where the point is made that melodrama serves powerfully as a means of dramatising feminism within the representation of patriarchal cultures (1999: 164–5).

Amongst other qualities, Cameron's films have become key to the construction of a number of film star personae. Whilst he had appeared in *Hercules in New York*, *Conan the Barbarian* and *Conan the Destroyer*, it was with Cameron's *The Terminator* that Arnold Schwarzenegger's screen persona crystallised. *Titanic* showcased two nascent film stars, Kate Winslet and Leonardo DiCaprio. Of the film star presence, as commodity and as conduit for ideological expression and representation, Richard Dyer has commented that 'stars relate to very general ideas about society and the individual' (2004: ix). In a sense, the film star becomes a fundamental part of the film's spectacle: seeing the particular performer in 'those' particular narrative conditions and within the illusion of the film is central to the audience's pleasure.

Setting a context for a discussion about Winslet's performance in *Titanic*, Thomas Austin and Martin Barker first consider her performance in *Jude* (Michael Winterbottom, 1996), a gritty adaptation of Thomas Hardy's *Jude the Obscure* (1895); they describe how, in *Jude*, she expresses 'rebellion physically, through her body, and it is through her naked body that Sue offers herself to Jude when the two set up house together despite their unmarried state' (2003: 110).

In terms of DiCaprio's role in the film, we can recognise Cameron's choice to cast a male lead who is not physically imposing or 'sturdy', in contrast to Schwarzenegger, Ed Harris in *The Abyss* or the performers portraying the Marines in *Aliens*. Indeed, DiCaprio's physical presence is very 'ordinary', even frail-looking at moments of particular jeopardy. As such Jake Sully's disabled body in *Avatar* would extend Cameron's image-making around physicalities apparently at odds with the extraordinary events unfolding around them. This contrasts with Sarah Connor in *Terminator 2: Judgement Day* who has built her body to a point where it is attuned for the experience she moves into.

The point has been made that Winslet's Rose is a typically headstrong female character as per the example of previous Cameron films. However, she also is consistent with a number of strong woman protagonists at the centre of contemporaneous Hollywood spectaculars with no Cameron connection, notably *Speed* (Jan DeBont, 1994), *Twister* (like Cameron's film *True Lies*, a movie of 'remarriage') and *Contact* (Robert Zemeckis, 1997). We might argue that with Sarah Connor and Ellen Ripley, Cameron's films assisted in developing a creative and representational space for these kinds of women to be characterised. *Speed*'s Sandra Bullock has more recently featured in the visually spectacular, dramatically taut piece, *Gravity* portraying a character not so far removed from Ellen Ripley in her resolve, adaptability and with a backstory that centres on maternal grief.

The film, then, was marketed quite emphatically as a DiCaprio star vehicle, the studio's marketing picking up on his established teen female following which had been 'with' the actor from *This Boy's Life* (Michael Caton Jones, 1993) and *What's Eating Gilbert Grape* (Jeremiah Chechik, 1993) through to *Romeo + Juliet* (Baz Luhrmann, 1996). We might say that DiCaprio is the performer who 'allows' the film to move between the forms of melodrama and action film. Peter Lehman and Susan Hunt suggest that '*Titanic* refashioned the body and characterization of the working-class lover and the male action hero in such a manner that a type of character that teenage girls normally cared little or nothing about suddenly became intensely attractive to them' (1999: 89). Indeed, looking to a post-*Titanic* cinema of spectacle, other male protagonists who find themselves in spectacular situations have more in common with DiCaprio than Stallone. In this regard we might cite the examples of George Clooney, Johnny Depp and Orlando Bloom. Cameron, then, countered expectation and, in a sense a part of his own casting tradition, by casting as Jack an actor who was not physically imposing.

We see the young and old physical body of Rose. Of this contrast, Lehman and Hunt note:

> In a culture that attributes much of women's power to their beauty, age, of course, is the enemy. Contrasting an elderly woman with her once youthful beauty is itself a form of punishment not unprecedented in recent Hollywood film ... To understand the success of *Titanic*, one must also understand the manner in which Cameron was able to modify it in a way that held particular appeal for teenage girls. In this story pattern, a conventionally attractive woman is discontented to the point of psychological instability, primarily because of her marriage of engagement to an intellectual man (often coded as upper class). ... by blocking the potential of the upper-class male to offer any intellectual, romantic (or technological) comfort to Rose, the film suggests that the only solution to Rose's oppression – to her very survival – lies in the anti-intellectual domain of frenetic bodily activity, and it is this aspect of the traditional mind/body split that holds such deep-seated appeal. (1999: 92, 98)

The Movie

The film begins with the Twentieth Century Fox studio logo and then we hear the sound of a lone female voice singing plaintively. We see the film's first image: 'fake' archive footage of the Titanic in dock. The camera pans left and the image dissolves across a set of shots showing crowds waving as the ship leaves the port of Southampton. There is then a dissolve to an image of a moonlit sea and the film's title fades in over the waves. The melancholy voice of the singer then fades away like a memory and another dissolve takes us to the seabed as a set of intensely bright beams of light are shining towards us. Momentarily, it feels like we are watching a spaceship approach. It is a moment that certainly recalls images from *The Abyss*. We are watching two exploration vehicles approaching and the camera tilts down to show the vessels descending ever-deeper into the ocean, their points of light lending them a similar sense of enchantment to the submarines in motion in *The Abyss*. The scene then cuts to an image of one of the vessels moving across the seabed, both mysterious and intriguing, followed by a shot that offers the audience a point of view from the vessel as it approaches the wreck of Titanic.

The action cuts to the submarine explorer Brock Lovett (Bill Paxton) looking out at the wreck. His facial expression registers awe and unease that can be seen on the faces of characters trapped beneath the ocean in *The Abyss*. The score becomes more prominent and conjures a feeling of mystery as we see the encrusted bow rail of the fallen ship. The scene is suffused with the same sense of mystery and suspense that Cameron deployed in *The Abyss*. Brock lies at the window of his vessel and narrates the moment of discovery, recording it on the video camera he wields at the portal. The recording of testimony, as in *The Terminator* and *Avatar*, is key to the structure of the storytelling and Brock's brief narration will soon be superseded by the elderly Rose as she recalls her experience on board the ship. A smaller vessel containing Brock and a pilot then explores the wreck, the lights of the craft piercing the gloom just as in the opening of *Aliens* when Ripley is discovered. It becomes apparent that Brock is hoping to locate sunken treasure and indeed he recovers a safe, which he and the crew are disappointed to find does not contain a particular necklace. However, a mud-caked object retrieved from the safe reveals a pencil sketch of a young woman wearing a necklace. Brock realises that the necklace they are seeking is the same as that in the drawing – 'the Heart of the Ocean'.

The action cuts to a domestic home and the elderly Rose Calvert (Gloria Stuart) sitting at a potter's wheel working on a new vase. She hears a TV report about Brock's exploration of the Titanic and sees the drawing of her a young woman. Brock receives a call from Rose who tells him she is the woman in the drawing. We cut to Rose and her granddaughter Lizzie (Suzy Amis) as they arrive on the exploration ship. Brock's crew are sceptical as to her intentions or even sanity (she is approaching her 101st birthday), but Brock, perhaps more in desperation than genuine belief, insists she must know something about the necklace. In the lab on board the ship we see Rose look down through the water in which the drawing of her still sits. She shuts her eyes and there is a very brief flashback of a young man's hand sketching a detail of the picture, as we hear Brock explain the history of the missing blue diamond from which the Heart of the Ocean was fashioned. Brock then shows Rose a number of items recovered from the state room on the ship and she picks up a broken hand mirror that had been hers; we see her face reflected in the mirror. The scientists interrupt Rose's reverie and explain how the ship hit the iceberg and was sunk using a computerised simulation of events, a pre-echo of the rather more sophisticated CGI that Cameron will utilise later in the film to dramatise the sinking. This scene also serves to offer the audience the necessary exposition about the ship. Critically, Cameron uses this exposition to give the audience a sense of the geography of the ship; knowledge that can be drawn upon two hours later when the film's action focuses on the spectacle of Titanic sinking.

'Of course, the experience of it was somewhat different,' Rose says of the trauma. She looks silently at the footage of the wreck on one of the lab's video screens and there is another brief image recalling 1914 on board the ship. 'It's been eighty-four years...' Rose says and plaintive music rises as we get a close-up of her, whilst over her shoulder we see an image of the sunken ship on a video screen, which morphs into the first shot seen of the Titanic in dock, ready to sail. The scene that follows showcases the anticipation of the ship's departure and also the rather painterly illusion of the photorealistic effects being used to recreate the Titanic. We see several glistening cars pull up among the crowds at the dock carrying two of the film's protagonists, Cal (Billy Zane) and Rose (Winslet), engaged and soon to be married. The camera drops down from a high wide shot to arrive at a close-up on Rose as she looks up from beneath the wide brim of her hat. 'God himself could not sink this ship,' Cal says to Rose. The hubris of excessive faith in technology as an element of dramatic tension that had also played its part in *The Terminator*, *The Abyss* and *Aliens* and would do so again in *Avatar*, also has a place in this movie. The scale of the recreation of the Titanic and its eventual sinking is rendered in the language of the epic movie. Amidst the wide shots of crowds of digitally created and amplified crowds, there is a fleeting eye-level shot that encapsulates a key issue behind the drama: in the background of a wide shot we see the wealthy boarding the ship, whilst in the foreground, the camera tracking past them to show third-class passengers being checked for the condition of their mouths and if they have lice in their hair. Like the shot of an arrow embedded in a tyre early in *Avatar*, the image functions as a motif.

We then hear the elderly Rose recalling that 'to me it was a slave ship ... inside I was screaming'. She says this as we watch her as a young woman (portrayed by Kate Winslet) walking towards the camera as she steps into the ship. From the luxury of her circumstances the action then cuts to a pub on the dock where we are introduced to the film's hero, Jack Dawson (DiCaprio), who wins third-class tickets on the Titanic for him and his friend Fabrizio (Danny Nucci) in a game of cards. Jack now has a means of getting home to America. Like Jake in *Avatar*, he will be taken out of his comfort zone and plunged into an alien culture, in this case of the upper-class passengers on board the ship.

'When you got nothing, you got nothing to lose', Jack says as he plays the card game in which he will win his ticket home. As such, he is as hopeless as Jake at the beginning of *Avatar*. Like Ripley in *Aliens* he is looking for a new start. There is a youthful intensity to his physicality as he celebrates his win and a bathetic dramatic irony as he then races to board the ship that we fear will become his tomb.

'We're practically goddamn royalty', Jack says as he and his buddy run to get on the ship. Jack's comment will be echoed later in the film by his antagonist, Cal. As the first two hours of the film unfold, Jack's bearing is presented as admirable, a counterpoint to Cal's selfish entitlement. There is then a sequence of shots that show the Titanic starting to embark on its journey. Inside the ship Jack and Fabrizio find their cramped cabin below decks which they share with two others, a stark contrast with the quarters that we then see Rose and Cal occupy, with their private promenade deck. The décor of flowers and elegant furnishing is almost too much, suffocating we might say. It becomes an outward expression of Rose's emotional and intellectual condition. Rose sorts through the modern art she has brought with her and she makes a comment that echoes something Cameron himself once said of his own creative *modus operandi*: 'There's truth but no logic.' One of the paintings that Rose has is a Picasso. A little later, she references Sigmund Freud, a name unfamiliar to her fellow travellers. Rose is clearly interested in a world beyond, and very different to, the one she finds herself about to be married into.

The scale of the engine room is unveiled by an upward tilt of the camera which reveals its space and immensity. It looks almost unearthly: the mechanical power of the machine in keeping with the mechanical power of certain environments and creations imagined in *The Abyss* and *Avatar*. The action then cuts to Jack and his friend up on the bow of the ship, the camera rising up above them to emphasise the enormous height of the Titanic as they look down at the water, the viewer being afforded a generous view of the ship as rendered via CGI. As Jack looks out at the sea he watches a (digitally created) school of dolphins outrun the ship; an early clue that nature cannot be beaten. An image then follows that emphasises the contrast between the wild and the delicacy and fragility of the civilised as we see the ship's captain Edward Smith (Bernard Hill), like Jack surveying the view, sipping from a dainty teacup. (The teacup as motif of civilisation also strikes a powerful note in Kevin Costner's western, *Open Range* (2003).) Standing on the rails, Jack then lets out a euphoric, wolf-like howl and declares: 'I'm the king of the world!' He is a primal figure like both Jake Sully in *Avatar* and Ripley as she moves towards the final sequence of *Aliens*. We then pull back and in a digitally created reverse zoom, the virtual camera moves back from the bow, across the deck, between the chimneystacks and on out beyond the stern. It is a moment that does not reflect any character's actual view of the ship, instead existing solely for the audience's pleasure. Contrasting with such an immense image is that shot of the teacup. The movie and the ship are equally spectacular visual experiences.

From Jack's 'barbaric yawp' (to borrow a phrase from Whitman's *Leaves of Grass*) the action cuts to Rose at dinner with Cal and a number of their fellow travellers, including Bruce Ismay (Jonathan Hyde), one of the ship's financial backers and the Titanic's designer, Thomas Andrews (Victor Garber). Cal partronisingly orders Rose's dinner for her, much to the amusement of fellow guest Molly Brown (Kathy Bates). Rose makes an outspoken comment that expresses her disdain for male chauvinists. This confidence in expressing her view also characterises Sarah Connor, Ellen Ripley

In *Titanic*, the mass of human-made machinery has a moment of harmony with the wilderness

and Lindsay Brigman in other Cameron films. 'I may have to mind what she reads,' Cal says dismissively of his fiancée. In just a couple of scenes, Cameron has economically, if unsubtly, brought to the fore issues of class and sexual politics, two themes generally under-represented in expensive Hollywood blockbusters.

The action then cuts to Jack out on the lower-class deck, drawing. He sees Rose in the most romantic of ways, the sunlight reflecting off her dress as she looks out to sea. One of Jack's Irish friends reminds him: 'You're as likely to have angels fly out of your arse as get next to the likes of her.' This expression of a sense of male camaraderie is more fully realised in *Aliens* and *The Abyss* than it is here. Indeed, Jack is the least macho of Cameron's male protagonists; perhaps even the ideal version of masculinity in his combination of physicality and a certain emotional sensitivity. From a distance, Jack then sees Cal walk Rose away from the deck and their body language confirms the tension between the couple.

In one of the film's key scenes we then see Rose at yet another lavish dinner and on the soundtrack we hear elderly Rose recall how she felt at that moment on the ship. Like Sarah Connor and Jake, Rose is recording her thoughts and feelings about an event: 'I saw my whole life as if I'd already lived it ... Always the same narrow people. The same mindless chatter. I felt like I was standing at a great precipice with no one to pull me back. No one who cared, or even noticed.' Like Sarah Connor in *The Terminator*, Rose recognises that a moment of change is imminent. As we hear the elderly Rose's recollection on the soundtrack, the camera holds on a mid-shot of her looking blankly at the plush dinner table. From this moment of stillness, the action cuts to a close-up of her feet running across the wooden deck of the ship. Jack is lying out under the stars, his face profiled in the foreground with the sky above as the background element. Jack recognises Rose as she runs by. She goes to the stern of the ship and stands on a rail, apparently determined to end it all. Jack sees her and goes to the bow of the stern and tells her that on account of his stopping her jumping, 'I'm involved now' – a statement that defines the essence of the Cameron hero. Jack is confident and physically adept. He talks about fishing with his dad on icy waters in Wisconsin and tells Rose: 'You seem like an indoor girl.' Indoor girls typically become outdoor girls in Cameron's movies, moving beyond the confines of the civilised world and out into the wilderness. Jack describes to Rose how cold icy water is: 'It hits you like a thousand knives stabbing you all over your body.' He is describing precisely how later in the film he and his fellow passengers will feel when the ship sinks.

Rose accidentally slips overboard, is caught and saved by Jack, but his heroism is misinterpreted by a crew member who presumes Jack is assaulting her. The misunderstanding resolved, Cal nonetheless treats Jack, the third-class passenger, with contempt. Cal's snobbery and sense of entitlement is an echo of Burke in *Aliens* and Ribisi's character in *Avatar*. These are not men of effective action: either in terms of choices or physical intervention. Cal eventually invites Jack for dinner the next night, supposedly a note of thanks for Jack's help but it is clearly a chance for Cal to mock Jack's class difference.

'Women and machinery do not mix,' says one of Rose and Cal's party rather dismissively as Rose's predicament resolves itself. It is a comment that might suggest something of the time in which the story is set but which pointedly contradicts the relationship between women and machinery that we would recognise in Cameron's films, such as the crucial story element of Ripley piloting the loadlifter in *Aliens*, eventually using this skillset to confront the alien Queen.

The action then cuts to Rose in her room, bathed in a golden light as a delicate tune plays on a music box. Cal comes in and talks with her: their conversation presented largely as a reflection in a mirror. The mirror serves as a simple motif of identity and ties the film into a detail of the genre of the melodrama. Rose and Cal are anticipating their engagement gala due to happen a week later. Rose does not look particularly excited or happy with the prospect, even after Cal gives her the 'Heart of the Ocean' necklace. She is suffocated by the world she is in, by the attitudes and the décor that externalises and physicalises this overbearing culture. (One might watch Martin Scorsese's adaptation of *The Age of Innocence* (1993) to see a similar *mise-en-scène* at work.)

Cal explains to Rose: 'We are royalty, Rose.' It is a statement that takes a very different meaning here compared to Jack's holler, 'I'm the king of the world!' Jack's declaration has none of the elitism present in Cal's association with royalty. Intriguingly, of course, for these American characters the notion of royalty should have no currency as they are from a republic. Indeed, we can make a connection between *Titanic* and Twain's novel *The Prince and the Pauper* (1881/2) which explores this tension between monarchy and republic, wealth and poverty.

The action then dissolves to a scene of Jack and Rose walking the ship's deck the next day, Jack carrying his folder of drawings. He explains how he 'lit on out of there' to travel, another Twain reference, this time to Huckleberry Finn. Rose thanks Jack for talking her down from the rails and for his discretion. Jack explains that he wants to know why she is feeling so sad. She tells him: 'It was everything. My whole world. And all the people in it. The inertia of my life.' Jack asks Rose if she loves Cal and she is disturbed by the directness of the question. Jack is plain-speaking, unsophisticated in his address, which a defensive Rose, who is perhaps not as uninhibited as she likes to think, interprets as rudeness. 'You don't know me, and I don't know you,' Rose says, offering a verbal motif that Cameron returns to in *Avatar* about seeing the authentic being. Rose then looks at the drawings that Jack has made of people he met and loved in Paris, including some nudes. The drawings remind us of how Cameron's films have celebrated the female body. As such, his movies play fully into the debate around the female and male gaze.

'You have a gift, Jack. You see people', Rose says as the scene cuts back and forth between close-ups of the young protagonists. 'You see me', she says of Jack's creativity. Indeed, this statement also becomes the most meaningful and affirmative statement that the lovers say to each other in *Avatar*. We might suggest that Rose is an avatar of herself: the well-to-do, polite Rose. She needs to connect with her authentic self in a renewed state. In *Avatar*, Jake's avatar identity allows him to connect with his authentic self anew. Moving beyond the artifice of our highly mediated, constructed and technological world (in terms of technology, class and gender roles) in order to recognise the most authentic parts of ourselves is the 'quest' that's being undertaken in the mythologically-informed terrain of Cameron's movies.

Following a scene of exposition where Captain Smith is urged by Ismay to push the Titanic harder ('This maiden voyage of Titanic must make headlines'), Jack and Rose are shown fantasising about being free and uninhibited in America before engaging in a spitting contest, to the disapproval of Rose's passing mother (Frances Fisher), to whom Jack is introduced. Molly Brown, immediately taken by Jack as a kindred spirit, provides Jack with evening dress for his dinner with Rose's party.

Brief though the dinner scene is, it establishes the geography of the upper-class quarters where much of the action will take place later and thematically attests to the urge of Cameron's characters to live in the fullest of ways, to entirely commit to an experience. Lindsey was committed to her work as an engineer in *The Abyss*. Sarah was entirely committed to her mission in *Terminator 2*. Grace is entirely committed to her work to understand the Na'vi in *Avatar*. It is an almost Thoreauvian sensibility that Jack explains, saying that even though he has little in a material sense he is able to live spontaneously: 'I figure life's a gift and I don't intend on wasting it,' he explains, directly alluding to Rose's suicide attempt. Having asserted his approach to daily life he then throws a box of matches across the table to Cal, thereby contravening all expected decorum but nonetheless charming his fellow diners. Affirming her newfound fascination, and concern, for Jack, Rose then raises her glass to Jack and his mantra of 'Making it count'. Cal looks miffed by the gesture. As dinner ends and Jack is escorted by Cal's manservant, Lovejoy (David Warner) from the dining room, he slips Rose a note. The action then cuts to Rose and Jack dancing to boisterous Celtic music, all fiddles and pennywhistles, in third class, the freedom of expression in marked contrast to the refined dinner above decks. They are secretly spied upon by Lovejoy, who recognises the threat Jack represents to Cal's future plans, even if Cal does not. In both *Titanic* and *Avatar*, singing and dancing/moving bind a community together.

The action shifts to the next morning and an evident tension between Rose and Cal. A furious Cal confronts Rose about her partying with Jack and demands that she 'honour' her future husband. Compounding this is the pressure that Rose is exposed to by her mother and her insistence that Rose not throw away marriage to Cal and the financial security it will bring her, an exchange that takes place as Mrs Calvert symbolically ties her daughter into a tight corset. It is a similar mercantile impulse that Burke uses to get Ripley on side in *Aliens*. Where Ripley recognises her authentic experience lies in being protective, in *Titanic* Rose will discover that her authentic experience will be to recognise her own self, to cite Walt Whitman again, 'to sound her barbaric yawp'. The image of the authentic life also drives *Avatar*. Jake's avatar condition allows him a certain kind of authenticity through artifice (just as movies do) but at the film's conclusion he moves beyond being an avatar and becomes an authentic Na'vi. In *The Terminator*, Sarah Connor is broken out of her stultifying life as a diner waitress by the authentic experience of future motherhood as well as a mission that in true heroic style sees her being required to move beyond what she considered possible. In *True Lies*, Helen is desperate to break out of the repetition of her suburban life and work life as an administrator.

Jack attempts to speak to Rose while she takes part in a church service, but he is ejected from the upper-class quarters on the orders of Lovejoy. He monitors her movements as she takes a turn around the ship (during which she helpfully notes the shortage of lifeboats in ratio to passengers) then admits he has feelings for her ('I'm not an idiot, I know how the world works … you're going to die if you don't break free'). A flustered Rose withdraws to take tea with her mother. Across the dining room Rose watches a little girl behaving properly and looks saddened by it as the little girl folds her napkin 'just so'.

The film then shifts to Jack alone on the bow of the ship. Rose comes out and joins him there ('I've changed my mind'), the sky a perfect, serene sunset (somewhat artificial in appearance). Jack's 'king of the world' moment is revisited, this time with Rose in his arms. In this, the film's emblematic scene, Jack and Rose stand on the bow of the ship, their arms outstretched against a rosy-fingered sky and a combination of the real and the artificial fuse. In this moment, the visual effect allows the emotional scope of the characters to be amplified, the expansive camera shot moving alongside the characters and then tracking around in front of them gives the moment an 'extraordinary' emotional reverberation. No surprise, perhaps, that this moment became emblematic of the film, emphasising not the historical frame of reference but instead its romance-genre dynamic.

There is a brief cut back to the present-day while Brock explains that, at this point, Captain Smith was taking the ship full steam ahead against his own better judgement, at the urging of Ismay. As in *Aliens* and *Avatar*, it is a bureaucrat who is the antagonist in the story. The elderly Rose looks at footage of an old fireplace in the wreck, which then morphs back to life on board the ship and we are back with young Rose, leading Jack into the room with the fireplace – her own quarters. Rose, the art collector, has a Monet on display. She asks him to draw her wearing her 'Heart of the Ocean' necklace – and nothing else: 'The last thing I need is another picture of me looking like a porcelain doll.' 'As a paying customer, I expect to get what I want,' says Rose, playfully reiterating their respective social positions. This sense of a female character wilfully striving to redefine herself again characterises other Cameron female protagonists. Cross-cutting between artist, model and picture, underscored by the film's theme played as a simple piano motif, cements their romantic bond, even though the older Rose is at pains to point out they did not consummate their relationship at this point.

We are then shown Cal and Lovejoy looking for Jack and Rose, while the Titanic ploughs on through the dark North Atlantic waters. Lovejoy returns to her cabin and Rose leads Jack away, but they leave his drawings behind in her safe. In much the same way as Ripley and Newt were stalked through the corridors of LV-426 by aliens, so too are Jack and Rose stalked, but this time by the monster of class entitlement, and the tone is light-hearted, accompanied by fiddle music. They hide out below decks in a motor car ('Where to, miss?' he asks, again foregrounding his lower-class status) and have sex, the aftermath of which is intercut with Cal's discovery of Jack's pictures, the crew's search for the couple and the watch's growing realisation that the ship is travelling dangerously close to an iceberg.

The film then moves to its final act as all hands try to turn the ship from its course, to the accompaniment of more urgent music. But to no avail – the Titanic strikes the iceberg and water immediately begins flooding the engine room. The action intercuts between increasingly concerned passengers and worried crew members, while Rose and Jack return to her quarters where Cal and Lovejoy frame Jack for stealing her necklace.

Thomas Andrews declares that the ship is certain to sink. The flooding of the ship begins and the film's action movie dynamic gets underway, with sardonic references to the wavering 'stiff upper lip' of the officer classes. Rose, aware of the ship's plight, leaves her mother and Cal (spitting in his face, as Jack has taught her) and races to find Jack, left for dead by Lovejoy while the room he has been imprisoned in starts to flood. It is a sequence that is structured with a similar sense of kineticism and increasing jeopardy that characterised the opening 'act' of *The Terminator* and the intercutting between troops exploring LV-426 whilst Ripley remains on board the tank in the early stages of *Aliens*. It also introduces to the film a succession of horror genre tropes (for what was undoubtedly a truly horrific situation), such as deserted corridors, failing light sources and, in Rose, an axe-wielding Final Girl.

Of Rose's rescue of Jack, David M. Lubin writes:

> In Kubrick's *The Shining*, the psychotic wife-abuser played by Jack Nicholson chops his way through a bedroom door that is the only obstacle between him and his terrified spouse. In *Titanic*, the axe is a benevolent instrument swung through the air on behalf of the heterosexual pairing rather than against it. Moreover, the bearer of the axe is female. In American lore, the wielding of an axe has always been regarded as a definingly male activity. (1999: 85)

Panic begins to take hold as the ship's officers use the threat of force to try to maintain control. There is an explicit reference to class uprising as the third-class passengers overwhelm the crew trying to keep them below decks. In his monograph about the film Lubin comments: 'The film produces social meanings out of the crash no less than did the original Titanic news reports, sermons, speeches and songs' (1999: 14).

In these latter stages of the film, Jack and Rose become rather like young lovers on the run, as with Kyle and Sarah in *The Terminator*. The presentation of the ship's destruction now trades on Cameron's well-established facility with 'engineering' visual spectacle. The soundtrack assumes particular power in this part of the film, supporting the images of what is essentially an apocalyptic moment. The wilderness is reclaiming civilisation. Jack and Rose, once plunged into the ocean, must struggle to survive the claim of the wilderness, just as Bud and Lindsey must in *The Abyss* and as the consciousness of Jake and of Grace in *Avatar* must also do.

Back on deck, and with the remaining women and children being pressed into the remaining lifeboats, Rose once again refuses to leave without Jack. A flare goes off behind Jack's sad face. Rose then gets out and back onto the ship to be with Jack. A cowardly but resourceful Cal fights his way onto a lifeboat, but not before chasing Jack and Rose deeper into the ship, she now wearing a coat containing the Heart of the Ocean necklace.

The ship's destruction is as apocalyptic as the conclusions to *Terminator 2* and *Avatar*. The Titanic breaks up amidst a great deal of technically impressive effects and emotionally intense sequences as Jack and Rose try to escape, culminating in the famous sequence of them at the stern of the broken-backed ship (where, Rose reminds Jack, they first met), which is now pointing vertically skyward. Throughout this exhausting, extended set piece of spectacle, the film merges the digitally produced and the 'actually' photographed, the spectacular (the destruction of the ship) with the affectingly naturalistic (the death of families in their cabins).

Once the Titanic goes down, Jack and Rose are cast adrift, holding onto a piece of wreckage, surrounded by the cries of the drowning. They are rather like Bud and Lindsey in *The Abyss* at this point as they keep each other alive amidst the threat and terror of nature that cannot be contained or controlled by human skill. A frozen Jack urges to Rose to hold on before letting go of her hand and sinking to his death, before Rose is eventually rescued.

Back in the present day, the elderly Rose finishes telling her story to the subdued crew of the exploration vessel, before a final 1912-set sequence shows the rescued Rose avoiding a searching Cal then arriving in New York harbour and giving her name as 'Rose Dawson'. Leaving her cabin, the elderly Rose tosses the Heart of the Ocean necklace overboard, the camera digitally following it down to the wreckage of the Titanic and in her dreams that night the ship is restored to its former glory, complete with a full crew and a waiting Jack.

Given the eventual commercial success of Cameron's film it is appropriate to note the spectre that was particularly fresh in studio executives' memories: the Universal Pictures production *Waterworld* from 1995. Like *Titanic*, *Waterworld* had been developed and duly promoted as an event movie, albeit an outright fantasy, though one which, like Cameron's *The Abyss*, sought to use its intensely generic mode as a means of dramatising and visualising a certain kind of 'eco-awareness'. Where *Titanic* proved to be an immensely successful commercial movie, *Waterworld*, whilst eventually turning a profit, was not considered to have been a success. Of interest here, and in terms of Cameron's *The Abyss* and *Avatar*, is the sub-genre of films that we could refer to as 'Hollywood green-films'. We could certainly count *Waterworld* amongst this cohort and also look to *The Thin Red Line* (Terrence Malick, 1998), *The Tree of Life* (Terrence

Malick, 2011) and perhaps even *Jurassic Park*, *Jurassic Park: The Lost World* (Steven Spielberg, 1997) and *Wall:E* (Andrew Stanton, 2008).

Of its relationship to the Hollywood studio system, the financial production context for *Titanic* crystallises the increasing move made by studios to share the production and distribution costs of the largest event films being produced. This financial 'norm' has come to increasingly characterise the contemporary Hollywood film production context. However, the ever increasing rise in the budgets and scale of the blockbusters that have succeeded *Titanic* – typically effects-driven comic-strip adaptations – poses just as much of a threat to the current industrial model as it promises huge rewards – a point of view aired, apparently without irony, by none other than Steven Spielberg and George Lucas, who, along with Cameron, are arguably the very architects of the current Hollywood eco-system.

CHAPTER EIGHT
Avatar (2009)

In *Visions of Apocalypse: Spectacles of Destruction in American Cinema*, Wheeler Winston Dixon quotes Paul Virilio: 'the cinema became the major site for a trade in dematerialization, a new industrial market which no longer produced matter but light, as the luminosity of those vast stained-glass windows of old was suddenly concentrated on the screen' (2003: 9). Virilio's poetic observation seems to take on particular resonance in relation to a film like *Avatar* with a production process, aesthetic and narrative that explore alternatives to tangible matter. The combination of the performance capture process used for filming the character interactions and the story's focus on real and fake 'identities' are underpinned by a fascinating sense of the virtual. A major entry in Cameron's oeuvre (we might propose *True Lies* and *Terminator 2* as minor titles) the film offers a rich case study in terms of its narrative, its production context and its cultural resonance at the moment, and thereafter, of its original theatrical release.

Battle Angel Alita was to have been Cameron's next project after *Titanic*. However, having had Twentieth Century Fox approve a four-and-a-half-minute proof of a concept sequence (produced at ILM) for the performance-capture technique, production moved forward on what became *Avatar* instead. Visual effects studio Weta, who had overseen the breakthrough motion-capture performance of Andy Serkis as Gollum in Peter Jackson's *Lord of the Rings* trilogy (2001–03), secured the contract (although ILM would become involved in the film eventually) and filming began in April 2007. Although principle live-action photography was a relatively short part of the production, the innovative techniques being used to visualise the world of *Avatar* meant production continued right up to its release, ending mid-November 2009.

Developing an image and narrative established in *The Abyss*, the film's promotion explicitly presented Cameron as 'The Visionary Director', marshalling hardware and software resources alongside an expansive crew. Coverage of the film extended to

Popular Mechanics, a demonstration of how Cameron's role as film engineer has been key to his persona.

As noted earlier, *Avatar* distils Cameron's commitment to an atavistic sensibility that has been so characteristic of the film worlds he has produced since his second feature film, *The Terminator* – white-American narratives about the relationship between people and wilderness. *Avatar* reverberates with something of the deep-rooted cultural preoccupation that Frederick Jackson Turner identified in his book *The Significance of the Frontier in American History* (1994: 116). American popular cinema, and, indeed, literature, has navigated the historical culture contact of the native culture with the white colonists of 'America's' early history. The genre of the western has dynamically, if complicatedly, dramatised these difficult and subtle historical engagements and experiences and mythologised them in cinema for a century now. Certainly, the point can be made that the western genre has seen elements of its semantic qualities being adopted and adapted by other genres and it is the science fiction genre that, in recent decades, has typically been understood as exemplifying this tendency.

During promotional activity, during a TED presentation soon after the release of *Avatar*, he recalled an aspect of his childhood: 'when I wasn't in school I was out in the woods, trying to understand the limits of possibility' (2010). Cameron's evocation of what sounds like an idyllic childhood takes us beyond his own autobiography and resounds with a sensibility attuned to the image of the explorer, and, by extension, the allure of narratives that have been central to the historical span of what became white North American experience and cultural expression during the age of European colonisation in the fifteen and sixteenth centuries. Indeed, Cameron's recollection of his childhood, wittingly or not, also carries with it something of two American literary icons, one imagined, one real: Tom Sawyer and Henry David Thoreau. For both, there was the promise of adventure offered by getting out of the house and into the wilderness.

In Cameron's recollection of the thunderous roar of water at Niagara Falls near his childhood home we can go some way to creating an image of how this particular filmmaker's work has been emblematic of the ways in which Hollywood movies represent the forces of nature, and the enormity of it in relation to human endeavour. It is a particular sensibility that has some antecedents in the visual art of the colonial and nineteen century in American painting. We have only to look at works such as those by Albert Bierstadt and Thomas Cole to make the correlation. Of the colonial and nineteenth-century American tradition of image-representations of wilderness, Robert Hughes has noted: 'Here, nature was incorrupt. No other part of the world that was being colonized by whites in the first half of the nineteenth century was so rich with promise. No wonder then, that in the nineteenth century Nature became America's national myth, and the act of painting it an assertion of national identity' (1999: 138). By extension and, ultimately, by contrast Wheeler Winston Dixon, in *Visions of Apocalypse*, explores how popular film and the broader culture now engages with the idea of the end of things.

Throughout its history, Hollywood films have told stories that place men and women against the 'forces of nature'. In particular, the western routinely visualises and dramatises this relationship and, more recently, science fiction. Particular films we may cite include: *Way Down East* (D. W. Griffith, 1920), *The African Queen* (John Huston, 1951), *The Searchers* (John Ford, 1956), *Silent Running* and *Jurassic Park*. Indeed, this latter film was originally considered by Cameron as a possible directorial project before Spielberg took it on.

If we wanted a motif with which to illustrate the broader narrative interests of *Avatar* we could cite a moment that occurs relatively early in the running time which would seem to draw on the woodland and waterfall reveries that Cameron had referred to from his own childhood whilst promoting the movie – the image of an immense tyre, on the immense wheel of an *even more immense* industrial machine, rumbling and pushing through the tangle of an unearthly jungle. As the machine's wheels roll their way left to right across the frame, we notice that a beautifully feathered arrow protrudes from one of the tyres. The arrow feathers are as iridescent as those of a peacock but the tyre and the wheel seem unimpeded by the piercing weapon. Whoever fired the arrow will need to do more than that to make an impact. It is a concentrated image, then, that encapsulates an emerging and essential story point *and* a broader dramatic conflict; and, by implication, a theme. Indeed, a similarly emblematic detail finds a place early on in another 'blockbuster' title released contemporaneously, *Indiana Jones and the Kingdom of the Crystal Skull* (Steven Spielberg, 2008). In this film's opening credit sequence we see the image of a pristine and highly reflective hubcap on a jeep, filled with Russian soldiers (disguised as American GIs), reflecting the image of a hotrod car crammed with rebellious, anti-authoritarian American teens rocking out to Elvis Presley's song 'Hound Dog' as they race in parallel, across the iconic American desert. The fleeting, location-setting scene condenses time, place and subject.

For all of its fantastical action and setting *Avatar* was quickly appropriated in both the ideological realm and in the realm of consideration of form. Was the film an example of animation? Was it all 'just' visual effects? Was it also perhaps a 'triumph' of make-up? *What* was it? Certainly, the film's formal interest marks a key moment in the evolving fusion of 'traditional' live-action filmmaking with animation and computer-

Ney'tiri, and the Na'vi, are fully connected to the wilderness

game aesthetics. In his essay 'Making Space' about Cameron's *Avatar*, and by extension digital cinema, Sean Cubitt writes that

> Anyone who has seen James Cameron's *Avatar* in 3D will have a clear idea of the significance of focal planes. Despite enormous technical achievement the film has to train its audience against one of the pleasures of the modern blockbuster spectacle: the opportunity to let your eyes roam over the whole of the screen. Here we see the universe of the monarchical seat in the baroque theatre: everyone occupies that perfect seat, but they must occupy it precisely as defined by the film's optical system, or suffer the consequent eyestrain. In *Avatar*, the layers … introduce schisms between foreground and background. (2010)

The film is replete with a sense of simulacra and its dramatic arc plays with these notions and the considerations about human connection and disconnection to the natural world.

Avatar elicited extensive print and online comment across mainstream and academic fields, regarding its 'meaning', its 'value' and its success financially and as a showcase for particular image-making technologies. The film, like many 'movie spectacles' before it, seeks to integrate the micro-level of a character's experience with the macro-level of a larger historical moment or expansive location. We might cite *Lawrence of Arabia* and *Saving Private Ryan* (Steven Spielberg, 1998) as indicative of this approach; both of them, like *Avatar*, turning on military engagements. The *Hollywood Reporter*, in a piece entitled 'Blue Men Group', describes Cameron's creative ambitions for *Avatar*: 'He wanted a picture as big as the epics of his youth, like *The Man Who Would Be King* and *Lawrence of Arabia*' (2009). But, typical of many Hollywood blockbusters, *Avatar*, for critic Daniel Mendelsohn, potentially houses an 'underlying hypocrisy of an apparent celebration on the part of a special effects-laden Hollywood blockbuster, of nature and of an accompanying polemic against technology and corporate greed' (2010).

Avatar was actually marketed for its theatrical release as *James Cameron's Avatar*, his name as important to the audience's initial engagement and expectation of how the subject might be treated as a sense of the film's possibilities. Certainly, the word 'Avatar' is a familiar one to computer gamers and users of social media and their assumed comfort with a digital persona. Indeed, the term 'digital native' has often been used to describe the generation born into a digital culture.

Like *Aliens* and *The Terminator*, the film apparently lent itself to a range of broader cultural appropriations, being seen variously as eco-destruction allegory, genocide allegory, post-colonial drama and perhaps even as an expression of our digitally connected world of virtual realities and the Internet. More resonantly, though, given Cameron's affinity for mythological tropes and devices, his use of the word avatar has its linguistic and cultural root in the ancient Indian term *avatara* used to identify a god-made human.

Avatar is Cameron's most recent narrative fiction feature film, re-released theatrically in North America with nine minutes of additional footage in August 2010. It is a film that generated a sizeable amount of pre-release media coverage in autumn 2009 – hype about the film had been developing for two years prior to its release – and, subsequent to its release, prompted further discussion beyond the film sections of print and online news media. Discourses around the film reinforced the romantic image of Cameron as a highly creative filmmaker working within the studio system, and as of this writing Cameron is developing sequel movies and novels in order to develop the transmedia application of his creative efforts.

It was certainly not the first film to engineer extensive media coverage for the scale and industry of its realisation for the screen, but Cameron's film was marketed as both spectacle and love story just as *Titanic* had been. Geoff King has noted that 'in some cases spectacle reinforces rather than interferes with, the work of narrative' (2000: 4). In an interview with *Popular Mechanics* at the time of *Avatar*'s theatrical release, Cameron noted that it was when he watched *The Lord of the Rings: The Two Towers* (Peter Jackson, 2002) that the viability of realising the film using performance capture crystallised. His recollection echoes the 'epiphany' that George Lucas described himself as experiencing upon seeing *Jurassic Park*, a film for which he had supervised post-production in the 'absence' of Spielberg who was in Poland filming *Schindler's List*. *Jurassic Park*'s digital creatures suggested that Lucas could bring to the screen his *Star Wars* 'prequels' (a marketing term rather than anything especially useful in terms of describing narrative).

In considering *Avatar*, from the moment of its announcement across the mainstream media and on through its production process, and eventually to its release and critical and commercial reception, it is worth citing Robin Wood on the subject of genre films and their function in the broader discourse. He wrote in his essay 'Ideology, Genre, Auteur' that 'at best they represent different strategies for dealing with the same ideological tensions' (2009: 594). In her essay 'The Masculine Subject of Science Fiction in the 1980s Blockbuster Era', Christine Cornea writes that 'a classic convention within science fiction films involves a more or less covert coverage of racial and ethnic tensions' (2007: 179). We can look to late 1960s titles like *Planet of the Apes* (Franklin J. Schaffner, 1968) and the TV show *Star Trek* as working allegorically to explore the racial conflict that was acutely felt and experienced in North America at the time. *Avatar* is but one of his latest variations on the subject of culture contact rendered as science fiction, a visualisation of the concept of the noble savage, a state of nature that has a historical narrative tradition in the writing of Jean-Jacques Rousseau. *Enemy Mine* (Wolfgang Petersen, 1985), *Predator* and *Alien Nation* (Graham Baker, 1988) are similarly focused science fiction films that were released as Cameron's filmmaking career was becoming established.

During the promotional press coverage, the *Los Angeles Times*, which provided something of a four-week countdown to *Avatar*'s release in late 2009, Rick Carter, the film's production designer, observed that 'Coming into *Avatar*, it took me about 3½ hours to read the script … As I started reading through it, there was a part – and it's a part, actually, that's not in the movie anymore – but one of the alien characters says "When you see everything, you see nothing." And I realised that I was so overwhelmed with all of what I was seeing that I was actually starting to see nothing. So in a very lyrical way I gave myself over to that idea that there was too much for me to see' (2009b). In an earlier interview he commented that 'I actually thought this movie is like *The Wizard of Oz* meets *Apocalypse Now*' (2009a). Such an observation immediately plugs *Avatar* into an association with two American classics that had functioned in excess of themselves: their characters, specific scenes and music extending to find lives in the culture beyond the actual experience of the film itself. They became narratives that expressed ideological tensions and dynamics.

Reaching as far back as *The Terminator*, Cameron's commitment to a knowing engagement with intensely generic antecedents and, indeed, with apparently 'trashy' subject matter synonymous with pulp writers found its ultimate expression in *Avatar*. When Cameron recalled, in an interview for *Cinefex* magazine at the time of the film's original release, the initial treatment of 1995 for what eventually became *Avatar*, key to his creative and entrepreneurial process had been 'to create iconic and memorable characters and creatures for pop culture, using new techniques much like the early days of Disney' (2009c: 68).

Avatar was produced at a moment when the fusion of live action with painting (digitally rendered) was becoming increasingly strong (both creatively and commercially) and blurred through the application of digital technology to the photography-based processes and aesthetics that had heretofore characterised cinema. That said, the capacity for movies to combine photography and moving illustration (animation) has a continuum reaching back to Winsor McCay and James Stuart Blackton and the Walt Disney-produced *Alice* short films.

Critically, *Avatar* extends the cyborg cinema concerns that are so central to Cameron's films *The Terminator* and *Terminator 2*. In *Cyborg Cinema*, Sue Short writes that 'cyborg protagonists breach the boundaries between the artificial and the organic, revising speculations regarding the nature of subjectivity, and provoking intense debate' (2011: 3). Short goes on to say that the cyborg is not tied to race or gender or class or sexuality, that it is 'a progressive symbol of change ... providing a vital means of transcending outmoded ways of thinking' (2011: 163). This understanding offers a useful handle on the central drama of *Avatar*.

Indeed, *Avatar*'s story and the industrial narrative detailing how the film's illusions were produced do, in fact, fuse, with the performance-capture technology used to modify and elaborate the human actors' performances being a form of avatar creation. Certainly, the performance-capture technique has, since the early 2000s, prompted a debate about what might or might not constitute an 'authentic' performance. Just as in films that do not explore performance capture, for this film the recording of human performance was central to its production. But *Avatar*'s promotional narrative emphasised performance capture in terms of an experience of the (pleasant) shock of the new. In fact, the performance-capture work for the film was only the next iteration of a technique that had moved into the American feature film mainstream with *Star Wars: Episode 1 – The Phantom Menace* in its realisation of the character Jar Jar Binks, a kind of intergalactic Sancho Panza. Another evolutionary step for performance capture was showcased in Robert Zemeckis's *The Polar Express* (2004). In Japan, *Final Fantasy: The Spirits Within* (Hironobu Sakaguchi, 2001) had been produced using the technology.

Zemeckis continued to work with performance capture for his adaptation of *Beowulf* (2007) and then *A Christmas Carol* two years later but, unlike *Avatar*, these films did not adopt a photorealistic aesthetic.

Performance capture, then, brings puppetry and animation into a new fusion with moviemaking as photography. The *Avatar* performance capture process revised the approach taken in Zemeckis's *A Christmas Carol* by introducing a camera mounted on a headband which is worn by each performer so that the detail of facial muscles in motion could be recorded. In an interview for *Cinefex* magazine, Cameron noted that 'the thing that would have to be cracked to do this movie, was real human facial response in CG' (2010: 72). Intriguingly, *Avatar* was produced at a time when certain computer-gaming aesthetics began to find expression in live-action cinema. We might cite *The Matrix* (Wachowski Brothers, 1999) as indicative of this development. Manohla Dargis, writing on blockbuster films, has noted, with a shot of irony, that

> These days highbrows dismiss movie blockbusters because they are often based in fantasy rather than reality, which is generally a bad thing unless the fantasy comes with a literary pedigree. Blockbusters tend to be made for adolescents instead of adults, which is also a bad thing because youngsters are untrustworthy cultural consumers. (2007)

Performance capture, then, has begun to assert a challenge to the idea of cinema as only being photographically-based realism. *Avatar* represents the evolution of cinema from photography in its fusion of forms and technologies to render characters and settings. Siegfried Kracauer commented of 'fantasy films' that 'from *The Cabinet of Dr Caligari* [1920] on, films or film sequences forgo the natural world in favour of the an imagined one which cannot deny its origin in the studio' (1997: 84). Kracauer goes on to reference the Michael Powell and Emeric Pressburger film *The Red Shoes* (1948), commenting that a filmmaker such as Powell, and by extension a filmmaker such as Cameron, works with the 'underlying belief that nature has no title to preferential treatment and that theatricality is as valid as in camera realism' (1997: 34).

Something of a culmination of formal aesthetic and socio-ideological elements across his previous films, *Avatar* is narratively familiar, relating as it does to American genre movies such as *Drums Along the Mohawk* (John Ford, 1939), *The Last of the Mohicans*, *Pocahontas* (Mike Gabriel and Eric Goldberg, 1995) and *Dances with Wolves* (Kevin Costner, 1990). Casting Wes Studi as father of the clan ties *Avatar* all the more strongly to both *Dances with Wolves* and its Native American theme and to *The Last of the Mohicans* (where Studi plays the Native American character, Magua).

In *Green Screen: Environmentalism and Hollywood Cinema*, David Ingram makes the point that if we go back to 1990 we can find the *Hollywood Reporter* commenting on 'film vert' – films with an ecological theme: *At Play in the Fields of the Lord* (Hector Babenco, 1991) and *FernGully* (Bill Kroyer, 1992), but also *Medicine Man* (John McTiernan, 1992) and a few years before this, *The Mosquito Coast* (Peter Weir, 1986) and *The Emerald Forest* (John Boorman, 1985). By extension, we can also include in this group of movies the *anime Princess Mononoke* (Hayao Miyazaki, 1997) which brings a specifically Japanese frame of reference to the dramatisation of the subject of the relationship between human endeavour (adventure and misadventure) and the wilderness. In *Jump Cut*, Todd McGowan provided a fascinating essay entitled 'Maternity Divided: *Avatar* and the Enjoyment of Nature' in which he says of the spirit Eywa in Cameron's film that she 'can take sides in a political struggle. When this happens *Avatar* undermines the ideology of completion that dominates up to this point and nature itself becomes politicised' (2010).

Yoking together the 'green film' sensibility and the war film, our thoughts are turned to the Vietnam War – a conflict undertaken mostly in a jungle environment. Vivian Sobchack writes in *Screening Space* that 'it is no accident that two related cinematic coincidences serve to mark both the mid-1970s renaissance of SF and its mid-1980s popularity as somehow entailed with the revisioning of America's history of failure and guilt in Vietnam' (2001: 228). Sobchack's observation not only suggests a way to read *Avatar* but also *Aliens* and the Cameron-scripted *Rambo: First Blood Part II*.

In assessing the popular appeal of Cameron's choices of subject and, broadly speaking, a way of creatively treating said subject, McGowan writes that 'despite Cameron's proclivity for making wildly popular films, his films scrupulously avoid granting the paternal figure his typical role'. In terms of this particular dynamic Cameron is compared and, therefore, contrasted with Spielberg for whom the father figure is the site of order and stability, although often a conflicted one: in *ET* the protagonist, Elliott, struggles to reconcile himself with his parents' divorce and his father's subsequent absence; in Spielberg's earlier film, *Close Encounters of the Third Kind*, which can be considered a significant influence on Cameron's *The Abyss*, the father figure, Roy Neary (Richard Dreyfuss), is the film's protagonist. Tellingly, Roy's obsession with meeting an alien culture results in him destroying his family and then abandoning the fragmented unit. Even in Spielberg's more recent film, *Lincoln*, the drama partly turns on the father/son dynamic.

The Movie

Avatar begins with the sound of percussive music, with only a black screen in view. The film then cuts to its first image: a point of view, we assume, (but whose?) as the camera rushes straight towards a mist-shrouded forest. We hear a voice-over delivered by the film's protagonist, Jake Sully (Sam Worthington), who explains: 'I was lying there in the VA hospital and I started having these dreams of flying. I was free.' Indeed, this scene that starts the film is not quite Jake's story, it functions more on a thematic level rather than as an inciting moment for the main plot; that occurs in the scene following. This first shot and voice-over function as a prologue. The emphatic reference here to flying stands in contrast with the motif of falling in *The Abyss*. Of the image of flying, and, by implication, of ascension, Gaston Bachelard has noted that 'anyone who flies feels that he has wings when he need no longer make an effort to fly. They appear at once, like a sign of victory, and then ... we can see the psychology of gliding unfold' (2011: 58).

The screen then goes to black, followed by a cut to an extreme close-up on one eye as Jake says: 'Sooner or later, though, you have to wake up.' The eye is shown under an intense blue light, a visual approach familiar from other Cameron movies. On the soundtrack we hear Jake in voice-over explain: 'In cryo you don't dream at all.'

There is then a cut to a wide shot showing a huge cryogenic chamber in which various people are being manoeuvered in an aerial ballet. Jake explains in voice-over that he is replacing his recently deceased twin brother, Tommy, on the avatar programme. 'Tommy was the scientist. Me? I'm just another dumb grunt going to a place he's going to regret,' Jake summarises, alluding to a class distinction in the workplace that will continue to be realised throughout the movie and which ties the film in with *Aliens*. These opening moments are followed by a brief scene in which bureaucrats discuss their financial investment in Tommy. The corporate impulse is in contrast with the individual and the moment evokes scenes between Burke and Ripley in *Aliens*.

The action then cuts to a beautiful shot of the spaceship near the planet of Pandora (like the use of the name Acheron for LV-426 in *Aliens*, Cameron calls on Greek mythology to suggest larger ideas at work in the narrative). Choral music on the soundtrack suggests something numinous about the earthly-looking Pandora. There is then a close-up of the furnace of the rocket that propels the ship into the Pandoran jungle. Forceful music accompanies this moment and the action cuts to the interior of the ship and we see a cohort of soldiers putting on face-masks, another moment that is akin to *Aliens*, and the soldiers being dropped onto LV-426. There is violence in the juxtaposition of the angular machines and the curvilinear forms of the forest. In *Star Wars: Episode 1 – The Phantom Menace* a more fleeting moment of deforestation occurs early in the action. Indeed, in Lucas's film the character of Boss Nass talks of the 'mekaneeks' (mechanics) who are invading the forest near to the underwater Gungan culture, upsetting the natural order. It is an image that is not so different to that of the placid forest being stirred up when airships land on Pandora. It is also a trope that is familiar from Vietnam War footage, particularly of helicopters landing in the jungle.

In a posthuman adventure, Jake's physical disability is the catalyst for an unexpected experience of mind and body

As the ship arrives on Pandora, all of the soldiers stand but the shot holds back on Jake (Sam Worthington) to reveal finally that he is a paraplegic wheelchair user.

We then follow the soldiers as they run down the ramp and a wide-shot shows the plane over a mining quarry in which huge machines are at work. 'There's no such thing as an ex-marine. I told myself I could pass any test that a man could pass,' Jake comments as we see him in medium wide shot grabbing his bag and preparing to wheel out. 'They can fix a spinal if you've got the money.' Jake's a working-class passenger, just like Jack in *Titanic*. Jake's monologue continues to set a context for the images as he explains: 'These guys were army dogs: marine – fighting or freedom. Out here they're just hired guns. Taking money; working for the company.' Jake explores and he sees wheels roll by pierced with arrows. Jake's look of concern registers the implication of a conflict of interests. 'The company' that Jake refers to is a corporation who are on Pandora to exploit the unobtanium reserves.

We then hear the voice of the film's antagonist, Colonel Quaritch (Stephen Lang) explaining to the new soldiers: 'You are not in Kansas anymore.' It is the film's most overt, but not its only, reference to *The Wizard of Oz* and it offers a sense of *Avatar*'s 'meaning' as a story about identity and finding a place to belong. L. Frank Baum's novel *The Wonderful Wizard of Oz* becomes a useful frame of reference for us in that, amongst other points of interest, it functions as an allegory of the conflict between the modern and the traditional. Quaritch's statement starts over the close-up of Jake and then cuts to the former's boots on the floor. We see Quaritch from behind, glimpsing his facial scars as he turns to be fully revealed for the first time. 'Out there beyond that fence, every living thing that crawls flies, or squats in the mud wants to kill you.' We hear him identify the Na'vi as Pandora's native population, as the camera fixes on Jake rolling to a stop and listening. Quaritch says that obeying the rules is how to survive and in this way he is an echo of Coffey in *The Abyss* where an unthinking following of the rules and status quo becomes his undoing.

Jake then meets Norm Spelman (Joel David Moore), a member of the avatar development team; Norm knew Jake's brother. As they move through the lab the camera tracks with them, immersing us in a central environment that the action will return to regularly throughout the film. Jake glimpses avatars floating in cylinders. On the soundtrack we hear what it is to be an 'avatar driver', manipulating the remotely-controlled bodies of the Na'vi avatars, grown from human DNA and then mixed with Na'vi DNA. In its deployment of such scientific terms, the scene has the kind of plausibility common from Cameron's other fantasy movies. Jake wheels across the lab and now confronts his avatar. A close-up on Jake's inquisitive gaze is engulfed by an ambient blue light. In the shot/reverse-shot sequencee we are able to recognise the avatar's facial similarity to Jake.

The action then cuts to a brief scene that shows Jake recording his first video diary, in which he explains how each driver and avatar have nervous systems in tune, just as in *The Terminator* Sarah committed her story to audiotape. 'We've got to get in the habit of documenting everything, what we see, what we feel,' explains Norm. Cut to a room with drivers emerging from their completed session, the camera focusing on Grace (Sigourney Weaver), as she emerges from her session. She is head of the avatar programme, and asks for a cigarette; this detail immediately makes Grace somehow 'ordinary' despite her academic credentials. She is introduced to Norm and Jake and her gesture and demeanour suggest something of the toughness of Ellen Ripley, also portrayed by Sigourney Weaver. As such, this connection might be considered to raise expectations from an audience familiar with Cameron and Weaver's existing collaboration. That said, Grace (as her name might suggest) does not become an aggressor as Ripley necessarily must in *Aliens*. Grace wears an ethnic necklace, suggesting an emotional affinity with Pandora's natives. But she is also dismissive of Jake, who does not have the scientific training of his brother. Objecting to the substitution, Grace threatens to kick the 'corporate butt' of the Resources Development Administration's (RDA) Parker Selfridge (Giovanni Ribisi), immediately establishing her anti-establishment credentials.

She goes on to explain how the entire wilderness of Pandora contains a network of intelligence. Grace even refers to it as 'a global network. And the Na'vi can access it – they can upload and download data – memories – at sites like the one you destroyed.' The bio-technology of Pandora echoes the 'world' of the NTIs in *The Abyss* and, more broadly, a recognition of what partly constitutes our proposed post-human experience as we connect increasingly through virtual means with, potentially, a waning regard for the connections across nature of which we are a part.

The scene then cuts to Selfridge playing golf by his desk. Grace approaches, the camera ahead of her capturing her anger at him and the larger bureaucratic ethos in a close-up: 'I need a researcher, not some jarhead dropout.' Selfridge is quickly sketched as a cynical colonialist who patronises the Na'vi, saying that they have taught them English and built them a school.

Grace returns her attention to Jake and helps him climb into his pod. We hear Jake's voice on the soundtrack as he explains: 'Maybe I was sick of doctors telling me what I couldn't do.' Here is a character who has the physical and emotional resilience that is typical of Cameron's protagonists as their bodies sustain physical trauma amidst experiences that serve to challenge their humanity. Coaxing us with anticipation for Jake's first 'drive', the music score rises and we are inside a pod with Jake. The scene then cuts to a doctor looking at a scan of Jake's brain as they monitor him. There is then an extreme close-up showing Jake closing his eyes and a brief, vivid moment of a colourful portal effect that fills the screen. We then see the doctors from Jake's point of view, then cut to their view of him, or rather of his avatar.

The shot that follows is handheld as Jake gets out of the bed. At this point we get a real sense of how much taller the Na'vi are. This is the first time that 'Jake' has been able to walk and he breaks out of the medical centre and runs. The action then cuts to Jake emerging outside. He starts to run rather like Clark Kent running at speed before launching into the air with 'a single bound' in *Superman Returns* (Bryan Singer, 2006). The score then builds with a sense of urgency. We see his body and his gait steady and momentarily we see him running in slow-motion. There is then a cut to a close-up of Jake, eyes shut in the chamber, and then back to an image of avatar Jake outside, feeling the dirt, as Grace, in her avatar form, approaches.

The action cuts to an image of the camp for avatars out in the forest underneath night skies. The avatar, as per the Na'vi, have white dots as part of their complexion and these dots make their faces look like starry night skies. The 'cosmic' connection between Na'vi and the wild (which extends to outer space) is condensed in this character design. We then see Jake awake in his avatar driver pod with his session at an end. Jake is then shown around the loading bay by Trudy Chacon (Michelle Rodriguez), who shows him the helicopter that she pilots, and then has an exchange with Quaritch who reminds Jake harshly: 'You get soft, Pandora will shit you out dead with zero warning.'

The scene's dramatic focus is rounded out by a *verité* sensibility as various incidental background characters and activities go about their business. It is akin to Lucas's aesthetic in the *Star Wars* movies in which framing would often accommodate principal characters in the central foreground of a given shot, with a range of background activity passing in and out of shot but without any 'cutaway' used to dwell on those details.

Quaritch is certainly akin to the Terminator in his relentless and singular sense of mission. His true danger lies in his disrespect or disregard for non-military personnel who he describes as 'limp-dicked science majors'. Quaritch's absence of sensitivity to other ways of seeing the worlds around him will, inevitably, prove his undoing. We watch him climb into one of the robo-suits. Seeing Quaritch the man now encased in a suit of mechanised armour recalls Ripley wearing the load-lifter in *Aliens* and also the female who comes to the rescue in Cameron's short film *Xenogenesis*. 'I want you to learn these savages from the inside,' Quaritch says to Jake. He goes on to explain that whilst theoretically (organisationally) Jake is to report to Grace, he is really to report to him. As he finishes talking, Quaritch executes a series of boxing moves with the robo-suit that illustrates how juvenile and unsophisticated his attitude is. Ultimately, Quaritch will become the quarry, as is hinted at by his name.

Quaritch proposes a Faustian pact to Jake – 'You get me what I need, I'll see that you get your real legs when you get back home' – then marches off in the bio-suit, leaving Jake alone. Of the film's presentation of disability Dana Fore, in her essay 'The Tracks of Sully's Tears', has written: 'The ways in which disabled bodies are presented to the audience suggest director James Cameron's sensitivity to *ableist* stereotypes. These ancient conceptions of disability valorize the undamaged "able" body as a universal standard of "normality" and perfection, while simultaneously assuming "natural" links between disability and extremes of either good or evil behavior' (2011). To this writer's mind, Cameron sees in the disabled Jake (physically and emotionally at the beginning of the film) a nascent heroism as he finds a way to survive the shock to his mind and body. It is this quality of survival, of determination, that characterises the essential Cameron hero.

The action then cuts to another driver session, with a wide shot showing a chopper flying across the water as a flock of birds fly alongside. Technology and nature harmonise, but as the chopper arrives in the jungle animals flee and armed soldiers, including Jake, move out into the Pandoran forest. Jake is on security detail for Grace and her assistant Norm. A still unimpressed Grace tells another soldier: 'Stay with the ship. One idiot with a gun is enough.' The camera follows the unit at low height so as to emphasise the expanse of the forest canopy above them. We might compare this visual treatment of colonisers in the wild with similar images in *Apocalypse Now* and *The New World*.

Cameron also deploys a handheld camera in this scene to emphasise a sense of uncertainty. Focus-pulls on foreground and background elements intensify the immediacy. Whimsical music plays on the soundtrack as the camera tracks through the canopy looking down at the tiny avatar forms. While Grace and Norm are engaged in their scientific work Jake is bored and goes wandering off. There is a cut and we are positioned behind Jake as avatar as he walks through the forest. He is confronted by a beast in a beast/'human' encounter similar to those in *Aliens* and *Jurassic Park*. Jake eventually escapes by leaping out and down into a river and, having lost his gun, he fashions a spear. This is when we meet the Na'vi native Neytiri (Zoe Saldana), who is watching Jake from above armed with a bow. Just as she is about to fire, a little forest sprite lands on top of her arrow, evoking something of the beneficent forest sprites in *Princess Mononoke*. She runs off.

Sunset falls and we see an image of a helicopter above the trees. Grace is on the vehicle trying to locate Jake who is lost in the forest. The action then cuts to the blue and purple of night on Pandora. Jake is clearly an able survivor in his avatar state. He lights a torch he has made and there is a point-of-view shot from the position of the 'monster' in the darkness approaching Jake. It is a briefly held moment that owes a debt to the B-movie sensibility that has informed all of Cameron's movies. It is an image of a primal condition and it offers a more elemental rendering of an image we have seen in *The Terminator* and *Aliens*, particularly when Ripley uses a flamethrower to confront the alien Queen.

Dogs surround Jake, but he is rescued by Neytiri. A spiritual moment follows in which the sprites gather around Jake; the camera delicately moves around him and Neytiri as she explains that they are looking at 'Seeds of the sacred tree. Very pure spirits.' The camera moves dreamily around Jake and Neytiri as she then leads him along the trunk of an immense tree and through the terrain. What we can consider the musical theme for the film is heard on the soundtrack, suggesting that this is an essential Pandoran experience for Jake in which the harmony of all natural energies is evident. Na'vi hunters then close in on Jake, sounding very like Native Americans, but Neytiri calms them. Tsu'tey (Laz Alonso) the hunter then instructs Neytiri to bring Jake to the village. The camera drops down as horses ride along towards the base of Hometree. The shot has a handheld quality to it, again suggesting a *verité* tone amidst such an artificial movie. The tribe watch Jake being pushed through to the leader of the tribe (Eytukan, portrayed by Wes Studi) who is Neytiri's father. His feathery adornment again suggests Native American culture. He calls Jake a 'dreamwalker'. Neytiti's mother then interjects. Neytiri explains that she is interpreting 'the will of Aiywa'. 'My daughter will teach you our ways.' Neytiri's mother (Moat, portrayed by CCH Pounder) says to Jake, 'We will see if your insanity can be cured.' The action then cuts back to the avatar chamber and Jake awaking from his most intense driver session. Grace asks him if the avatar is safe.

In the rest and recreation room, Grace, Jake and the others are chatting. Norm looks concerned. Jake tells Quartich that he is in with the clan. Quaritch is pleased.

'Just find out what the blue monkeys want', says Selfridge angrily. He then explains that the Na'vi village is located on the richest unobtanium deposit, which Jake recognises as the Hometree. Quaritch is given three months to move the tribe from Hometree.

Grace then briefs Jake on the clan hierarchy, this expository information being equally important to the viewer in providing them with necessary information from this point onward.

The action then cuts to a sequence set in the clan community. Jake's avatar is shown learning to ride a horse and becoming increasingly comfortable with the Na'vi culture, more so than with the human culture he has been placed in. Grace, Norm and Jake travel by helicopter to a research station in a relatively inaccessible part of Pandora. In the station Jake sees pictures that Grace has taken of the young natives. Jake explains that he knows Grace is aware he is in with Quaritch but that Jake can also be her way back into the clan. At the camp they plug into their avatars.

The action then cuts to Jake and Neytiri as they walk high up in one of the trees on the floating rocks. The camera moves freely out over the edge of the rocks. In this sequence, the film's romantic storyline between Jake and Neytiri begins to cohere, the two of them, like Rose and Jack in *Titanic*, separated by cultural difference. Neytiri has the physical and mental resources of Sarah Connor and Ripley and also of Mace from the Cameron-scripted *Strange Days*. Jake and Neytiri glimpse the tail of a dragon under the cover of a tree's foliage. Neytiri commands the dragon and rides it effortlessly.

The action then moves to a scene focused on Jake recording another videoblog, which assumes the quality of a confessional. Jake's videoblogs resonate with our collective experience of connecting with the world online via a range of media software, again screening the world around us, rather than writing it. Jake is shown in the foreground and Grace in the background working. 'The days are starting to blur together. The language is a pain. It's like field-stripping a weapon: just repetition, repetition.' We then see a sequence showing Neytiri training Jake in how to negotiate life on Pandora. The action then cuts to Norm and Jake talking about a particular phrase that the Na'vi use, namely 'I see you'. It will become the film's critical line of dialogue.

Jake settles into his avatar life with the Na'vi. He becomes agile and at one with the wild. Grace encourages Jake to see the forest through Neytiri's eyes. 'With Neytiri it's learn fast or die,' Jake acknowledges. We then see Jake and Na'vi male warriors tame and ride a number of banshees. The sequence becomes emblematic of a broader motif occurring throughout the movie, that of flight and liberation. Grace in her avatar form sees Jake accepted. There is an overhead shot of all of the arms of the Na'vi reaching out to Jake at the centre of their web.

Neytiri and Jake make love and at this point, after a moment of tenderness, the mining company's bulldozers move in on Hometree. Indeed, this counterpoint of tenderness followed by the prospect of imminent destruction echoes the structural pattern evidenced in *Titanic* and *True Lies*. Jake cannot wake because he is not plugged in for a driving session. Jake 'awakes' in his avatar form just in time and tries to stop the bulldozer. At the company base, Quaritch watches video of Jake smashing cameras and he states that he is going to ride in and bring Jake's rebellion to an end. At Hometree the tribe prepares a war party and Grace insists: 'This will only make it worse.'

The cross-cultural conflict is as true of the class divide and clash in *Titanic*. *Avatar* takes the Cameron-Milius-Hill connection to a particularly potent place. John Milius and Walter Hill had collaborated on *Geronimo* about the genocide of the Native Americans and their attempts at resisting colonisation. As such, both *Geronimo* and *Avatar* articulate the concerns that Richard Slotkin exhaustively explores in his study *Regeneration Through Violence*. Slotkin's book was originally published in 1973 and its exploration of aspects of American history, culture and national identity provides a resonant and relevant set of contexts in which we can regard not only Cameron's movies but also, we might say, probably all American-produced war films and westerns.

Jake tries to explain to the Na'vi who their enemy is. Quaritch and a patrol unit are then shown arriving at the research station and Quaritch shuts the system down. Grace's avatar collapses and then so does Jake's. Tsu'tey is not sympathetic and says to the tribe: 'See? It is a demon in a false body.' There is then a cut that shows Jake waking up. Quaritch is there and he punches Jake back down and then removes him from the research station into the Pandoran air, which as a human he cannot breathe. Grace and Jake are taken back to the base by Quaritch, who calls Jake a traitor. Just as Rose is regarded to have betrayed her class in *Titanic*, so Jake is considered to have betrayed his race.

Grace explains that the trees under threat are sacred to the clan but also an essential component of the planet's eco-system: 'I'm not talking about some pagan voodoo here. We think there's some kind of electro-chemical connection like synapses between neurons.' Her impassioned description is met by Selfridge's scepticism ('They're just goddamn trees'), just as Burke shrugged off Ripley's concern in *Aliens* and just as the crass hotelier does with Anne's caution in *Piranha 2*. Grace goes on to explain that the forest is a network of memories for the Na'vi. In *Avatar*, memory is communal whereas in *The Terminator* films, the function of memory works much more personally for Sarah Connor and in *The Abyss*, Bud and Lindsey's memories of their love and feeling for each other are both threatened, and ultimately, redeemed by the technological/industrial threat to their lives.

Quaritch then explains that because a deal cannot be made with the Na'vi it is time to take the Hometree by force. He assures Selfridge that there will be minimal casualties. It is a promise that seems hollow. Aware of what Quaritch now plans, Trudy Chacon alerts Jake and Grace. The narrative now is propelled by a race against time. Grace confronts Selfridge to try to stop him, with something of the same feeling that Ripley displays in *Aliens* when pleading with the corporation not to ignore the threat of the alien, but is ignored. Jake and Grace then plug in to their avatar drivers. Jake explains to the Na'vi that Hometree is now under imminent threat and explains how his loyalties have changed, how he fell in love with the forest, with the clan and then with Neytiri.

Choral, percussive music underscores the beginning of the assault, intensifying the emotion and also making connections with the tribal, ancient nature of the conflict. Jake and Grace are then tied up for their betrayal as the offensive against Hometree commences. There is a crash zoom that shows airships drifting in over the mountainside to fire on the tree, conjuring the effect of immediacy, of newsreel footage from combat zones that we might recognise. Hometree is destroyed and Neytiri's father and many other Na'vi are killed.

The image fades to black and we hear pounding drums. Norm, Grace and Jake are imprisoned at the base camp. Trudy frees them, transporting them to the floating mountain research station. Grace is seriously injured by a gunshot. Jake goes back to the tribe, who have retreated to the sacred Tree of Souls, and explains that he will serve the clan and his return to his new 'home' is depicted against a setting of golden, sunset light that invests him with a newfound heroism.

The injured Grace is brought to the tree. There is a shot of her looking upwards and it recalls a similar image from *The Abyss* when Lindsey sees an NTI for the first time, its purple luminescence reflected in the visor of her diving helmet. Grace is connected with the tree. Neytiri's mother then explains that Grace must pass through the eye of Aiywa and into her avatar. It is a sensibility that embodies the film's pantheistic, 'green' credentials and espousal of something akin to James Lovelock's Gaia Hypothesis. However, Grace dies before she can be healed by the tree.

Jake asks Tsu'tey for permission to address the clan and a scene ensues that is redolent of scenes in *Henry V* (Kenneth Branagh, 1989), *Robin Hood* (Kevin Reynolds, 1991), *Braveheart* and *The Lord of the Rings: Return of the King* (Peter Jackson, 2003) as Jake musters the support of the tribe. He makes a particularly resonant American comment saying that 'This is our land', evoking the American folk singer Woody Guthrie. Rather than a Guthrie-inflected twang, though, Jake's address and the tribes' gathering is emphasised and ennobled further by an expansive percussive drum beat and choral soundtrack. There is then a wide shot of the night sky as countless Na'vi riders fly in whilst on the ground 'the horse clans of the plain' ride in. The final battle then ensues which concludes with Jake and Quaritch confronting each other, Jake in his avatar form and Quaritch armoured in his AMP-suit, a less elegant avatar condition, we might say, in which the human body fuses with technology.

Quartich closes in on the research station where Jake lies in his avatar driver chamber. Neytiri rides in to stop Quaritch and discordant music accompanies the moment on the soundtrack. Like Spielberg, Cameron recognises the 'operatic' potential of action sequences. Quaritch derides Jake's loyalty to the Na'vi, just as Cal is repulsed by Rose's affection for the lower-class Jack in *Titanic*.

Jake's avatar weakens and the scene cuts to Jake struggling to breathe in the research cabin. Finally, an arrow fired by Neytiri kills Quaritch. Neytiri then goes to Jake in the pod, finding him exhausted and near death. Neytiri puts an oxygen mask on Jake and his condition steadies. 'I see you', Neytiri says to Jake, her ability to now see the authentic Jake echoing a similar connection between Rose and Jack in *Titanic*. Jake is able to breathe, both literally and metaphorically, and a close-up of Neytiri never quite lets us know if we are watching an image that is photographed or digitally 'illustrated'.

In the film's epilogue Jake's voice-over explains: 'The aliens went back to their dying world.' We watch the fallen company men being marched off as Norm, Jake and Neytiri stay on Pandora. Back in an avatar driver room Jake commits what seems to be his final video-log to file, explaining that it is time to go. The sequence then cuts to an image of the clan gathered together.

Percussive and choral music underscores the action and we see Jake lying at the base of the Tree of Souls with his avatar body lying beside him. Jake is connected to his avatar body through the tendrils of the tree. The spirits dance around him. There is a close-up on his face as his avatar eyes snap open: he is properly in the Na'vi body now and so is no longer an avatar but an authentic self.

Reception

The film's release was an immense marketing and promotional event across the autumn of 2009 and press coverage was extensive, before, during and after the film's release. It was received with both extensive approval and dissent. Criticism of the film rested on its perceived inconsistency of attitude. In his piece 'The Wizard', for the *New York Review of Books*, Daniel Mendelsohn wrote that the film was 'visually ravishing and ideologically awkward' and criticised it for an incoherent subtext in that the Na'vi are both 'admirably precivilised and admirably hypercivilised' (2010).

In January 2010, *Avatar* won the Golden Globe for Best Picture (Drama), a validation of sorts, we might argue, by the popular critical establishment, for science fiction and fantasy cinema, which have historically not been considered as a prestige format. At the more prestigious Academy Awards, however, Cameron lost out in the major categories to his ex-wife Kathryn Bigelow and her Iraq War drama *The Hurt Locker* (2009). *Avatar*'s cluster of award wins nonetheless built on the Oscar for Best Picture given for *Lord of the Rings: The Return of the King* in 2004. Indeed, Jackson's trilogy had indicated that the previously 'niche' genre of high fantasy could find much broader commercial appeal than had hitherto been thought. Only Lucas's *Star Wars* serial had really effectively found mainstream acceptance beyond its original 'target' audience. The proof of this integration into the mainstream moment occurred when *Vanity Fair* magazine, in early 2001, featured a production photo of the main cast of Hobbits gathered for a group photo. *Avatar* then, arguably, bolstered the perception that the fantasy genre and the science fiction genres are accessible and not inevitably too obscure for the mainstream audience. Key to this 'revival' of the legitimacy of the science fiction movie genre were the conditions of the film's release.

In the latter part of 2009, and into 2010, the film and entertainment industry press discussed *Avatar*'s production and presentation as a 3D film. Swiftly, Cameron became the figurehead for advancing the legitimacy of choosing to shoot certain kinds of films in 3D. Critically, he was also clear in advocating only native-3D filming (where the action is captured on a 3D camera during filming) rather than converting footage shot in the traditional way during post-production. In the *New York Daily News*, referencing the *Hollywood Reporter*, a story, by Nicole Lyn Pesce, ran that charted the film's box office success, partly in relation to the forms of the film's exhibition. The article explains that 'in fact, more than 80% of *Avatar*'s domestic business was done in 3D theatres, which represent less than half of its runs' (2010). Just two weeks later, the *Hollywood Reporter*, the same paper ran a piece entitled 'All about the endgame: how Cameron and Company delivered *Avatar* to the screen and changed the rules forever', which explored how 18 different versions of the film had been produced for the US release and 92 different versions (languages and so on) for international release. *Avatar* was exhibited in 17,604 35mm theatres, 7,832 digital 2D screens, 553 digital 3D screens and 272 IMAX 3D screens in the USA (2010).

But not only was *Avatar* a an expensive blockbuster release, with all the usual attendant financial risks, it was also saddled with the hopes of the industry looking to turn a recent re-emergent fad for 3D into something more permanent and lucrative. In a piece entitled '*Avatar* as Technological Tentpole', Charles R. Acland wrote:

> So, while extraordinarily conventional in story and characterization, *Avatar* is celebrated and promoted to stand out as a flagship work beckoning the next wave of industrial and consumer technologies and entertainments. With *Avatar*, we have 3D filming processes, 3D exhibition, digital exhibition, and 3D home entertainment all counting on the film's appeal for their own advancement. And given that corporate participants in the making of *Avatar* span from Quebec's Hybride to New Zealand's Weta Digital, the film is a good example of a transnational economic entity. *Avatar* is a technological tentpole under which we find not only other movies and appended commodities, but media formats and processes that slide into our lives as supposedly essential. Technological tentpoles introduce and promote hardware and media systems; such entities advance the very notion of a reconstructed cinematic apparatus as well as that of a wider audiovisual environment. (2010)

As Jorg Heiser noted in a piece for *Frieze* magazine:

> *Avatar* is an amalgam, as if in a strange dream ... you can look at it as being very clever[ly] calculated to capture the widest possible audience globally, playing many cards at once; but by way of the very same strategy, it also could be seen as capturing the widest possible 3D panorama shot of collective anxieties about the future (ecology, war, loss of social love and security, etc). And in the same contradictory way, it is this all-encompassing ambition that is interesting about it, but also what is off-putting. (2010)

In the wake of the film's immense popularity, the media's image of Cameron shifted from representing him as 'visionary' engineer to an icon of the *zeitgeist*; Cameron had been transformed from a B-movie filmmaker to a mainstream conduit for world affairs. *Avatar*'s popular culture expressivity and resonance was perhaps best encapsulated when, in the summer of 2010, the Iroquois lacrosse team were in need of financing to travel to a sporting event. Cameron intervened to provide the money on account of the connection between the Iroquois and, by extension, first nation cultures and the fictional Na'vi culture of *Avatar*.

The immense commercial success of the film also legitimised the use of stereoscopic filmmaking for spectacles. George Lucas announced in autumn 2010 that his *Star Wars* films would be re-formatted for 3D presentation, commencing in 2012 with *The Phantom Menace*. Critically, the film's 3D element has led to a wider debate about the 'integrity' and aesthetic and technological limitations and possibilities of the form.

In January 2011, renowned sound designer and editor Walter Murch wrote a piece entitled 'Why 3D doesn't work and never will', originally published as a letter to film critic Roger Ebert.

Avatar, then, gave a high profile to a new way in which digital technology was impacting on the traditional idea of the actor, and yet in another way it took us back to the ancient idea of actors in masks to create characters; Cameron described the project as 'an actor-driven process'. Around the time of the film's release, he explained in an article entitled '*Avatar*'s Animated Acting' in the *Los Angeles Times*:

> I'm not interested in being an animator ... That's what Pixar does. What I do is talk to actors. 'Here's a scene. Let's see what you can come up with,' and when I walk away at the end of the day, it's done in my mind. In the actor's mind, it's done. There may be a whole team of animators to make sure what we've done is preserved, but that's their problem. Their job is to use the actor's performance as an absolute template without variance for what comes out the other end. (2009)

The film as an event movie showcasing the potential for a new iteration of the form as business model was significant, more so than its story, to the film industry at the level of production and distribution. During *Avatar*'s original theatrical release advertisements were to be found in industry trade-papers such as this one placed by the film lab DeLuxe in the *Hollywood Reporter*: 'A film about the future just changed it forever.' The implication is that the film industry has been immediately transformed through various applications of digital technology.

Beyond its textual interest, the film's primary interest is arguably as a venue for discussions of the expressive value and potential in 3D presentation of event movies. *Avatar*'s 3D element has led to a wider debate about the 'integrity', aesthetic and technological limitations and possibilities of 3D. In *The Hobbit* trilogy we have a suitable case study for the impact of digital technology on production and distribution. When *The Hobbit: An Unexpected Journey* (Peter Jackson, 2012) was released one of its major marketing points was that it had been shot at a higher frame rate of 48 frames per second (fps) rather than 24 fps which has been the 'standard' for much of cinema to date. However, there was a general sense of dissatisfaction with the 'real' look of the 48 fps presentation that said much about the inherent 'fantasy' of film as of a photochemical process. Both higher frame rate and 3D presentation have been much discussed and utilised in recent years but currently there seems to be some uncertainty about the financial viability of both processes and very recently Cameron has suggested in *Variety* that 3D was being wrongly used by Hollywood film studios and that a sense of its appropriate expressivity needed to be reasserted (2014).

Throughout Cameron's films, then, the human body has been a source of meaning. It was perhaps no surprise that in 2010, he announced that he was to collaborate with the performance troupe *Cirque du Soleil*. Cameron had in fact consulted with the company in terms of developing the movement he wanted for the Na'vi characters in *Avatar*. In a statement Cameron's offices announced:

> Shooting with the *Cirque du Soleil* team has been one of the most enjoyable experiences of my professional life. For years I've been a fan, both of their celebration of human physical performance and for their wild imagination in the designs of characters, costumes, music and unparalleled theatrical staging.

Cameron's comment about the company's foregrounding of 'human physical performance' makes a critical connection with his own film work and its foregrounding of the human body as a site of meaning and value.

Amidst the spectacle of sound and image in *Avatar* is a critical, climatic scene in which the fusion of the painted and the photographed achieve a real synthesis. Cradling Jake Sully in her lithe arms, towering over his much smaller, frail form, the character of Neytiri appears utterly photorealistic. In this moment, Neytiri provides a visual echo to Ripley in *Aliens* protecting Newt from the monstrous. In *Avatar*, the gesture is romantically charged, bringing into particular focus Cameron's career-long interest in the love story as the basis for ventures into the genres of science fiction, horror and war.

How interesting it will be to see how Cameron engages with the world of *Avatar* in the proposed three sequels that, as of this writing, are in pre-production. In a recent online news report for Yahoo News, Gwynne Watkins notes that these sequel projects already suggest not only the broad narrative interests of the new films but also the possibility that Cameron may seek to apply and develop existing virtual reality hardware and software in terms of the films' screenings. The audience may well find Cameron's story interest in bio-tech fusion reaching out to them (2014).

The paradox of *Avatar* and, indeed, of all films, is the use of illusion for the simulation of authentic experience. *Avatar* is about body and soul. It is a lavish rendition of the idea behind *Pinocchio*: what does it take to be real, or, rather, really human?

CHAPTER NINE
Cameron's Documentaries

Film scholar Bill Nichols has usefully made the observation that 'it is worth insisting that the strategies and styles deployed in documentary, like those of narrative film, change: they have a history ... the comfortably accepted realism of one generation seems like artifice to the next' (1985: 259). James Cameron has to date made two sea documentaries, *Ghosts of the Abyss* and *Aliens of the Deep*, which provide 'real world' corollaries to his fantasy dramas and which also deploy a palette of visual effects that elaborate on the sensibility of the marine-focused documentaries of a key influence on Cameron's sensibilities, Jacques Cousteau.

In the post-*Titanic* years to date, Cameron has committed much of his energy to deep-sea exploration; a setting that is not without a narrative fiction antecedent for him, of course. In spring 2013, Cameron was interviewed by *National Geographic* magazine and asked why the ocean, and not outer space, fascinated him more as a site for exploration outside of his filmmaking work. He explained:

> They both do. I love space exploration as well. But the difference between space exploration and ocean exploration – whether it's the shallow diving on scuba or deep-diving stuff I do now – ocean exploration is something I can do. There's not a firm line between science fiction and reality [for me] – it's a continuum. The more I can step over that line and see the alien world that we have on Earth, the more exciting it is. (Quoted in Lee 2013)

This statement sits consistently with Cameron's project in *Avatar*, in a promotional DVD extras piece for which, Cameron said of its technological demand (and, by extension, its aesthetics), 'We were way out in the unknown. I mean that's cool. That's where I want to be' (2010).

Ghosts of the Abyss (2003)
Ghosts of the Abyss is just under an hour in duration and charts the exploration of the wreck of the Titanic using two newly created small cameras that can enter the heart of the wreck. The film focuses around Bill Paxton, who played the explorer Brock Lovett in *Titanic*, as a conduit for the audience. Visual spectacle is key to the film as visual effects that restage events are overlaid onto new footage of the wreck. Like Cameron's fiction films, much is made of pushing the boundaries of available technology for the narrative purposes of the documentary project. At one point, aesthetics lead the effort: Cameron goes back down to the wreck in the sub just to light the windows from outside to evoke some sense of how sunlight would have fallen through the beautiful, early-twentieth-century design. The film also anthropomorphises its two robot cameras and they find themselves in their own mini-rescue story. Joel McNeely's score interpolates the traditional hymnal 'For Those in Peril on the Sea'. It is undoubtedly effective.

The film also finds itself applying the tragedy of the Titanic to another, more recent tragedy, which in turn, makes an eerie connection to certain elements of Cameron's fiction films. The documentary follows a day in the period of visits to the wreck and there is footage of one of the crew saying that the date is 11 September 2001. Footage then follows of the crew on deck receiving the news of the terrorist attacks on US soil.

Aliens of the Deep (2005)
Early in his career, Cameron spoke of his deep affinity for the work of underwater documentarist Jacques Cousteau. *Aliens of the Deep*, like *Ghosts of the Abyss*, allows the director an opportunity to invoke the Cousteau sensibility, although the film's title is more reminiscent of the kind of projects that were being produced by Roger Corman's studio during the late 1970s and early 1980s when Cameron worked there.

Aliens of the Deep fuses 'fact' with vividly realised imaginative speculation. As such, it is highly consistent with the 'fiction informed by fact' of Cameron's narrative features. It begins by exploring the world of deep sea life that does not require sunlight but which instead is 'fuelled' by the heat that vents from the ocean bed. The film then extrapolates the world observed in deep sea in order to speculate on the life that may exist beneath the icy surface of Europa, one of Jupiter's moons. It revels in the science fiction of it all, which is to say the possibilities suggested by the technology being deployed to explore the ocean bed and also to record it. Indeed, Cameron is very much presented as the director of the marine exploration and his two 'characters' are young scientists: a man and a woman.

The film's opening credits run over 'abstract' swirls of forms that are perhaps best described as otherworldly. We see images of the human race that suggest *Koyanisqaatsi* (Godfrey Reggio, 1982) and then the film cuts to a visual effects simulation of solar flares on our sun. It clarifies the way in which most life on earth is solar-powered. The film then cuts to Cameron in one pod and to the PhD student in another. The orchestral score plays and there is a sense of spectacle and awe that recalls the presentation of submarine life in *The Abyss*. Some of the life forms we are shown indicate the influence

Artifice, imagination and scienctific documentary fusion

of Cameron's deep-sea work on the design of environments for *Avatar*. He makes the point in voice-over: 'I love this. Way more exciting than Hollywood special effects.'

When the film shows us deep-sea life we hear choral music and there is a shot that tilts up to reveal an immense tower of rock. The film overtly engages with relationships between humans and technology through a discussion about who would go to Mars if they could and the personal life ramifications of that decision. The film makes the observation that in the era in which we created nuclear missiles we also were able to create mass communication, bringing up the idea of destruction and creation/coming together, a concept that Cameron dramatises in his feature films. *Aliens of the Deep* also refers to the humans exploring the seabed: in that context we are the 'outsiders'.

The film's final sequence begins with a mid-shot of a pod in which the two scientists ride: it is a blue-screen shot and in the reflection of the pod's screen we see an 'alien' of the deep approach and touch the glass. The camera then pulls back and turns to reveal a wave of 'aliens of the deep'; just beyond them lies an immense underwater city, almost identical to the city that we see the NTIs occupying in *The Abyss*.

Cameron's film shows us marine researchers and astrobiologists together on the team and Cameron talks about the 'most insane alien life forms' to be discovered beneath the ocean's surface. The film is, to some degree, about filmmaking as a group endeavour, pragmatism, a shared ambition and a way to visualise your view of the world.

CHAPTER TEN

Cameron as Writer and Producer

In the tradition of his near-contemporaries Steven Spielberg, George Lucas and Robert Zemeckis, James Cameron has a number of projects as a writer and/or producer to his name. There are also a number of feature film projects that he developed in various capacities.

Rambo: First Blood Part II (1985)
While writing the screenplay for *Aliens*, Cameron had also been commissioned to write what became the original draft of the sequel to *First Blood* (Ted Kotcheff, 1982). Cameron's script was entitled *Rambo: The Mission*. Whilst Cameron would ultimately share screen credit with the film's star, Sylvester Stallone, he has offered several reflections on his involvement with the project and the finished film certainly has elements of Cameron's films as writer/director. Directed by George Pan Cosmatos, the film prompted an outcry about the level of violence at the time of its release in 1985.

Set in East Asia, and telling of a one-man rescue mission by the Vietnam veteran John Rambo (Stallone) to retrieve his former commander from imprisonment, the film revels in a military sensibility and Stallone's muscular presence. Rambo was considered to be a character that embodied the *zeitgeist* of Ronald Reagan's conservative America.

Of the Rambo character, Stallone, when asked in an online Q&A, 'What's the appeal of the action hero?', replied: 'Action films, past, present and future are really a device for maintaining modern mythology. In reality, evil quite often triumphs over good and its effects have devastating longevity. So I believe the action film supplies an outlet for optimism and the unwavering belief that heroes, under great physical threat, rise and vanquish the oppressors' (2010).

Endurance, stamina and the spectacle of combat frame the story with countless images showing Rambo armed and running wild in the wilderness; an image explicitly invoking the mythology of the white colonist in the American wilderness of the eighteenth and nineteenth centuries. The original *First Blood* (with a screenplay credited to Stallone, Michael Kozoll and William Sackheim from the 1972 novel by David Morrell) was a taut thriller, akin to *The Fugitive*, set in the northwestern forests of the United States, its narrative and images evoking stories such as James Fenimore Cooper's novel *The Last of the Mohicans*. (This wilderness aesthetic can be seen as reaching its elaborate climax in Cameron's oeuvre with *Avatar*.) Stallone re-wrote Cameron's draft for the sequel and, in Cameron's eyes, moved it away from the more thoughtful approach he had developed to examine a war veteran, which in his draft began with Rambo as a patient at a psychiatric hospital.

Of the eventual film, Cameron, in an interview with *Monsterland* magazine in October 1986, commented: 'It was quite a different film from *First Blood*, apart from the continuation of the Rambo character. The first one was set in a small town, it had a different social consciousness from the second one, which was a very broad, stylized adventure. It was a little more violent in execution than I had in mind in the writing' (1986). Cameron also called the final film's conclusion 'breathtaking in its stupidity' (ibid.).

Of the commission, Cameron explained in an interview with Jean-Marc L'Officier, now archived online: 'One of the things that interested me is that there are a lot of soldiers from Vietnam who have been in intensive combat situations who re-enlist to go back again, because they had psychological problems that they had to work out. It's like an inner demon to be exorcised. I did a bit of that in *Rambo*, but it didn't get used' (1985).

Point Break (1991)
With the director Kathryn Bigelow, Cameron wrote an uncredited draft of the original screenplay by Peter Ilif for *Point Break*. The film is a thriller set in the world of surfboarding. The film's protagonists Johnny Utah (Keanu Reeves) and Bodhi (Patrick Swayze) are typical Cameron-esque characters, particularly Bodhi with his love for nature and the wilderness of the sea. The film became famous for both its kinetic action sequences and the homoerotic tension between the leads.

Strange Days (1995)
Strange Days was directed by Kathryn Bigelow from a screenplay by Cameron and Jay Cocks. More specifically, Cameron had written a 'scriptment', a fusion of script and prose treatment document. Cocks wrote the actual screenplay; he had once been a film critic and had long been close with the Lucas/Scorsese circle, collaborating with Scorsese on *Mean Streets* (1973) and *The Age of Innocence* (1993) and, in due course, *Gangs of New York* (2002). Issues of gender and race are powerfully dramatised and visualised in *Strange Days* and the film is a fascinating collision of ideas and approaches. In his Introduction to the published 'scriptment', Cameron explained its genesis: 'Lenny Nero was born in 1985 when I decided to write a film noir thriller

Strange Days: Lenny Nero and Mace in a tech-noir world of compromised identities

taking place on New Year's Eve in 1999. I was fascinated by the dramatic and thematic potential of the millennium, and the idea of doomsday as a backdrop for the redemption of one individual' (1995: vi).

The film is a thriller that is predicated upon a future technology whereby people's point-of-view memories can be recorded then experienced by others. The plot hinges on a bootleg tape of a rape and murder and on its release the film was compared to *Peeping Tom*. A telling phrase in Cameron's treatment, as he builds impressions of the world in which *Strange Days* occurs is his description of the world in which the story is set: 'Reality shows and amateur video shows dominated TV programming. It is the age of scopophilia, voyeurism and vicarious living … We like to watch. It is a surveillance culture…' (1995: 18).

Strange Days, then, is very much a film about filmmaking, and in their study *The Cinema of Kathryn Bigelow: Hollywood Transgressor* Deborah Jermyn and Sean Redmond note that Bigelow is 'a filmmaking artist who is able to transcend the collective, industrial and commercial constraints of the Hollywood cinema machine to individually author her films in innovative and transgressive ways … her political play with genre and gender is self-conscious and the signs of her authorship are a knowing presence in her film work' (2003: 2). They go on to state that 'Bigelow's cinema of transgression, then, is a contradictory or paradoxical activity. On the one hand, Bigelow subverts the codes and conventions of dominant film form, in part through employing a range of art cinema devices (self-reflexivity, self-conscious camera work, the corporeal traces of her authorship), and on the other she accepts (and pays homage to) these codes and conventions by revelling in this exploration and execution' (2003: 3).

Dark Angel (2000–2002)

Dark Angel was broadcast on American television between 3 October 2000 and 3 May 2002 and starred Jessica Alba. James Cameron created the series. The premise centres on a character called Max, a genetically-enhanced human prototype hunted by her former military handlers through the edgy, underground street-life version of twenty-first-century America. Max is aided in her quest, both to avoid capture and reunite with her 'siblings' scattered in the aftermath of their escape. Cameron directed the final two episodes of the second, and final, series.

Shortlived though the series was (and produced during the immediate aftermath of Cameron's involvement in a proposed Spiderman adaptation coming to a conclusion) it brought to TV a drama that was replete with Cameron's feature film 'characteristics'. The cyberpunk interests of Stange Days are revisited in this series in which a genetically enhanced soldier named Max Guevara escapes from a military centre as a child with the wish to live a normal life. In this briefest of outlines the situation suggests the dramatic scope that the series sought to explore around the idea of the 'posthuman' experience that has been so central to Cameron's cinema. Max embarks on a quest to find her 'family'. The series, then, has connections with *The Terminator* and *Avatar* particularly in terms of what constitutes human when the body and mind are so enmeshed with the technological. Like *Aliens* and perhaps even reaching back to the influence of *Escape from New York* (on which Cameron worked as a visual effects artist) there is also the narrative interest of a government acting covertly and with a certain capacity for compromise. At the level of narrative structure, the series shares with *The Terminator* particularly, a propulsive sense driven by a main character being pursued.

Spider-Man (unproduced)
In the early 1990s Cameron was attached to write and direct a new film adaptation of Stan Lee's Marvel Comics character, Spider-Man. In contrast to the often playful film that Sam Raimi eventually directed from David Koepp's screenplay (2002), which derived in part from reworking content in Cameron's development work, Cameron's 'scriptment' includes his by-now familiar mixture of seriousness and self-consciously rendered mythography. The studio behind Cameron's proposed adaptation was Carolco, who had enjoyed commercial success in the early 1990s with films such as *Total Recall* (Paul Verhoeven, 1990), Cameron's *Terminator 2* and *Cliffhanger* (Renny Harlin, 1993). When they went bankrupt the material was bought by Columbia Pictures.

Jose Arroyo has explained that there is a pertinent connection between Cameron and the Marvel Comics tradition: 'Marvel Comics such as *X-Men*, *Spiderma*n and *Daredevil* depict a corrupt world characterized by conflict between species (as in *Aliens*); rampant and ruthless corporate interests which value profit over human life; stupid and careless government representatives. As in Cameron's films, narration in Marvel Comics alternates between spectacular action and a troubled domestic sphere in which surrogate families are created as alternatives to traditional ones and as a buffer to troubled love relationships – families that are glimmers of utopia in otherwise dystopian worlds' (2000: 41).

Solaris (2001)
Solaris is a 1961 novel written by Stanislaw Lem in which an astronaut named Kris Kelvin encounters an alien culture during an interstellar mission. In 1972, Andrei Tarkovsky directed a famous feature film adaptation, although this was not the first: there had also been an adaptation directed by Boris Nirenburg and released in 1968.

Cameron secured the rights to the novel in the late 1990s and for a while contemplated directing a version before acting as producer to the eventual director, Steven Soderbergh, who took on the project with the ambition to make an adaptation of Lem's novel that was more faithful than Tarkovsky's take to the source material. In an interview to promote the film's theatrical release, Soderbergh commented that the film offered a counterpoint to the tendency in Hollywood-financed 'science fiction' films: 'I feel since *Star Wars* they've tilted pretty far into the action genre and I'm not really interested in technology or gadgets' (2003). Certainly, the film concentrates Cameron's brand of cerebral science fiction interests that find expression in his own directorial projects but which jostle for attention amidst the overt visual spectacle and event movie sensibilities.

Sanctum (2011)
Cameron was the executive producer of this modestly-scaled thriller about divers trapped in an underwater cave. The film was promoted very much as a 'James Cameron production' but its release and commerical success was muted. Typical of the film's reception is found in this comment from Roger Ebert who wrote that '*Sanctum* tells the story of a terrifying adventure in an incompetent way ... If this were a "James Cameron film", I suspect it would have fewer flaws and the use of 3D would be much improved' (2011).

Cirque du Soleil (2011)
Cameron produced a film presentation of a live *Cirque du Soleil* show in 2011.

FILMOGRAPHY

As Writer-Director

Piranha 2: The Spawning (1981)
Production Company: Chako Film Company
Producers: Chako van Leeuwen
Director: James Cameron
Screenplay: James Cameron
Cinematography: Roberto D'Ettore Piazzoli
Editor: Robert Silvi
Original Music: Steve Powder
Main Cast: Tricia O'Neil (Anne Kimbrough), Steve Marachuck (Tyler Sherman), Lance Henriksen (Police Chief Steve Kimbrough)

The Terminator (1984)
Production Company: Orion
Producers: Gale Anne Hurd
Director: James Cameron
Screenplay: James Cameron & Gale Anne Hurd
Cinematography: Adam Greendberg
Editor: Mark Goldblatt
Original Music: Brad Fiedel
Main Cast: Arnold Schwarzenegger (The Terminator), Linda Hamilton (Sarah Connor), Michael Biehn (Kyle Reese), Paul Winfield (Lt. Ed Traxler), Lance Henriksen (Detective Hal Yukovich), Rick Rossovich (Matt Buchanan), Shawn Schepps (Nancy), Dick Miller (Pawn Shop Clerk)

Aliens (1986)
Production Company: Twentieth Century Fox, Brandywine Productions
Producers: Gale Anne Hurd
Director: James Cameron
Screenplay: James Cameron
Cinematography: Adrian Biddle
Editor: Ray Lovejoy
Original Music: James Horner
Main Cast: Sigourney Weaver (Ellen Ripley), Carrie Henn (Rebecca 'Newt' Jorden), Michael Biehn (Corporal Hicks), Paul Reiser (Carter Burke), Lance Henriksen (Bishop), Bill Paxton (Private Hudson), Jenette Goldstein (Private Vasquez), William Hope (Lt. Gorman), Al Matthews (Sergeant Apone)

The Abyss (1989)
Production Company: Twentieth Century Fox
Producers: Gale Anne Hurd
Director: James Cameron
Screenplay: James Cameron
Cinematography: Mikael Solomon
Editor: Conrad Buff IV
Original Music: Alan Silvestri
Main Cast: Ed Harris (Bud Brigman), Mary Elizabeth Mastrantonio (Lindsey Brigman), Michael Biehn (Lt. Hiram Coffey), Leo Burmester (Catfish), Todd Graff ('Hippy'), John Bedford Lloyd (Jammer), Kimberley Scott ('One Night')

Terminator 2: Judgement Day (1991)
Production Company: Carolco
Producers: James Cameron
Director: James Cameron
Screenplay: James Cameron & William Wisher
Cinematography: Adam Greenberg
Editor: Conrad Buff IV
Original Music: Brad Fiedel
Main Cast: Arnold Schwarzenegger (The Terminator), Linda Hamilton (Sarah Connor), Edward Furlong (John Connor), Robert Patrick (T-1000), Joe Morton (Miles Dyson), S. Epatha Merkeson (Tarissa Dyson)

True Lies (1994)
Production Company: Twentieth Century Fox / Lightstorm Entertainment
Producers: James Cameron & Stephanie Austin
Director: James Cameron
Screenplay: James Cameron, based on the screenplay La Totale by Claude Zidi, Simon Michael & Didier Kaminka
Cinematography: Russell Carpenter
Editor: Conrad Buff, Mark Goldblatt and Richard A. Harris
Original Music: Brad Fiedel
Main Cast: Arnold Schwarzenegger (Harry Tasker), Jamie Lee Curtis (Helen Tasker), Art Malik (Aziz), Tom Arnold (Gib), Grant Heslov (Faisal), Tia Carrere (Juno Skinner), Charlton Heston (Spencer Trilby)

T2:3D: Battle Across Time (short film, 1995)
Production Company: Landmark Entertainment & Lightsorm Entertainment
Producers: Chuck Comisky, Jessica Huebner, Frank Kostenko Jr., Andrew Millstein & Scott Ross
Director: James Cameron, John Bruno & Stan Winston
Screenplay: James Cameron, Gary Goddard & Adam J. Bezark
Original Music: Brad Fiedel
Main Cast: Arnold Schwarzennegger (The Terminator), Edward Furlong (John Connor), Linda Hamilton (Sarah Connor), Robert Patrick (T-1000)

Titanic (1997)
Production Company: Twentieth Century Fox / Lightstorm Entertainment
Producers: James Cameron & Jon Landau
Director: James Cameron
Screenplay: James Cameron
Cinematography: Russell Carpenter
Editor: Conrad Buff, James Cameron, Richard A. Harris
Original Music: James Horner
Main Cast: Leonardo DiCaprio (Jack Dawson), Kate Winslet (Rose DeWitt

Bukater), Billy Zane (Cal Hockley), Kathy Bates (Margaret 'Molly' Brown), Frances Fisher (Ruth DeWitt Bukater), Bernard Hill (Captain Edward John Smith), Jonathan Hyde (J. Bruce Ismay), David Warner (Spicer Lovejoy), Bill Paxton (Brock Lovett), Gloria Stuart (Elderly Rose)

Ghosts of the Abyss (2003)
Production Company: Walden Media and The Walt Disney Company
Producers: John Bruno, James Cameron, Chuck Comisky, Janace Tashjian & Andrew Wight
Director: James Cameron
Cinematography: Vince Pace & D.J.Roller
Editor: David C.Cook, Ed W.Marsh, Sven Pape and John Refoua
Original Music: Joel McNeely & Lisa Torban

Aliens of the Deep (2005)
Production Company: Walt Disney Pictures
Producers: James Cameron & Andrew Wight
Director: James Cameron & Steve Quale
Cinematography: James Cameron, Vince Pace & Ron Allum
Editor: Matthew Kregor & Fiona Wight
Original Music: Jeehun Hwang

Avatar (2009)
Production Company: Lightstorm Entertainment / Twentieth Century Fox
Producers: Jon Landau
Director: James Cameron
Screenplay: James Cameron
Cinematography: Mauro Fiore
Editor: John Refoua, Stephen Rivkin and James Cameron

Original Music: James Horner
Main Cast: Sam Worthington (Jake Sully), Zoe Saldana (Neytiri), Sigourney Weaver (Grace Augustine), Stephen Lang (Quaritch), Michelle Rodriguez (Trudy Chacon), Giovanni Ribisi (Parker Selfridge), Joel David Moore (Norm Spellman), CCH Pounder (Moat), Wes Studi (Eytukan), Laz Alonzo (Tsu'tey), Dileep Rao (Dr Max Patel)

As Writer – Producer

Point Break (uncredited as writer) (1990)
Production Company: Twentieth Century Fox
Producers: Peter Abrams, James Cameron, Rick King, Robert L. Levy, Michael Rauch
Director: Kathryn Bigelow
Screenplay: Rick King, Peter Iliff
Cinematography: Donald Peterman
Editor: Howard E.Smith
Original Music: Mark Isham
Main Cast: Patrick Swayze (Bodhi), Keanu Reeves (Johnny Utah), Gary Busey (Pappas), Lori Petty (Tyler), John C.McGinley (Ben Harp), James LeGros (Roach)

Strange Days (1995)
Production Company: Twentieth Century Fox
Producers: James Cameron & Steven-Charles Jaffe
Director: Kathryn Bigelow
Screenplay: James Cameron & Jay Cocks
Cinematography: Matthew F.Leonetti
Editor: James Cameron & Howard E.Smith
Original Music: Graeme Revell
Main Cast: Ralph Fiennes (Lenny Nero), Angela Bassett (Mace), Juliette Lewis

(Faith), Tom Sizemore (Max Peltier), Vincent D'Onofrio (Burton Steckler), Michael Wincott (Philo Gant)

James Cameron's Dark Angel (2000–2002)
TV Series
Series Creator: James Cameron and Charles H.Eglee

Cast: Jessica Alba (Max Guevara), Michael Wetherly (Logan Cale), Richard Gunn (Calvin 'Sketchy' Theodore), J.C MacKenzie (Regan 'Normal' Ronald), Valarie Rae Miller (Cynthi McEachin), John Savage (Donald Lydecker)

BIBLIOGRAPHY

Abramowitz, Rachel (2009) 'Avatar's Animation Acting', *Los Angeles Times,* 18 February; http://articles.latimes.com/2010/feb/18/entertainment/la-et-avatar-actors18-2010feb18.

Abrams, Janet (2000) 'Escape From Gravity', in Jose Arroyo (ed.) *Action/Spectacle Cinema: A Sight and Sound Reader.* London: British Film Institute, 106–13.

Acland, Charles R. (2010) '*Avatar* as Technological Tentpole', 22 January; http://flowtv.org/2010/01/avatar-as-technological-tentpole-charles-r-acland-concordia university/.

Altman, Rick (1999) *Film/Genre.* London: British Film Institute.

Andrew, Geoff (1989) 'Review of *The Abyss*', *Time Out*; http://www.timeout.com/london/film/the-abyss-1989.

____ (1991) 'Review of *Terminator 2: Judgement Day*', *Time Out*: http://www.timeout.com/london/film/terminator-2-judgment-day.

Arroyo, Jose (ed.) (2000) *Action/Spectacle Cinema: A Sight and Sound Reader.* London: British Film Institute.

Austin, Thomas and Martin Barker (2003) *Contemporary Hollywood Stardom.* London: Arnold.

Bachelard, Gaston (2011) *Air and Dreams: An Essay on the Imagination of Movement.* Dallas: Dallas Institute of Publication.

Barker, Chris (2008) *Cultural Studies.* London: Sage.

Bartlett, Andrew (2004) 'Nuclear Warfare in the Movies', *Anthropoetics*, 10, 1 ; http://www.anthropoetics.ucla.edu/ap1001/bartlett.htm.

Baudrillard, Jean (1994) *Simulacara and Simulation: The Body in Theory: History of Cultural Materialism.* Michigan, IL: University of Michigan Press.

Bettelheim, Bruno (1991) *The Uses of Enchantment: The Meaning and Importance of Fairy Tales.* London: Penguin.

Block, Alex Ben (2010) '*Avatar* may get second wind, with new scenes, summer release', *The Globe and Mail,* 12 March; http://www.theglobeandmail.com/arts/avatarmay-get-second-wind-with-new-scenes-summer-re-release/article4309810/.

Bly, Robert (2001) *Iron John: Men and Masculinity*. London: Rider.
Bochenksi, Matt (2010) 'Interview with Francis Coppola', 24 June, *Little White Lies*, 29; http://www.littlewhitelies.co.uk/features/interviews/a-z/f.
Bould, Mark (2009) *The Cinema of John Sayles: A Lone Star*. London and New York: Wallflower Press.
Bordwell, David (1985) 'Classical Hollywood Cinema: Narrational Principle and Procedures', in David Bordwell, Janet Staiger and Kristin Thompson, *The Classical Hollywood Cinema: Film Style and Mode of Production to 1960*. New York: Routledge, 17–34.
____ (1988) 'ApPropriations and ImPropprieties: Problems in the Morphology of Film Narrative', *Cinema Journal*, 27, 3, 3–17.
____ (2007a) 'Anatomy of the Action Picture'; http://www.davidbordwell.net/essays/anatomy.php.
____ (2007b) 'Live with it! There'll always be movie sequels. Good thing, too', 20 May; http://www.davidbordwell.net/blog/2007/05/20/live-with-it-therell-always-bemovie-sequels-good-thing-too/.
____ (2007c) *Poetics of Cinema*. New York: Routledge.
____ (2008) 'It's the 80s, stupid', 20 November; http://www.davidbordwell.net/blog/2008/11/20/its-the-80s-stupid/.
____ (2013a) 'All Play, No Work? Room 237', 7 April; http://www.davidbordwell.net/blog/2013/04/07/all-play-and-no-work-room-237/.
____ (2013b) 'Pandora's digital box: End Times', 12 May; http://www.davidbordwell.net/blog/2013/05/12/pandoras-digital-box-end-times/.
Boucher, Geoff (2009) 'Jim Cameron vs. Robert Zemeckis? An Insider's View of the Rivalry', *The Los Angeles Times*, 26 November; http://herocomplex.latimes.com/uncategorized/jim-cameron-vs-robert-zemeckis-theinside-scoop-on-the-rivalry/.
Boyd, Brian (2009) *The Origin of Stories: Evolution, Cognition and Fiction*. Cambridge: Belknap Press.
Bradshaw, Peter (2009) 'Review of *Avatar*', *The Guardian*, 17 December; http://www.theguardian.com/film/2009/dec/17/avatar-james-cameron-film-review.
Braidotti, Rosi (2011) *Nomadic Subjects: Embodiment and Sexual Difference in Contemporary Feminist Theory*. New York: Columbia University Press.
____ (2013) *The Posthuman*. London: Polity Press.
Burroughs, Norris (2011) http://kirbymuseum.org/blogs/kinetics/2011/01/01/spatial-relationships/ www.kirbymuseum.org.
Cameron, James (1986a) 'Interview', *Galactic Journal*; http://www.jamescameronline.com/Rambo2.htm.
____ (1986b) 'Interview with Randy and Jean-Marc L'Officier in *Starlog*'; http://www.lofficier.com/cameron.htm.
____ (1986c) Interview with *Monsterland* magazine'; http://www.jamescameronline.com/Rambo2.htm.
____ (1989) 'Interview', *Movieline* interview with Cameron by Michael Dare; http://archive.today/dbhoW.

____ (1994) 'Iron Jim' interview with *Premiere* magazine, August 1994, reprinted in Brett Dunham (ed.) *James Cameron: Interviews*. Jackson, MI: University of Missisippi Press, 63.

____ (1995) *Strange Days: Original Text*. London: Pocket Books.

____ (1997) 'Back to *Titanic*', *Cinefex*. December, 16.

____ (1999) *Titanic: James Cameron's Illustrated Screenplay*. London: Boxtree.

____ (2009a) 'Interview', *Playboy*; http://www.playboy.com/playground/view/playboy-interview-james-cameron.

____ (2009b) 'Ghost in the Shell'; http://www.theguardian.com/film/2009/oct/19/hollywood-ghost-in-the-shell.

____ (2009c) 'The Seduction of Reality', *Cinefex*, 120, 68.

____ (2009d) 'Avatar's Animated Acting', *The Los Angeles Times*; http://articles.latimes.com/2010/feb/18/entertainment/la-et-avatar-actors18-2010feb18.

____ (2010) 'Before *Avatar* ... a curious boy', TED; http://www.ted.com/talks/james_cameron_before_avatar_a_curious_boy.html.

____ (2011a) *James Cameron: A Life in Pictures*, BAFTA interview with Francine Stock; http://www.bafta.org/film/features/james-cameron-a-life-in-pictures,2327,BA.html.

____ (2011b) 'not to trust the fabric of reality', 20 December, BAFTA Film, *James Cameron: A Life in Pictures* BAFTA interview with Francine Stock, http://guru.bafta.org/james-cameron-interview-video.

____ (2012) 'James Cameron Talks Jurassic Park', *Empire,* 14 September; http://www.empireonline.com/news/story.asp?NID=35206.

____ (2014) *Variety*; http://variety.com/2014/film/news/james-cameroncalls-on-bolder-use-of-3d-by-all-filmmakers-1201132122/.

Campbell, Joseph (2004) *Pathways to Bliss: Mythology and Personal Transformation*. Novato: New World Library.

Carroll, Noel (1990) *The Philosophy of Horror or Paradoxes of the Heart*. London and New York: Routledge, Chapman and Hall.

Carter, Rick (2009b) 'James Cameron vs. Robert Zemeckis?', *Los Angeles Times*, 26 November; http://herocomplex.latimes.com/uncategorized/jim-cameron-vs-robert-zemeckis-the-inside-scoop-on-the-rivalry/

Cavell, Stanley (1988) *Themes Out of School: Effects and Causes*. Chicago, IL: University of Chicago Press.

Chabon, Michael (2000) 'Comics Came First', *The New York Times*; http://www.nytimes.com/books/00/09/24/reviews/000924.24buz.html.

Charity, Tom (1986) 'Review of *Aliens*', *Time Out*; http://www.timeout.com/london/film/aliens.

Cleaver, McKelvey Thomas (1994) 'How To Direct a Terminator', *Starlog*, 89, 56.

Clyne, James (2009) 'Concept Designer James Clyne Talks Avatar and Battle Angel!', 24 April; http://marketsaw.blogspot.co.uk/2009/04/concept-designerjames-clyne-talks.html#.Uu6oAHm4nHg.

Coehlho, Paulo (2010) 'Character of the Week'; http://paulocoelhoblog.com/2010/08/11/character-of-the-week-the-mountain/.

Conrich, Ian and David Woods (2004) *The Cinema of John Carpenter: The Technique of Terror*. London and New York: Wallflower Press.
Cook, Pam and Mieke Bernink (1999) *The Cinema Book*. London: British Film Institute.
Cornea, Christine (2007) *Science Fiction Cinema: Between Fantasy and Reality*. Edinburgh: Edinburgh University Press.
Cubitt, Sean (2010) 'Making Space', December; http://sensesofcinema.com/2010/feature-articles/making-space/.
Dare, Michael (1989) 'Life's Abyss and then You Die', *Movieline*; http://archive.is/dbhoW.
Dargis, Manohla (2007) 'Defending Goliath: Hollywood and the Art of the Blockbuster', 6 May, *The New York Times*; http://www.nytimes.com/2007/05/06/movies/moviesspecial/06darg.html?fta=y&_r=0.
Dixon, Wheeler Winston (2003) *Visions of the Apocalypse: Spectacles of Destruction in American Cinema*. London and New York: Wallflower Press.
Duncan, Jody (2010) 'The Seduction of Reality', *Cinefex*, 120, January, 70–145.
Dunham, Brent (2012) *James Cameron: Interviews*. Jackson, MS: University of Mississippi Press.
Dutka, Elaine (1992) 'The Toys in his Attic', *The Los Angeles Times*, 13 December; http://articles.latimes.com/1992-12-13/entertainment/ca-3759_1_barry-levinson.
Dyer, Richard (2004) *Heavenly Bodies: Film Stars and Society*, 2nd edition. London and New York: Routledge.
Ebert, Roger (1977) 'Top Secret Steven Spielberg on the Brink of the Close Encounters Premiere', *Chicago Sun Times*, 1 May; http://www.rogerebert.com/interviews/top-secret-steven-spielberg-on-the-brink-of-the-close-encounters-premiere.
____ (1986) 'Review in *Chicago Sun Times* of *Aliens*', 18 July; http://www.rogerebert.com/reviews/aliens-1986.
____ (1991) 'Review of *Terminator 2*', *Chicago Sun Times*, 3 July; http://www.rogerebert.com/reviews/terminator-2-judgment-day-1991.
____ (2011) 'Review of *Sanctum*', 2 February; http://www.rogerebert.com/reviews/sanctum-2011.
Elliot, Andrew B. (2011) '"She's a goddam liar": Perspectives on the Truth in *Aliens* and *Titanic*', in Matthew Wilhelm Kapell and Stephen McVeigh (eds) *The Films of James Cameron: Critical Essays*. Jefferson, NC: McFarland, 72–90.
Fore, Dana (2011) 'The Tracks of Sully's Tears: Disability in James Cameron's *Avatar*', *JumpCut*; http://www.ejumpcut.org/archive/jc53.2011/foreAvatar.
Fossati, Giovanna (2009) *From Grain to Pixel: The Archival Life of Film in Transition*. Amsterdam: Amsterdam University Press.
Freeland, Cynthia (1996) 'Feminist Frameworks for Horror Films', in Leo Braudy and Marshall Cohen (eds) *Film Theory and Criticism*. Oxford: Oxford University Press.
French, Sean (1996) *The Terminator*. London: British Film Institute.
Geuens, Jean-Pierre (1996) 'Through The Looking Glasses: From the Camera Obscura to Video Assist', *Film Quarterly*, 49, 3, 16–26; http://www.clas.ufl.edu/users/

burt/%20%20%20%20%20%20Kiaorostami%20Shakespeare%20Amy%20 Scott-Douglas/cinephilia%20film%20preservation%20and%20archive%20pdfs/ Film%20theory%20preservation%EF%80%A8/1213467.pdf.

Giardina, Carolyn (2010) 'How *Avatar* changed the rules of deliverables', *The Hollywood Reporter*, 25 March; http://www.hollywoodreporter.com/news/how-avatarchanged-rules-deliverables-22027.

Gledhill, Christine (1999) *The Cinema Book*. London: British Film Institute, 164–5.

Grant, Barry Keith (2004) 'Disorder in the Universe: John Carpenter and the Question of Genre', in Ian Conrich and David Woods (eds) *The Cinema of John Carpenter: The Technique of Terror*. London and New York: Wallflower Press, 10–21.

Grant, Michael (2000) *The Modern Fantastic: The Films of David Cronenberg*. Westport, CT: Greenwood Press.

Gravett, Paul (2010) 'Moebius and Jean Giraud: Leading a Double Life; http://www.paulgravett.com/index.php/articles/article/moebius_jean_giraud_2.

Gross, Larry (2000) 'Big and Loud', in Jose Arroyo (ed.) *Action/Spectacle Cinema: A Sight and Sound Reader*. London: British Film Institute, 3–9.

Gunning, Tom (1986a) 'The Cinema of Attractions: Early Film, Its Spectators and the Avant Garde', *Wide Angle*, 8, 3-4, 64.

____ (1986b) 'An Aesthetic of Astonishment'; http://elenarazlogova.org/hist452w07/gunning.pdf.

Hammond, Robert (2002) 'Some Smothering Dreams: The Combat Film in Contemporary Hollywood', in Steve Neale (ed.) *Genre and Contemporary Hollywood*. London: British Film Institute, 62–77.

Haraway, Donna (1991) 'A Cyborg Manifesto: Science, Technology and Socialist Feminism in the Late 20th Century', in *Simians, Cyborgs and Women: The Reinvention of Nature*. London: Routledge.

Hayward, Susan (2012) *Cinema Studies: The Key Concepts*, 4th edition. Oxford: Routledge.

Hourigan, Peter (2009) 'On Abel Gance's *J'Accuse* and *La Roue*', *Senses of Cinema*, February; http://sensesofcinema.com/2009/49/abel-gance-jaccuse-la-roue/.

Huddleston, Tom (2009) 'Review of *Avatar*', *Time Out*, 15 December; http://www.timeout.com/london/film/avatar.

Hobbs, Angie (2000) *Plato and the Hero: Courage, Manliness and the Impersonal God*. Cambridge: Cambridge University Press.

Hodgens, Richard (1999) 'A brief tragical history of the science fiction film', in Pam Cook and Mieke Bernink (eds) *The Cinema Book*. London: British Film Institute.

Hughes, Robert (1999) *American Visions: The Epic Story of Art in America*. London: Harvill.

Hyman, Wendy Beth (2011) *The Automata in English Renaissance Literature*. London: Ashgate.

Ingram, David (2000) *Green Screen: Environmentalism and Hollywood Cinema*. Exeter: University of Exeter Press.

Isaacs, Bruce (2011) 'Art, Image and Spectacle: High Concept Cinema', in Matthew Wilhelm Kapell and Stephen McVeigh (eds) *The Films of James Cameron*. Jefferson, NC: McFarland, 90–109.

Jeffords, Susan (1993) *Hard Bodies: Masculinity in the Reagan Era*. New Brunswick, NJ: Rutgers University Press.

Jermyn, Deborah and Sean Redmond (eds) (2003) *The Cinema of Kathryn Bigelow: Hollywood Transgressor*. London and New York: Wallflower Press.

Jones, Kent (1999) 'American Movie Classic', *Film Comment*, January/February; http://www.theofficialjohncarpenter.com/pages/press/filmcomment0199.html.

Kapell, Matthew Wilhelm and Stephen McVeigh (2011) 'Surveying James Cameron's Reluctant Political Commentaries', in Matthew Wilhelm Kapell and Stephen McVeigh (eds) *The Films of James Cameron: Critical Essays*. Jefferson, NC: McFarland.

Kaufman, Roger (2011) 'Terminators, Aliens and Avatars', in Matthew Wilhelm Kapell and Stephen McVeigh (eds) *The Films of James Cameron: Critical Essays*. Jefferson, NC: McFarland, 167–86.

Kavanagh, James (1990) 'Son of a Bitch: Feminism, Humanism and Science in Alien', in Annette Kuhn (ed) *Alien Zone: Cultural Theory and Contemporary Science Fiction Cinema*. London: Verso, 73–92.

Keller, Alexandra (1999) 'Size Does Matter', in Kevin S. Sandley and Gaylyn Studlar (eds) *Titanic: Anatomy of a Blockbuster*. New Brunswick, NJ: Rutgers University Press, 132–55.

Kellner, Douglas and Michael Ryan (2004) 'Technophobia/Dystopia', in Sean Redmond (ed.) *Liquid Metal: The Science Fiction Film Reader*. Wallflower Press, 57–64.

King, Geoff (2000) *Spectacular Narratives: Hollywood in the Age of the Blockbuster*. London: IB Tauris.

Kracauer, Siegfried (1997) 'The Redemption of Reality', in *Theory of Film: The Redemption of Physical Reality*. Oxford: Oxford University Press, 27–39.

Kramer, Peter (1999) 'Women First', in Kevin S. Sandley and Gaylyn Studler (eds) *Titanic: Anatomy of a Blockbuster*. New Brunswick, NJ: Rutgers University Press, 108–32.

Kubrick, Stanley (n.d.) http://btbennett.wordpress.com/2013/09/25/a-non-verbal-experience-kubricks-2001-a-space-odyssey/comment-page-1.

Larson, Doran (2004) 'Machine as Messiah: Cyborgs, Morphs and the American Body Politic', in Sean Redmond (ed.) *Liquid Metal: The Science Fiction Film Reader*. London and New York: Wallflower Press, 191–205.

Lebeau, Vicky (2008) *Cinema and Children*. London: Reaktion.

Lee, Jane (2013) 'Filmmaker James Cameron Reflects on Exploration', *National Geographic*; http://news.nationalgeographic.com/news/2013/13/130319-james cameron -deepsea-challenge-ocean-science/.

Lehman, Peter and Susan Hunt (1999) 'Something and Someone Else: The Mind, the Body and Sexuality in Titanic', in Kevin S. Sandley and Gaylyn Studlar (eds)

Titanic: Anatomy of a Blockbuster. New Brunswick, NJ: Rutgers University Press, 89–108.

Lem, Stanislaw (2002) 'The *Solaris* Station'; http://english.lem.pl/arround-lem/adaptations/soderbergh/147-thesolaris-station?start=1.

Lloyd, John Bedford (2001) 20th Century Fox DVD.

LoBrutto, Vincent (1998) *Stanley Kubrick*. London: Faber and Faber.

L'Officier, Randy (1986) 'Interview with James Cameron and Gale Ann Hurd about the production of *Aliens*'; http://www.lofficier.com/cameron.htm.

Lubin, David M. (1999) *Titanic*. London: British Film Institute.

Lynch, Jane (2002) 'Steven Soderbergh: Space Invaders'; http://www.close-upfilm.com/features/Interviews/stevensoderbergh.htm

Maslin, Janet (1984) 'A Horror Director Creates a Magical Alien', *Los Angeles Herald Examiner*, 14 December; http://www.theofficialjohncarpenter.com/pages/press/laheraldex841214.html.

Masters, Kim (2013) 'Darren Aronofksy, Paramount Spar Over *Noah* Final Cut, 15 October, *Hollywood Reporter*; http://www.hollywoodreporter.com/news/darrenaronofsky-paramount-spar-noah-648777.

Mathijs, Ernest and Xavier Mendik (2008) *The Cult Film Reader*. Maidenhead/New York: Open University Press/McGraw-Hill Education.

Mathison, Melissa (2002) *ET: From Concept to Classic – The Illustrated Story of the Film and the Filmmakers*, ed. Laurent Bouzereau, London: Pocket Books

McCabe, Colin (1985) *Theoretical Essays: Film, Linguistics, Literature*. Manchester: Manchester University Press.

McCarthy, Helen (2011) 'Gods and Monsters: Birthday Greetings to Tezuka and Godzilla', 6 November; http://helenmccarthy.wordpress.com/2011/11/06/gods-and-monsters-birthday-greetings-to-tezuka-and-godzilla/.

McGowan, Todd (2010) 'Maternity Divided: *Avatar* and the Enjoyment of Nature', *JumpCut*; http://www.ejumpcut.org/archive/jc52.2010/mcGowanAvatar/.

Melville, Herman (1987 [1851]) *Moby Dick*. London: Penguin.

Mendelsohn, Daniel (2010) 'The Wizard', *The New York Review of Books*, 25 March; http://www.nybooks.com/articles/archives/2010/mar/25/the-wizard/?pagination=false.

Milius, John (2009) 'Interview'; http://www.youtube.com/watch?v=rg3ahYUswd8.

Morris, Nigel (2007) *The Cinema of Steven Spielberg: Empire of Light*. London and New York: Wallflower Press.

Mulvey, Laura (1975) 'Visual Pleasure and Narrative Cinema', *Screen*, 16, 3, 6–18

Murch, Walter (2011) 'Why 3D doesn't work and never will', 23 January, *Chicago Sun Times*; http://www.rogerebert.com/rogers-journal/why-3d-doesnt-work-and-never-will-case-closed.

____ (2012) 'Josh Melnick and Walter Murch in Conversation', *Paris Review*, 7 February; http://www.theparisreview.org/blog/2012/02/07/josh-melnick-and-walte-rmurch-in-conversation/.

Nichols, Bill (1985) 'The Voice of Documentary', in Bill Nichols (ed.) *Movies and Methods: Volume II*. Berkeley, CA: University of California Press.

O'Riordan, Kate (2009) 'Human Cloning in Film: Horror, Ambivalence, Hope'; http://dx.doi.org/10.1080/09505430802062919.

Palmer, Martin (2009) *In Our Time* (BBC Radio

Parker, Mark and Deborah Parker (2011) *The DVD and the Story of Film: The Attainable Text*. London: Macmillan.

Parisi, Paula (1998) *Titanic and the Making of James Cameron*. London: Orion.

Peachment, Chris (1984) 'Review of *The Terminator*', *Time Out*; http://www.timeout.com/london/film/the-terminator.

Perkins, V. F. (1993) *Film as Film: Understanding and Judging Movies*. New York: DeCapo Press.

Perry, Hugh (2001) 'John Carperneter', in Yoram Allon, Del Cullen and Hannah Patterson (eds) *Wallflower Press Critical Guide to North American Filmmakers*, London and New York: Wallflower Press, 70–1.

Pesce, Nicole Lyn (2010) '*Avatar* may return to theatres for summer re-release, with additional scenes', *New York Daily News*; http://www.nydailynews.com/entertainment/tv-movies/avatar-return-theaters-summer-re-release-additional-scenes-article-1.166954.

Pierson, Michele (2002) *Special Effects: Still In Search of Wonder*. New York: Columbia University Press.

Pirani, Adam (1986) 'Attack of the Exotic Aliens', *Starlog*, 109.

Prince, Stephen (1996) 'True Lies: Perceptual Realism, Digital Images and Film Theory', *Film Quarterly*, 49, 3, 27–37; http://fdm.ucsc.edu/~landrews/film178w09/Film_178_THE_RECONSTRUCTED_IMAGE_files/True%20Lies-%20Perceptual%20Realism.pdf.

____ (2009) *Firestorm: American Film in the Age of Terrorism*. New York: Columbia University Press.

Quinlivan, Davina (2012) 'Prometheus', 31 May, *Times Higher Education*; http://www.timeshighereducation.co.uk/420110.article.

Rebello, Stephen (2009) 'Interview with James Cameron', *Playboy*; http://www.playboy.com/playground/view/playboy-interview-james-cameron.

Richardson, John (1994) 'Iron Jim', in Brent Dunham (ed.) *James Cameron: Interviews*, Jackson, MI: University of Mississippi Press, 57–71.

Richardson, Niall (2010) *Transgressive Bodies: Representation in Film and Popular Culture*. London: Ashgate.

Riley, Brooks (2014) 'Heart Transplant: *Apocalypse Now*'; http://filmcomment.com/article/apocalypse-now-heart-transplant.

Robey, Tim (2013) 'Interview with Roger Corman', 6 November, *The Daily Telegraph*; http://www.telegraph.co.uk/culture/film/10426947/Roger-Corman-interview-Audiences-will-turnaway-from-gory-films.html.

Rodriguez, Clara E. (1997) *Latin Looks: Latinas and Latinos in the US Media*. Boulder, CO: Westview Press.

Sandler, Kevin S. and Gaylyn Studlar (1999) 'Introduction: The Seductive Waters of James Cameron's *Titanic*', in Kevin S. Sandler and Studlar Gaylyn (eds) *Titanic: Anatomy of a Blockbuster*. New Brunswick, NJ: Rutgers University Press, 1–14.

Schatz, Thomas (2004) *New Hollywood Violence: Inside Popular Film*. Manchester: Manchester University Press.

Sennett, Richard (2008) *The Uses of Disorder: Identity and City Life*. New Haven, CT: Yale University Press.

Shone, Tom (2012) 'Woman: The Other Alien in Alien', *Slate*; http://www.slate.com/articles/arts/culturebox/2012/06/prometheus_why_are_academics_so_obsessed_with_ridley_scott_s_alien_and_its_sequels_.html.

Shay, Don (1997) 'Back to Titanic', *Cinefex*, 72, December, 15–176.

Short, Sue (2011) *Cyborg Cinema*. Basingstoke: Palgrave Macmillan.

Slotkin, Richard (2000a [1973]) *Regeneration Through Violence: The Mythology of the American Frontier 1600–1860*. Norman, OK: University of Oklahoma Press.

____ (2000b) 'The Fall into Guns', *The Atlantic*, 1 November; http://www.theatlantic.com/past/issues/2000/11/slotkin.htm.

____ (2001) 'Unit Pride: Ethnic Platoons and the Myths of American Nationality'; http://muse.jhu.edu/login?auth=0&type=summary&url=/journals/american_literary_history/v013/13.3slotkin.html.

Sobchack, Vivian (2001) *Screening Space: The American Science Fiction Film*. New Brunswick, NJ: Rutgers University Press.

Soderbergh, Steven (2003) 'Interview with Nev Pierce'; http://www.bbc.co.uk/films/2003/02/24/steven_soderbergh_solaris_interview.shtml.

Sontag, Susan (1965) 'The Imagination of Disaster'; http://americanfuturesiup.files.wordpress.com/2013/01/sontag-the-imagination-of-disaster.pdf.

Spielberg, Steven (2009) 'Introduction', in Jan Harlan and Jane M. Struthers (eds) *Artificial Intelligence: From Stanley Kubrick to Steven Spielberg: The Vision Behind the Film*. London: Thames and Hudson.

Stallone, Sylvester (2006) 16 December; http://www.aintitcool.com/node/30932.

____ (2010) 28 July; http://www.aintitcool.com/node/45937.

Telotte, J. P. (2001) *Science Fiction Film*. Cambridge: Cambridge University Press.

Thompson, Anne (1994) '5 True Lies About James Cameron'; http://www.ew.com/ew/article/0,,303109,00.html.

Thompson, Kristin (2007) *The Frodo Franchise: The Lord of the Rings and Modern Hollywood*. Berkeley, CA: University of California Press.

____ (2010) 'Motion-capturing an Oscar', 23 February; http://www.davidbordwell.net/blog/2010/02/23/motion-capturing-an-oscar/.

____ (2011) 'Has 3D already failed?', 20 January; http://www.davidbordwell.net/blog/2011/01/20/has-3d-already-failed-the-sequel-part-one-realdlighted/.

Todd, Erica (2013) 'Depicting Love in Cinema', in *Passionate Love and Popular Cinema*. Basingstoke: Palgrave Macmillan.

Traub, Susanne (2012) 'Dancing is thinking: On the relationship between philosophy and dance'; http://www.goethe.de/kue/tut/tre/en8820849.htm.

Trumbull, Douglas (2012) http://www.icgmagazine.com/wordpress/2012/04/04/exposure-douglas-trumbull.

____ (2013) 'Interview', 5 February; http://www.craigskinnerfilm.com/douglas-trumbull-interview/.

Turner, Frederick Jackson (1994) *The Oxford History of the American West*, eds. Clyde A Milner, Carol O'Connor and Martha A Sandweiss. Oxford: Oxford University Press.
Twain, Mark (1987 [1884]) *The Adventures of Huckleberry Finn*. London: Penguin.
Verhoeven, Paul (2010) http://moviesblog.mtv.com/2010/04/14/paul-verhoevenrobocop-christ-story-remake-update/.
Warner, Marina (1979) 'What the Virgin of Knock Means to Women,' September; http://www.marinawarner.com/Magill.pdf.
____ (1995) *From the Beast to the Blonde: On Fairy Tales and Their Tellers*. Vintage: London.
Watkins, Gwynne (2014) 'New *Avatar* Sequels Will Require Big Effects and Big Bucks', 16 June; https://www.yahoo.com/movies/new-avatar-sequels-will-require-big-effects-and-big-88967038312.html.
Weaver, Sigourney (1986) 'Attack of the Exotic Aliens', *Starlog*, 109.
Wells, Paul (1998) *Understanding Animation*. London: Routledge.
Williams, Linda (1991) 'Film Body: An Implantation of Perversions, Explorations', in *Film Theory: Selected Essays for Cine-Tracts*, Bloomington, IN: Indiana University Press, 46–72.
Wood, Robin (1989) *Hitchcock's Films Revisited*. London: Faber and Faber.
____ (2002) 'The American Nightmare: Horror in the 70s', in Mark Jancovich (ed.) *Horror: The Film Reader*. London: Routledge, 25–32.
____ (2003) *Hollywood: From Vietnam to Reagan*. New York: Columbia University Press.
____ (2009) 'Ideology, Genre, Auteur', in Leo Braudy and Marchall Cohen (eds) *Film Theory and Criticism: Introductory Readings*. Oxford: Oxford University Press.
Wollen, Peter (2000 [1993]) 'Theme Park and Variations', in Jose Arroyo (ed.) *Action/Spectacle Cinema: A Sight and Sound Reader*. London: British Film Institute.
Wyatt, Justin (1994) *High Concept: Movies and Marketing in Hollywood*. Austin, TX: University of Texas Press.
Wyatt, Justin and Katherine Vlesmas (1999) 'The Drama of Recoupment: On the Mass Media Negotiation of Titanic', in Kevin S. Sander and Gaylyn Studlar (eds) *Titanic: Anatomy of A Blockbuster*. New Brunswick, NJ: Rutgers University Press.
Xavier, Ismail (1999) *Allegories of Underdevelopment: Aesthetics and Politics in Modern Brazilian Cinema*. Minneapolis, MN: University of Minnesota Press.
Zakaria, Fareed (2012) 'The Heirs of Reagan's Optimism', *Time*, 6 September; http://fareedzakaria.com/2012/09/06/the-heirs-of-reagans-optimism/.
Zipes, Jack (2011) *The Enchanted Screen: The Unknown History of Fairy Tale Films*. Oxford: Routledge.

INDEX

Abyss, The 3, 5, 11, 17, 20, 23–4, 31–2, 48–9, 52, 6–41, 68–9, 75–90, 95, 106–8, 110–13, 115–17, 119–22, 124, 127, 129, 136, 138–9, 143–4, 149–51
Age of Innocence, The 123, 154
AI: Artificial Intelligence 9, 40, 50
Akira 89, 91
Akira Kurosawa's Dreams 89
Alien 43, 45, 57, 58, 60, 62–3, 65, 69, 71, 78–9
Aliens 5, 8, 13, 16, 18–9, 27, 30–3, 39, 43, 48–9, 52–3, 55, 57–61, 64–6, 68–73, 75, 77–8, 81, 83–4, 86–8, 90, 92, 95–7, 106, 108, 110, 113, 116–17, 119–23, 126, 132, 136–7, 139, 140–1, 143, 148–9, 153, 156
Aliens of the Deep 77, 82, 149–51
Andrew, Geoff 87, 97, 114
angels 79, 83–5, 122
animation 4, 8, 22–4, 40, 61, 91, 99, 116, 131, 134–5
Arnold, Tom 106
Arroyo, Jose 12, 46, 95, 156
At Play in the Fields of the Lord 135
authorship 21–4, 54, 155
Avatar 2–6, 8–11, 13, 15, 17, 20–1, 23, 25, 27, 30–2, 39–41, 46, 48–9, 52–3, 55, 57–8, 60–8, 71, 75–7, 79, 81–2, 84, 86–8, 91–2, 94, 98–101, 103–4, 108, 110–11, 113, 117, 119–21, 123–5, 127, 129–49, 151, 154, 156

Bachelard, Gaston 3, 78, 86, 136
Battle Beyond the Stars 7, 30, 43–4
Baudrillard, Jean 39
Biehn, Michael 43, 46, 66, 82, 94
Bigelow, Kathryn 2–3, 19, 22–3, 145, 154–5
Big Wednesday 19–20
Blade Runner 14, 31, 40, 45–6, 54, 91
blockbuster 11–13, 22, 24, 35, 105, 112, 122, 131–3, 135, 146
Bordwell, David 4, 8, 10, 14, 16, 22, 47, 72
Boyd, Brian 4–5
Braidotti, Rosi 55, 76
Brother From Another Planet 30–1, 94
budget 2, 7, 19, 23, 29, 43, 54–5, 71, 100, 105, 128
Burroughs, Norris 61
Burton, Tim 17, 22–4, 73

Campbell, Joseph 59, 107
Carpenter, John 18–9, 31, 38–40, 69, 71, 97
Carter, Rick 16, 133
Charity, Tom 72
Christmas Carol, A 15, 84, 135
Cinefex 100, 116, 134–5
Cocks, Jay 154
Commando 42, 45, 90, 104
Conan the Barbarian 19–20, 24, 41–2, 45, 90, 104, 117
Conan the Destroyer 43, 45, 117

Corman, Roger 7, 22, 30, 150
Cornea, Christine 3, 11–12, 36, 60, 96, 133
Cosmatos, George Pan 46, 153
Cruise, Tom 2
cult film 72
Curtis, Jamie-Lee 106
cyborgs 2, 39, 41, 46, 50–1, 65, 90–3, 96, 98–9, 108, 134

Dante, Joe 7–8, 18, 31, 38, 87
Dare, Michael 78
Dargis, Manohla 10, 135
Dark Angel 155
Day After Tomorrow, The 89
DiCaprio, Leonardo 25, 117–18, 120
digital 1, 4, 9, 10, 15, 23–4, 27, 30, 39, 45, 47, 80, 85, 92, 98–100, 103–4, 115–16, 120–1, 127, 132–4, 144, 146–7
disability 14, 137, 140
Disney, Walt 9, 22–3, 25, 76, 91–2, 99, 113, 134
Dixon, Winston Wheeler 89, 129, 130
documentary 19, 22, 77–8, 82, 84, 98, 149–51
Drums Along the Mohawk 135
Dushku, Eliza 110
Dyer, Richard 17

Ebert, Roger 72, 76, 98, 147, 157
Edge of Tomorrow 2
Edison, Thomas 23, 113
Elysium 17, 46–7
Emerald Forest, The 136
Enemy Mine 133
Escape from New York 14, 18, 31, 156
exoskeleton 1, 47, 71, 94, 97
extraterrestrial 84, 86

FernGully 135
Fiedel, Brad 45, 106
Ford, John 22, 131, 135
Fore, Dana 41, 140
Frakes, Randall 115
French, Sean 36, 38
Furlong, Edward 93

Galaxy of Terror 7
gender 60, 65, 81, 83, 92, 104, 114, 115, 124, 134, 154, 155,

genre 2, 3, 5, 6, 8, 10, 13, 14, 16–9, 22, 24–7, 29, 30, 35, 37–40, 44, 54–5, 57, 59–61, 69, 71, 75–6, 78, 80, 83, 89, 90, 92, 99, 103–5, 109–11, 113, 117, 123, 125–7, 130, 133, 135, 145, 148, 155, 157
Geronimo 57, 143
Geuens, Jean-Pierre 15
Ghost in the Shell 89, 90–1
Ghosts of the Abyss 77, 82, 84, 149, 150
Giraud, Jean 'Moebius' 78–9
Gledhill, Christine 117
Goldstein, Jenette 65, 93
Gorbachev, Mikhail 78
Grant, Barry Keith 18
Gravett, Paul 79
Griffith, D.W. 24, 31
Gross, Larry 11, 72, 107
Gunning, Tom 13, 98

Hamilton, Linda 43, 47, 93
Hammond, Robert 6, 58
Harris, Ed 78, 82, 117
Henry V 144
Hercules in New York 41, 45, 117
heroism 8, 27, 123, 140, 144,
Heslov, Grant 106
Heston, Charlton 108
Hill, Walter 18, 43, 45, 57, 143
Hobbit, The 145, 147
Hollywood Reporter, The 80, 132, 135, 145, 147
Horner, James 61–2, 71, 117
Howard, Ron 22, 23, 73, 76, 79, 99, 116
Howling, The 8, 38
Hughes, Robert 130
Hugo 16
Hurd, Gale Anne 43–4
Hurt, John 69

ideology 37, 41, 133, 136,
Independence Day 89
Indiana Jones and the Kingdom of the Crystal Skull 131
Industrial Light and Magic (ILM) 98
Ingram, David 135
Isaacs, Bruce 13, 96

Jackson, Peter 9, 17, 23, 99, 129, 133, 144–5, 147
Jeffords, Susan 42

Jurassic Park 17–8, 38, 61, 98–9, 128, 131, 133, 141

Kapell, Matthew Wilhelm 105, 109, 110
Keller, Alexandra 12, 108
Kellner, Douglas 14
Kindergarten Cop 90, 104
King, Geoff 12, 13, 23, 133
Koepp, David 156
Kozoll, Michael 154
Kracauer, Siegfried 9, 135
Kramer, Peter 71
Kubrick, Stanley 24, 62, 77, 100, 126
Kurosawa, Akira 24, 89

Larson, Doran 46, 98
Last of the Mohicans, The 115, 135, 154
Last War, The 89
Lawrence of Arabia 11, 61, 132
Lean, David 11, 24, 38, 132
LeBeau, Vicky 67
L'Officier, Randy 13, 58
Lord of the Rings, The 129, 133, 144–5
Los Angeles 5, 43–6, 49, 64, 93, 100
Lubin, David M. 5, 126
Lucas, George 6–8, 14, 18–9, 21–3, 29, 36–7, 44, 97–100, 133–4, 137, 140, 145–6, 153–4
Lumière Brothers, the 13, 38, 98

Malik, Art 108
Mann, Michael 115, 135
masculinity 25, 26, 41–2, 90, 107–8, 110, 114, 122
Maslin, Janet 39
Mastrantonio, Mary Elizabeth 78, 81
Mastubayashi, Shuei 89
McCabe, Colin 80
McGowan, Todd 136
McLaren, Norman 4
McNeely, Joel 150
McVeigh, Stephen 105, 109–10
Medicine Man 135
Méliès, Georges 13, 16, 98
Melville, Herman 75–6, 85
Mendelsohn, Daniel 132, 145
Mendik, Xavier 7
metaphor 3, 27, 42, 53, 55, 58–9, 63, 65, 77–8, 84, 86, 110, 144
Metropolis 45, 66
Milius, John 18–20, 104, 143

Morrell, David 154
motion capture 16, 129
Mosquito Coast, The 135
Murch, Walter 50, 147
Muren, Dennis 85
Murikami, Jimmy T. 7, 89
mythology 6, 27, 35, 137, 153–4

Near Dark 22
New World Pictures 7, 18, 43,
New York Review of Books, The 145
Nichols, Bill 149
nuclear 36, 64, 78, 80, 89, 92–4, 103, 108, 112, 116, 151

Orion Pictures 43–4, 54, 72
O'Riordan, Kate 25
Outland 14

Paxton, Bill 66, 107, 119, 150
performance capture 23, 40, 116, 129, 133–5
Perkins, V.F. 23
Pierson, Michelle 16, 24
Piranha 7, 31
Piranha 2: The Spawning 7, 25, 31–3, 143
Pirani, Adam 75
Pocahontas 135
Point Break 19, 23, 154
posthuman 27, 76, 111, 156
Postman, The 89
Prince and the Pauper, The 123
Princess Mononoke 89, 136, 141
Prometheus 65

Rambo: First Blood Part II 26, 42, 45, 48, 57, 58, 63, 136, 153
Reagan, Ronald 36, 42, 78, 153
Rebello, Stephen 6, 39
Reeves, Keanu 154
Reitman, Ivan 90, 104
representation 2, 3, 8, 10, 14, 15, 17, 19–20, 25–7, 36–7, 41–2, 46, 64–5, 92, 104, 107–9, 111, 114, 117–18, 130
Rhapsody in August 89
Ribisi, Giovanni 123, 139
Richardson, Niall 41
Rodriguez, Michelle 140
Romeo + Juliet 118
Romero, George A. 18
Ryan, Michael 14

Sackheim, William 154
Sanctum 22, 157
Sayles, John 7, 12, 30–1, 94
Schatz, Thomas 35
Schwarzenegger, Arnold 25, 37, 41–7, 54–5, 90, 93–5, 98–9, 104, 106, 112–13, 117
Scorsese, Martin 5, 16, 21, 123, 154
Scott, Ridley 6, 33, 43, 45–7, 65, 87, 96, 99, 111
Sennett, Richard 49
Short, Sue 50, 92, 134
Slotkin, Richard 27, 35, 47, 64, 66, 43
Soderbergh, Steven 78, 157
Solaris 78, 156
Sontag, Susan 36, 80
spectacle 8–13, 16, 24, 26, 38, 42, 45–6, 71, 75–6, 84, 98, 100, 103, 107, 109, 112, 114–15, 117–18, 120, 127, 129, 132–3, 146, 148, 150, 154, 157
Spielberg, Steven 5, 6, 8–9, 17–9, 31–2, 36–40, 49–50, 54, 70, 75–6, 81, 90, 104–5, 109, 112, 128, 131–3, 136, 144, 153
Spiderman 156
Stallone, Sylvester 26, 42, 45, 118, 153–4
Starlog 58, 60, 75, 80
Stone, Oliver 6, 22, 58, 72
Strange Days 2–3, 22–3, 31, 47, 54, 91, 111, 142, 154–5
Stuart, Gloria 119
surveillance 106, 110–11, 155
Swayze, Patrick 154

technology 1–3, 8–11, 14–15, 23, 25, 27, 29–30, 36–40, 44, 47, 52, 55, 66–7, 75–6, 80–4, 91–2, 97, 99–100, 103–4, 106–7, 110–11, 115, 120, 124, 132, 134–5, 139–40, 144, 147, 150–1, 155, 157
Terminator, The 1, 2, 8, 11, 14, 17–18, 21, 23, 25, 27, 29–33, 35–57, 60–1, 63–4, 66–8, 70–2, 75–9, 81, 84, 86–7, 89–90, 92–4, 96–7, 100, 106, 108–10, 112, 116–17, 119–20, 122, 125–6, 130, 132, 134, 138, 141, 143, 156
Terminator 2: Judgement Day 9, 11, 16, 23, 30–2, 48, 63–4, 81, 87, 89–101, 103–6, 110–12, 118, 124, 127, 129, 134, 156

T2: 3D 99–101
Thatcher, Margaret 78
Thing, The 19, 38, 40, 69
This Boy's Life 118
Thompson, Kristin 15, 23
3D (technology) 16, 24, 100, 101, 132, 145–7, 157
Time Out 54, 72, 87, 97, 114
Titanic 2–3, 5, 8–9, 10, 12–3, 17, 19–25, 53, 62, 69, 70, 75, 80–1, 84–7, 94, 98, 101, 107, 110–29, 133, 138, 142–4, 149, 150
True Lies 11, 16, 42, 75, 78, 87, 101–114, 118, 125, 129, 142
Trumbull, Douglas 12–13, 82–3, 100, 131
Twain, Mark 2, 123
Twentieth Century Fox 21, 55, 71, 81, 106, 119, 129
Twins 90, 104
Twister 113, 118

Visual effects 7–9, 15–18, 23–4, 29–31, 75, 80, 82, 85, 92, 97–100, 115–16, 129, 131, 149–50, 156

Weaver, Sigourney 60, 62–3, 92, 139
Wells, Paul 40
What's Eating Gilbert Grape 118
When the Wind Blows 89
Whitman, Walt 125
Williams, Linda 16, 42, 96
Winslet, Kate 117, 118, 120
Winston, Stan 38, 40, 52, 61, 69
Wood, Robin 14, 37, 42, 54, 60, 72, 103, 106, 112, 133
Woods, David 18
Worthington, Sam 99, 136, 138
Wyatt, Justin 22, 24,

Xavier, Ismail 27
Xenogenesis 7, 29–30, 66, 100, 140

Zakaria, Fareed 36
Zane, Billy 120
Zemeckis, Robert 11, 15–16, 22–4, 36, 65, 73, 116, 118, 134–5, 153
Zipes, Jack 59

GPSR Authorized Representative: Easy Access System Europe, Mustamäe tee
50, 10621 Tallinn, Estonia, gpsr.requests@easproject.com

www.ingramcontent.com/pod-product-compliance
Lightning Source LLC
Chambersburg PA
CBHW021950290426
44108CB00012B/1016